AMONG *THE* JANEITES

AMONG

THE

JANEITES

A JOURNEY
THROUGH THE WORLD OF
JANE AUSTEN FANDOM

———

BY

DEBORAH YAFFE

———

A MARINER ORIGINAL

𝔐𝔞𝔯𝔦𝔫𝔢𝔯 𝔅𝔬𝔬𝔨𝔰

HOUGHTON MIFFLIN HARCOURT

BOSTON • NEW YORK

2013

Library of Congress Cataloging-in-Publication Data is available.
ISBN 978-0-547-75773-5

Book design by Alex Camlin

Printed in the United States of America
DOC 10 9 8 7 6 5 4 3 2 1

For Alastair
I have loved none but you

CONTENTS

———

THE TAROT OF JANE AUSTEN

THE JANE AUSTEN TAROT CARD I am holding in my hand shows a series of small images — a young woman tending to children, fetching soup, performing domestic tasks.

Anne Elliot, in Persuasion, *selflessly running her lazy sister's household?* I guess. *But how does that answer my question?*

I know nothing about the tarot, and believe less, but I've played along anyway, following the tarot grand master's instructions to think of an open-ended question about my life and then draw a card from the deck. I am here in Philadelphia to attend the Jane Austen Society of North America's Annual General Meeting, and I have asked the cards to tell me whether I should write the book about Jane Austen fans that I've been mulling for months. *Could I do the project justice?* Now that the cosmos is supposedly giving me an answer, however, I can't figure out what it means. Typical.

This conference session on Jane Austen tarot cards is standing room only, despite the competition from the Regency ball in full swing next door, and I'm not the only audience member with a question about her card. I wait my turn to ask for help from the tarot grand master who created the Jane Austen deck — Diane

Wilkes, a jolly woman with auburn hair falling past her shoulders. Yes, she confirms at last, my pictures do show Anne Elliot. The card illustrates the sentiment that Captain Wentworth, Anne's lost love and future husband, expresses halfway through the novel: "No one . . . so capable as Anne."

Despite my militant skepticism, the hairs on my neck prickle as the Jane Austen tarot cards yield an answer so perfectly suited to my question. And could it be coincidence that my middle name is Anne? Or that my literature-loving parents chose it from *Persuasion*? In spite of myself, I laugh.

"That's pretty interesting, considering my question," I tell Wilkes.

"I thought it would be," she says.

The summer I was ten, I inserted a tiny key into the lock of my diary, turned to the gilt-edged page reserved for July 28, and wrote, "I woke up at 5:30 and read 'Pride and Prejudice.' We went to Central Park after breakfast, and I read some more."

That bicentennial summer of 1976, we were visiting relatives in New York, at the end of a family vacation during which I'd spent every spare minute inhaling a suitcase's worth of books. Next to the cot in my grandfather's apartment, I had stacked a few last volumes to tide me over the long days until the flight home to Colorado. My father was a college English professor and inveterate book buyer, and it was he who had added *Pride and Prejudice* to my stack. History will record that this was my first Jane Austen novel. I was about to become a junior Janeite.

I was a bright, bespectacled child, with a head of wiry, unmanageable dark curls that refused to grow into the waist-length cascade I longed for. I lived in sleepy Colorado Springs, in an old white house with red shutters; my bedroom window framed the snow-capped summit of Pikes Peak. Through sixth grade, I weathered the big team-taught classes in the open-plan rooms of the neighborhood public school, where, one year, most of the girls had a crush on a teacher with groovy '70s sideburns named — yes, really — Mr. Darcy. Then my parents transferred me to a crunchy-granola private school, where camping in the mountains was part of the curriculum and we called all the teachers by their first names. As far back as I can remember, I earned good grades, hated gym class, and read with a ravenous hunger.

I was the ultimate literature nerd. Dickens, Thackeray, Trollope, George Eliot, H. G. Wells, Arthur Conan Doyle, Charlotte and Emily Brontë, Mary Shelley, Rudyard Kipling, Robert Louis Stevenson, Edith Wharton: throughout my tweens and teens, I mainlined classic fiction, finishing one thick novel only to start another, like a chain smoker lighting her next cigarette from the embers of its predecessor. "I finished 'Hard Times,' began 'The Last Chronicle of Barset,' and went to the dentist," ran a typical diary entry by my eleven-year-old self. A month later: "I have started a book called 'Black and Blue Magic' for school, because Katie recommended it. For pleasure I am reading 'Can You Forgive Her?' by Trollope."

By fifth grade, I was spending every recess sitting cross-legged on the playground, engrossed in a book, while the other kids played foursquare. My teacher prohibited me from reading during the time set aside for wholesome physical activity, and, good girl that I was, I initially obeyed. But addicts have no morals. Soon I was sneaking books outside under my coat and pursuing my disreputable habit in dark corners of the playground, one eye cocked for patrolling adults. I finished *A Tale of Two Cities* that way, curled up in a doorway during lunch period, weeping over Sydney Carton's noble sacrifice.

My laconic diary entries and fragmentary memories provide few clues to what I loved in all these books, and I can't remember when Jane Austen's witty courtship novels emerged from the illustrious pack to become something special. Perhaps it was the winter's day when, age eleven, I finished *Mansfield Park*, arguably Austen's least accessible novel, and told my diary, "It is a wonderful book. I love Jane Austen." Or perhaps it was the summer I was sixteen, when my parents and I visited Chawton cottage, the house in southern England where Austen wrote or revised all six of her novels and which is now a museum of her life. I spent hours wandering through the quiet rooms, reading every label, gazing at the household objects she might have touched, steeping in a magical sense of connection.

Back home that September, I persuaded a teacher at my high school to add *Emma* to the syllabus of her Women in Literature class. (I'm not sure how the other kids liked the book. One fellow student, unfamiliar with nineteenth-century language, read Austen's account of Mr. Elton "making violent love" to the heroine and thought he was committing rape, not proposing marriage.) Sometime that fall, my parents bought me a membership in the three-year-old Jane Austen Society of North America, and a year later I took a weekend off during my first semester of college to attend JASNA's fifth annual convention in nearby Philadelphia. I think I was the youngest participant—one woman told me I looked "charming" in the black velvet dress I wore to the banquet—but by then I had been reading Austen nearly half my life, and it was thrilling to meet two hundred other people who wanted to talk about her. Still, I felt mildly surprised when JASNA's president rose to his feet at the conclusion of the conference and reminded us that our efforts to honor Austen were more for our benefit than hers—that, by now, she was so famous that she didn't need us to keep her name alive. *Jane Austen — famous?* I wondered. Somehow I had always thought of her as my own private possession.

That illusion was easier to maintain back when I first discovered Jane Austen. In July 1976, she had been dead for exactly 159 years — her novels were published during the period known as the Regency, the nine years from 1811 to 1820 when the future George IV served as acting king, or regent, during his father's disabling illness — but she was not yet the global brand she would become. Nearly twenty years would have to go by before Austenmania's Big Bang — the shot of a wet white shirt clinging seductively to the chest of the British actor Colin Firth, in the BBC's 1995 production of *Pride and Prejudice.* As much as I loved the novels, back then I could not buy Jane Austen tote bags, mugs, board games, T-shirts, or bumper stickers, let alone the Jane Austen Action Figure (five inches of molded plastic, complete with quill pen). I could not watch and rewatch movie versions of her books, or devour dozens of literary spinoffs and sequels, or log on to the Republic of Pemberley at midnight to post my analysis of a key passage in *Persuasion.* All that would come later, after the world had caught up to my obsession.

In the years after college, my Austen-love percolated just below the surface, as I launched a journalism career, moved to suburban New Jersey, and started a family. (My husband is British — he even read Austen in high school — but we met not at a ball, but over cold toast in the dining hall of an Oxford college.) I rushed to all the Austen movies and tuned in to all the miniseries, and I reread the books whenever my life needed a bracing dose of Austen's clarity and wit. When the JASNA conference came to Colorado Springs, I flew home, dropped my toddler son with his grandparents, and, with nary a backward glance, spent a joyful weekend absorbed in *Emma.*

A few years later, inspired by Karen Joy Fowler's novel *The Jane Austen Book Club,* I roped five neighbors into reading the novels with me once a month, over tea and cake. We had a great time, and they liked the books, but—well, they didn't like them quite the way I did. They didn't seem to put themselves to sleep at night by composing dialogue for Mr. Darcy and Elizabeth Bennet to say during the climactic *Pride and Prejudice* proposal scene, which Austen sketches with characteristic indirection ("He expressed himself on the occasion as sensibly and as warmly as a man violently in love can be supposed to do"). They showed no inclination to memorize the passionate love letter ("You pierce my soul. I am half agony, half hope") that Captain Wentworth gives Anne Elliot in the climactic scene of *Persuasion.* They didn't worry about whether Marianne Dashwood is really happy at the end of *Sense and Sensibility.* In other words, they weren't nuts.

It was only a matter of time before I found my way to the Republic of Pemberley, the Internet's largest Jane Austen fan community. The first time I read Pemberley's epigraph ("Your haven in a world programmed to misunderstand obsession with things Austen"), I knew I was home.

In 1894, the British literary critic George Saintsbury coined a new term to describe Jane Austen's adoring fans, and ever since—sometimes affectionately, sometimes derisively—we've been called "Janeites." New Janeites are born all the time. Some, like me, fall in love young. One summer in the early 1990s, nearly a generation after I first cracked open *Pride and Prejudice,* a bookish teenager named Darrell Sampson finally gave in to his mother's urging and read the novel during a family road trip from Decatur, Illinois, to Washington, D.C. The witty, self-assured Elizabeth Bennet captivated him; in his thirties, as a gay high school guidance counselor in northern Virginia, he joked to a local newspaper that if his life were a book, its title would be *Confessions of a Jane Austen Addict: My Eternal Search for Mr. Darcy.* He kept a Jane Austen Action Figure, still in its original packaging, on his desk at work and reread two or three of the novels every year. And the day he flew home to say goodbye to his dying mother, he took a copy of *Emma* to read as he sat by her hospital bed. "I knew it would be a comfort to me," he said, "but I also wonder if I grabbed it because I will always associate Austen with my mother, as she was the one who introduced the novels to me."

Other Janeites come to their obsession later in life. Around the time I was corralling my neighbors into reading Jane Austen with me, seventy-three-year-old Mary Previte was wrapping up a distinguished career that had taken her from running a juvenile detention center in the impoverished city of Camden, New Jersey, to serving four terms in the state legislature. Casting around for something to do in retirement, she borrowed her daughter Alice's copy of *Pride and Prejudice.* Alice is still waiting to get her book back. Then Mary borrowed Alice's DVD of *Pride and Prejudice,* wet-shirt version. Alice never got the DVD back either. In the years that followed, the two women traveled together to the Jane Austen Festival in Bath, England, where, in 2009, dressed in homemade gowns of purple Dupioni silk (Alice) and blue cotton velveteen (Mary), they helped the festival set a Guinness World Record for the largest gathering of people in Regency attire. When I visited the Prevites in late summer 2010, they were busy preparing for a return trip to Bath, shuffling through pictures of the previous year's festival, reminiscing about the friends they had made. Here, for example, was Edwin, from Holland.

"He had his boots handmade, because he couldn't find boots that he liked," Alice said.

Mary peered at the photo. "They look exactly like the ones that Darcy takes off when he jumps into the water," she said.

Alice had kept in touch with one woman from northern England who was sewing not only her own Regency gown but also outfits for her brother, her daughter, and her husband, a police officer.

A British cop who's into Jane Austen?

"Well, no," Alice said. "He's into *her*. *She's* into Jane Austen. He's into rescuing bats."

The Prevites' story points up the big difference between my journey and those of today's Janeites. Back when I was discovering Jane Austen, it wasn't so easy to find other fans. Without Twitter accounts and online communities, Austen obsession was more likely to remain a solitary pursuit, or one shared with, at most, a few relatives or close friends. Today, no junior Janeite need curl up alone with her book in a dark corner. She can start a blog, join the online Janeites discussion group, or hang out at the Republic of Pemberley. She won't feel isolated in her love because nowadays Jane Austen is everywhere. Sequels to Austen's six novels stack up in bookstores; film adaptations of her work fill the DVD racks; pithy, out-of-context quotations from her books adorn coffee mugs, T-shirts, and engagement calendars; and blogs, web communities, and Facebook pages devoted to her worship proliferate in cyberspace. One year, a small publisher struck it rich by adding zombie scenes to the text of *Pride and Prejudice*. The following summer, the Internet made a viral hit out of "Jane Austen's Fight Club," a short, hilarious video featuring women in Empire-line dresses doing needlework, practicing the piano, and slugging each other silly.

Austen's commercial potential is so compelling that even those who barely know her books fearlessly appropriate her long-out-of-copyright brand. In 2009, in upstate New York, Joanna Manring, a classical singer who supported herself by teaching voice, was looking for ways to stay afloat in the midst of economic collapse. She decided to expand her group lessons by preparing teenage girls to perform the music of the late eighteenth and early nineteenth centuries. The Jane Austen Singing School for Young Ladies was born. During rehearsal breaks, the students drank tea and watched movie adaptations of Austen's novels; at their concerts, they performed wearing high-waisted gowns. Was Manring an Austen fan? "This is a secret: I have not read any Austen books," she admitted. "I do have a book of her complete works, so that is waiting for me. That is on my cosmic to-do list."

Of course, other artists have ardent admirers; other fan clubs run wild on the Internet; other subcultures have clubby conventions where grownups play dress-up. But still, there's something about Jane. Hip college professors may lecture on *Star Trek* and edit collections of essays on *The Big Lebowski,* but no one confuses those works with artifacts of high culture. By contrast, nearly two centuries after her death, Jane Austen has a secure home in two very different worlds: the solemn pantheon of classic English literature and the exuberantly commercial realm of pop culture. She is the ultimate crossover artist, equally welcome at Yale and on YouTube.

Welcome to the party, Janeites! Fandom loves company. After all, what could be more fun than spending an hour, or a weekend, with fellow devotees, hashing over the age-old question of whether Elizabeth Bennet is subconsciously attracted to Mr. Darcy even while claiming to dislike him? What a relief to be among people who know without being told who Tom Lefroy, Martha Lloyd, and Harris Bigg-Wither were! (Jane Austen's youthful crush, lifelong friend, and rejected suitor, respectively.) Who wants to love in solitude? Literature nerd can be a lonely way to spend an adolescence.

And yet . . .

Truth be told, I didn't mind my teenage isolation all that much. I cherished my solitary passions as marks of individuality, even distinction. That tug of surprise I felt at my first JASNA convention, when I realized that Austen-love was hardly an esoteric taste, wasn't entirely pleasant. Part of me didn't want to share Jane Austen — or, at least, not with too many other people. And other Janeites seem to feel the same way. "To this day, Jane Austen will, most likely, remain an enigma," wrote one participant in the online Janeites discussion list, "and, ironically, who is also imagined to be only-truly-known by each of us reading her." This tension between the desire for community and the desire for exclusivity probably lies at the heart of any fandom, but because of Austen's unique standing in both high culture and popular culture, that conflict has a sharper edge among Janeites. It's not just the tension between privacy and community, self and other; it's the tension between people who truly *understand* Jane Austen — people like me! — and those other, lesser fans who like her for all the wrong reasons, because of the movies, or the zombies.

Perhaps because Jane Austen is one of the most accessible of great writers — easy to read, easy to love — the drawing of such distinctions has a long history. Henry James sneered at sentimental, commercialized Austen-love as far back as 1905. "Are there any other writers who have seemed so vulnerable to being loved by so many in so wrongheaded a way?" the English-literature scholar Deidre Lynch wrote in 2000. "Repeatedly over the last 190 years, certain admirers of her novels have seen fit to depreciate the motives and modes of everyone else's admiration." Still, those tensions have come into clearer focus since a wave of Austen movies hit screens in the 1990s, globalizing Austen's brand. Once, calling yourself a Jane Austen fan seemed to signify a truly refined taste, the ability to appreciate biting irony and subtle characterization. Today, it's just as likely to signify a healthy lust for handsome Brits in tight breeches. Merely calling yourself a Janeite is no longer enough to mark your superior powers of discrimination. Now you have to spell out what kind of Janeite you are.

Although they are often caricatured as middle-aged, tea-drinking spinster librarians who knit sweaters and keep cats, Janeites are in some ways a rather diverse bunch. A 2008 survey of forty-five hundred Austen fans found an air traffic controller, a zookeeper, and a Dominican friar among the ranks, as well as a fair number of teachers and, yes, librarians. The vast majority of survey respondents were female—though presumably not the Dominican friar—and most were also college-educated, with ages ranged across the spectrum. (Respondents weren't asked about their race or ethnicity, but at the JASNA events I've attended, most of the participants have been white.) Despite these commonalities of gender, educational attainment, and perhaps racial background, the survey results showed what any attendee at a JASNA conference already knew: Janeites are college students and grandparents, evangelical Christians and secular feminists, academics who condescend to bonnet-wearing enthusiasts and unabashed swooners who love ogling Colin Firth in a wet shirt at least as much as they love rereading *Pride and Prejudice.*

What all these diverse enthusiasts share is a quality of engagement with Austen and her works that goes beyond mere admiration. For as long as Austen fans have been called Janeites, the word has signified more than a simple fondness for the six great novels. A Janeite is someone who feels an intensely personal affection for the writer and her books. Janeites love Austen's novels, but they also feel close to the author herself, whom they often call "Jane," as if she were a neighbor whose kitchen door they could knock on to borrow a cup of sugar.

The retired New Jersey legislator Mary Previte is a Janeite like that. She spent part of her childhood in a Japanese prison camp, lost a hand in a buzz-saw accident as a teenager, and faced down bureaucrats and lobbyists during her career in public service, but when we talked over green tea and zucchini bread, a Jane Austen biography lying open on the stack of books at her feet, what really got her angry were Austen's early experiences in the publishing world. "Every biography, when I get to that part" — the decibel level of Mary's clipped, emphatic voice began to rise above the ladylike — "that she can't get anyone to publish her books, and one publisher takes it, and it sits for, what, ten years, and she has to buy it back — I just want to *weep* with *rage* at the disrespect for such talent!" Separated from her husband in the 1970s, with a teenage daughter to support, Previte had gone back to work after years as a stay-at-home mother. She never remarried, and now, immersed in her late-life passion, she thought a lot about Austen's own life as a single woman in a culture that made little provision for the support of women without husbands. "You sort of see some of your own issues in her life, playing out still," Mary said.

If the connection that fans feel with Jane Austen seems surprisingly intimate, given that she lived in an alien, barely industrialized world and died before their great-grandparents were born — well, that's nothing compared to the connection they feel with Jane Austen's characters. At least Jane Austen was a real person. What to make of the sentiment, expressed by one participant in the online Janeites discussion list, that it was a shame Sir Thomas Bertram, the stern patriarch of *Mansfield Park*, couldn't file a defamation suit against a filmmaker who portrayed him as a rapist? "Yes, I know he is a created character and not real," she added. "All the more reason to leave him as he was created." Another online discussion group was repeatedly convulsed by epic debates over the merits of the mousy heroine of *Mansfield Park,* battles so heated that they became known as "the Fanny Price wars." And how to account for the animosity with which Alice Previte talks about some of Austen's villains? "Aunt Norris just makes me nuts," Alice said. "Lucy Steele—I want to scratch her eyes out." The gold-digging, manipulative Lucy Steele of *Sense and Sensibility* belongs to a category that might be called Jane Austen's Poisonous Bitches, female characters who lie, scheme, and bully their way through the genteelly vicious struggle over men, money, and social standing. No question she's a piece of work, but still—scratch her eyes out? Janeites are rational people, perfectly capable of drawing firm lines between fiction and reality, and yet that distinction seems to melt into insignificance when they begin thinking about Jane Austen's characters.

In Austen's stories, Janeites find not just entertainment but an inexhaustible source of wisdom, comfort, and insight. Austen can be a support in adversity, to be read beside a sickbed, or a moral beacon in a murky world. Laurie Michael, a Maine resident in her twenties who was homeschooled by evangelical Baptist parents, found in Austen's novels a clear commitment to the values inculcated in her devoutly Christian upbringing but sometimes neglected in twenty-first-century life. "I appreciate a man who is a gentleman, and so Jane Austen's heroes especially speak to me in that way," Laurie said. "And then the heroines for their purity and modesty, as well as their wit and intelligence. They connect with things that I'm taught in the Bible, virtues that are to be cultivated."

Me? I almost never refer to our author as "Jane"—like the characters in *The Jane Austen Book Club,* I find that "more intimate, surely, than Miss Austen would wish," and perhaps a bit condescending too, as if Austen deserves less deference than the male members of the literary pantheon. (Do we call Shakespeare and Dickens "Will" and "Chuck"?) I like the movies, but I think the books are better. I don't read with an eye to political or social history—I care very little about the Napoleonic Wars or the availability of sugar in the early nineteenth century—but I love the characters with an intensity reserved for few people in my real life. I would gladly talk all night about whether Anne Elliot or Captain Wentworth is more to blame for their eight-year estrangement. Come to think of it, I might scratch out Lucy Steele's eyes myself.

But however much Janeites have always treasured her books, it's really the wet shirt that morphed Austen from a much-loved classic into an international phenomenon. The BBC had produced previous adaptations of *Pride and Prejudice,* including a 1980 version with a screenplay by the feminist novelist Fay Weldon, but the new writer, Andrew Davies, set out to emphasize "sex and money and physicality, really, rather than all that buttoned-up-to-the-neck scene-setting," he told a JASNA audience years later. "So I was looking for opportunities to get the characters out of their clothes, to be frank." Midway through the story, Davies invented a scene —unaccountably omitted by Austen herself—in which a hot, tired Darcy rides up to his palatial estate, Pemberley, sheds his constricting jacket and cravat, and dives into a convenient pond. Moments later, a fetchingly damp and disheveled Colin Firth strolled into Janeite history.

The show was a hit both in Britain, where it aired in the fall of 1995, and in the United States, where it was broadcast on the A&E Network in January 1996. Visits to Austen's home at Chawton doubled, from twenty-eight thousand in 1995 to fifty-seven thousand the next year. Three other Jane Austen adaptations—a British TV film of *Persuasion,* starring Amanda Root; a feature film of *Sense and Sensibility,* starring Emma Thompson; and the movie *Clueless,* which updated *Emma* to high school in Beverly Hills — showed in American movie theaters around the same time, and over the next year and a half, as two more versions of *Emma* arrived on the big and small screens, JASNA's membership grew by more than a third, from twenty-five hundred to thirty-five hundred.

Sociological explanations for the explosion of Janeite enthusiasm multiplied as quickly as journalists could write punny headlines ("Jane Addiction," "Austen Powers") or find new ways to finish a *Pride and Prejudice*-inspired lead sentence beginning, "It is a truth universally acknowledged . . ." Perhaps Austen represented a simpler, slower-paced era that appealed to a public exhausted by 24/7 bad news. Or perhaps women longed for romantic courtships conducted by chivalrous men who would fall in love without expecting so much as a kiss in return. Was it the elegance of Austen's language, or the sharp edge of her social satire, or her strong heroines, or her happy endings? Were the inhabitants of Britain's former colonies indulging their latent Anglophilia? Or did everyone just want an excuse to dress up in Empire waists and long gloves? Why Jane Austen?

Curiously, that's a question that may be harder to answer the more you love Jane Austen. Long before the wet-shirt days, Edith Lank heard a version of it every year. Edith had discovered Austen right after World War II, when she was teaching at a small college in Maine and decided to while away the cold New England winter by reading her way through the library, starting with the A's. In later years, she raised three children, worked in her husband's real estate business, and wrote a syndicated real estate column and a series of real estate textbooks. She collected Jane Austen translations in languages from Farsi to Icelandic, and every year, after their annual visit to the JASNA conference, her husband would turn to her and ask, "So, what is it about Jane Austen?" Finally, she gave him the answer that Louis Armstrong had offered when asked to define jazz: "Man, when you got to ask what is it, you'll never get to know."

I read all those mid-'90s articles about the Austen phenomenon, of course (what Janeite could resist a headline like "Jane Spotting"?), but I found all the pat explanations for her popularity deeply unconvincing, or perhaps just beside the point. Partly, it was that none of them seemed adequate to the size and diversity of the phenomenon. Austen is a great writer, but she's not the *only* great writer. Nineteenth-century English literature is filled with vivid characters and exquisite prose, chaste courtships and long gloves, but no one is buying George Eliot tarot cards.

Mostly, though, like Edith Lank quoting Louis Armstrong, I found that none of the explanations seemed to capture the essential. If you asked why I love my husband, I could pile up complimentary adjectives — *smart, funny, kind, supportive* — but all those words would never account for the element of the unexplainable at the heart of any true love. I feel the same way when I'm asked why I love Jane Austen. If you're not a Janeite, nothing could possibly explain this — the dressing up, the repeated viewings of the wet-shirt scene, the endless discussions of the doings of people who are *not real*. If you are a Janeite, it hardly needs explaining. What else could be as fascinating as this? The sociological interpretations may have merit, but they inevitably give us a bird's-eye perspective on Austen-love, a view from the outside. We miss something essential about a consuming passion if we don't look at it from the inside. Sociology can tell us a lot, but it can't tell us what stories can, and every Janeite has a love story as distinctive as that of Elizabeth Bennet or Anne Elliot.

So, with the approval of the Jane Austen tarot cards, nearly thirty-five years after I first became a Janeite, I set out to examine Janeite obsessiveness from the inside, and maybe to figure out along the way what kind of Janeite I was myself. I didn't go looking for a single Big Theory that would make sense of Jane Austen's appeal; I wasn't planning to collect quantifiable data and fashion it into an explanation rigorous enough to satisfy a social scientist. My task was more impressionistic: to explore what Austen obsession looks like and feels like for people who are living with it, and perhaps to tease out some of the common threads that weave this diverse array of individuals into a community. I'd spent enough time immersed in online Austen discussions to know how differently her works could be read by people who all considered themselves Janeites. Were all of us just seeing what we wanted to see, finding ourselves reflected in an Austen-shaped mirror? Or did our divergent interpretations reflect something real about Austen herself?

Although Austen-love is an international phenomenon by now —there are Jane Austen societies in Argentina, Australia, Brazil, Japan, and the Netherlands, as well as in Britain—I focused on North American Janeites, the most numerous branch. I attended JASNA conferences with notebook in hand, interviewed Janeites from more than twenty U.S. states and two Canadian provinces, toured Austen sites in England with a group of fellow Americans, and scoured the Internet for Austen-related blogs. I met the people you'll find in these pages, among them a Canadian speech pathologist who thinks Austen wrote about autism, a Florida lawyer who is pursuing a byzantine theory about hidden subtexts in the novels, a Texan with a closetful of Regency gowns, an academic couple whose first conversation was an argument about *Mansfield Park,* and a writer of Jane Austen fan fiction who found her own Mr. Darcy while reimagining *Pride and Prejudice*. I read dozens of sequels, spinoffs, and updates of Austen's stories, played a rather tedious Austen-themed video game, watched the Mormon movie version of *Pride and Prejudice* and the Tamil and Latina versions of *Sense and Sensibility,* and even scored a rare Jane Austen bobble-head doll.

And then there was The Dress.

PART I

IN
JANE AUSTEN'S
FOOTSTEPS

CHAPTER 1

DRESSING THE PART

THE BOTTOM DRAWERS of Baronda Bradley's dresser are filled to overflowing with kid gloves, ballet slippers, stockings, feathers, lace collars, nineteenth-century coins, smelling salts, period playing cards, drawstring reticules, a vintage sewing kit — all the accessories with which she augments the breathtaking Regency outfits she wears to each year's Annual General Meeting of the Jane Austen Society of North America. A walk-in closet holds her thirty size 6 gowns — the green-and-orange with striped silk overlay, which premiered in Seattle in 2001; the flowered silk brocade day dress, from Los Angeles in 2004; the square-necked, pale-pink georgette with hand-embroidered bodice; the dark red with cutout sleeves and matching long velvet coat; the lace-and-silk confection so daringly low-cut that, at the Vancouver ball in 2007, she armed her friends with a code word ("Shakespeare!") to deploy if they noticed a hint of areola peeking out.

By mid-2011, when I visited Baronda at the ranch house in Fort Worth, Texas, that she shares with three children, two cats, and a large boa constrictor named Honeybun, she had become a near-icon of the JASNA AGM — "Baronda of the two thousand dresses," as she had been dubbed at Milwaukee in 2005. She was hardly the only person to attend the AGM in period attire — many dressed up for the Saturday night ball, and some also wore bonnets or morning dresses to the daytime lectures and discussions — but Baronda took JASNA costuming to a completely different level. In 2004, seven years after her first AGM, she had begun wearing Regency outfits not only throughout every moment of the conference but even en route, from the minute she left home until the minute she returned several days later. Wearing her bonnet onto the airplane was easier than finding space for it in a suitcase, and besides, she liked the stir she caused strolling through the airport in a floor-length, Empire-waist day dress. In her elegant gowns and headdresses, she felt different. "I'm no longer the usual mom, out there playing soccer or being graceless," she says. "I know that as soon as I step out the door, I'm on display, and people are watching." For JASNA conference regulars, anticipating Baronda's new outfit had become part of the familiar yearly ritual.

It hadn't always been this way. Back in 1983, when I attended my first JASNA conference, the Saturday night program featured a sober lecture on *Emma* delivered by a distinguished Jane Austen scholar. No one cleared away the tables after the banquet so we could promenade through English country dances in high-waisted gowns, feathered turbans, and opera-length gloves. Not until the early twenty-first century did a Regency ball, period costumes optional, become a regular feature of JASNA's AGM. But over the years, perhaps influenced by the visions of silk and lace in all those Austen movies, more and more people began dressing the part. Even the men, rare birds at a JASNA AGM, were squiring their be-gowned wives and girlfriends in cutaway coats, knee breeches, and brocade waistcoats. These days, a costume parade through the streets surrounding the conference hotel, with bystanders snapping cell-phone pictures of dressed-up Janeites, often preceded the dancing.

My reaction to these developments could be summed up in a single sentence: *I will not be caught dead wearing a period costume to a Jane Austen ball.*

I have always had a vexed relationship with clothes. I find shopping at best dull, at worst depressing — a recurrent reminder of how far my real-life body diverges from the ideal. I buy off-the-rack separates in dependable solid colors, own as few shoes as possible, and accessorize so rarely that when I had my ears pierced for the first time on my fortieth birthday, my brother dubbed this uncharacteristic fit of eccentricity my "midlife crisis." Playing dress-up in costume is just as unappealing to me. As a child, I never much liked Halloween; the sugar rush couldn't fully redeem the weeks of angst over what to wear. As for the adults who attended the JASNA ball in Regency attire — well, I was quite sure I was Not That Kind of Jane Austen fan. Yes, Baronda looked stunning in her many gowns, but to me dressing up seemed the province of the goofy, nostalgic types who were ready to trade modern life, with its antibiotics and feminism, for some imagined ideal of elegant living.

And yet, one spring day, there I was on eBay, searching for Jane Austen–style Regency gowns. *How did I get here?* I wondered helplessly, as I rejected the "1960s — VELVET — brown — BABYDOLL — Jane AUSTEN — Hippie — Dress," which appeared to be so short that even Elizabeth Bennet's wild sister, Lydia, would have hesitated to wear it in public.

The answer, of course, was research for that book the Jane Austen tarot cards had urged me to write. If I was going to discover what made my fellow Janeites tick, if I was going to experience the Janeite world in all its glorious diversity, I would have to immerse myself in aspects of the fandom that had never appealed to me. Interviewing Baronda of the two thousand dresses wouldn't be enough. I would have to overcome a lifetime of resistance to dress-up and wear a Regency gown to the JASNA ball. And with that ball less than six months away, I couldn't dither much longer.

Baronda Bradley wasn't used to being admired for her appearance. Growing up in a lower-middle-class family in a small town near Fort Worth, she often felt invisible, or out of place. Her parents, who had blended their first names, Ron and Barbara, to create hers, exacted harsh discipline at the end of a belt. "They were very much 'spare the rod, spoil the child' people," Baronda says. Saddled young with adult responsibilities for her two younger brothers and for the children who used her mother's in-home babysitting service, Baronda felt more comfortable with adults than with her peers. She sang, played the piano, excelled in school, and developed consuming interests that she stoked with intensive research. She read everything in the house—her father's car books, her mother's dog books, whatever was stacked on the top shelf of her closet. One summer, she checked out every one of the public library's books on cats. She was the smart girl, and the smart girl doesn't get to be the pretty girl.

With no college-going tradition in her family and no money for tuition, Baronda knew she would have to make her own way. When she earned scholarships that would help pay her costs at the University of Texas, the congregants in the conservative Southern Baptist church her family attended were torn: some feared she would lose her way in the den of iniquity that was Austin, Texas, but others envisioned their bright girl, with her gift for languages, making a wonderful missionary's wife. At college, Baronda studied psychology and French and played percussion in the band. Gradually, she drifted away from the no-drinking, no-dancing, submit-to-your-husband values she had grown up with. And she worked, paying the costs her scholarships didn't cover with earnings from an array of different jobs. Eventually, she was working twenty to thirty hours a week.

It was all too much — the long hours at work, the academic course load, the depression that began to creep over her as she confronted the emotional fallout from her childhood. In more than one course, she squandered good grades when she fell into a funk and skipped the final exam. After three and a half years in college, her GPA was so low that she was on academic probation. Her college boyfriend was already attending medical school, and she decided to drop out, join him in Galveston, and get married. She started therapy and took a job as a 911 dispatcher, sending ambulances and police cars to emergencies and fielding less-than-urgent calls from lonely people who just wanted to talk. Her coworkers were smart and capable, but none of them had aspired to this job; their lives, like hers, had somehow veered off track. "That was what helped me to determine I needed to go back and get my degree, or I'd be around people who were underachievers all my life," Baronda says. She went back to school, finishing with a major in French and minors in psychology and classical civilizations. Reading and writing, she realized, were what she most enjoyed. When her husband's training took them to Indianapolis, Baronda found a diverse, intellectual Methodist church to attend, took a day job with a software company, and began studying for a graduate degree in English at night school. A professor recommended Jane Austen.

Baronda's Jane Austen was a swift, ironical satirist, a writer who could sketch a character in one or two tart, definitive sentences. In *Persuasion,* whose heroine gets the chance to reverse a life-changing, long-regretted decision taken at the behest of a family friend, Baronda found an added resonance, a reflection of her own journey from the constricting world of her childhood to the greater freedom she had begun to find in college. "It's the story of being told one thing and making choices around that, but then being given an opportunity to exercise your own desires," she says. "Kind of like my life."

Despite my eBay frustrations, I figured it couldn't be that hard to find a Regency gown. Jane Austen managed it, and she didn't have the Internet.

The post-Firth upsurge of interest in Austen's life and works has carved a niche for merchants selling everything from reticules to spencers (or, for the uninitiated, from drawstring purses to short buttoned jackets), and on the World Wide Web, every Janeite cottage entrepreneur can find a home and a customer base. Years before there was an Internet, Jennie Chancey was a teenager who started sewing her own clothes because she yearned to look like the title character in the *Anne of Green Gables* miniseries. In college, in the 1990s, her old-fashioned clothes earned her the nickname "the Anne girl," and she launched a small sewing business catering to young women with similar tastes. With the advent of the Internet, she took her company online, named it Sense and Sensibility Patterns, in tribute to the writer she loved, and began selling designs for Regency gowns to women who wanted to make their own. In an Austen-worthy irony, modern technology facilitated a return to a pre-industrial handcrafted aesthetic.

By 2010, Chancey was selling as many as two hundred patterns a week and netting $20,000 to $30,000 a year. Although she sold patterns from other historical periods too, she estimated that 70 to 80 percent of her customers were Regency enthusiasts, many of them planning outfits for Jane Austen festivals or evenings of English country dance. Eventually, Chancey took more than a dozen of her customers on a summer tour of Austen sites in England. On the bus, they watched a movie version of *Persuasion,* pausing the DVD now and then to critique the costuming. "Somehow, putting on the clothing of the time lets you step into somebody else's experience," Chancey says. "And I think that's the experience that Jane Austenites are looking for—how can I step into Jane's period as much as is possible and just feel a little part of what it's like to be in the Regency."

I certainly wasn't going to sew my own gown—reattaching lost buttons is about the extent of my expertise with needle and thread—but the whole Regency costume enterprise was turning out to be much more complicated than I had realized. Finding a gown, I had learned, was only half the battle; with Regency clothing, the big question is what lies beneath. The Regency silhouette features breasts pushed up to an impossible height—"the shelf look," it's called—and held there by a boned corset that laces up the back. Modern underwear that I'd never heard of (the balconette bra? Who knew?) could approximate the look, but only imperfectly. "It is impossible to achieve a historically accurate look without the proper corset or stays for your time period," one costume website lectured. "A proper corset will make the difference between looking like a princess who has stepped out of an historic painting or looking like someone on their way to a modern costume party." Of course, I *was* on my way to a modern costume party, but still, who wouldn't rather look like a princess?

Luckily for me, the Regency corset wasn't meant to achieve a Scarlett O'Hara–style eighteen-inch waist—that look became fashionable later in the nineteenth century—but it was still hard to imagine actually wearing this bizarre and probably uncomfortable undergarment, especially since I didn't employ a lady's maid who could help me into it on the night of the ball. I imagined wandering half-dressed through the halls of the conference hotel, looking for a sympathetic Janeite to lace me up before the clock struck midnight and my coach turned back into a pumpkin. Were there period-correct alternatives? Several costumers told me about so-called short stays, which resemble a sports bra and were rumored to be fairly comfortable. But when I investigated further, I learned that short stays were recommended for the young and slender, a category that most definitely did not include me. Rebecca Morrison-Peck, a Janeite costumer from Vancouver, Washington, mentioned the boned-bodice petticoat, a historically accurate undergarment that you could, just barely, put on by yourself. "It's buttoned at the top of the back very, very tightly, and you can pull it around and button it in the front and then swing it round and squeeze your arms in the very tight little straps," Morrison-Peck said. "I've done it, and it's like a monkey with a deck chair. It's not a pretty sight."

All right, I told myself. *The corset is out. The balconette bra is in.*

But after a few dispiriting hours scrolling through websites I had never imagined visiting (Frederick's of Hollywood?), looking at come-hither pictures of models in low-cut satin push-up bras, I was depressed and dissatisfied. All these conversations with costumers; all these hours spent at websites with names like Austentation, window-shopping through pictures of seed-pearl hair combs and cameo brooches; all this talk of stepping into the Regency experience: it had done something to me. *If I'm going to do this, I might as well do it right,* I found myself thinking. The corset was back in.

In fact, I realized, I was becoming slightly obsessed with corsets. I seemed to be working them into every conversation. At lunch one day, I told my husband about how proper Regency evening-wear called for breasts elevated practically to chin level and necklines low enough to display show-stopping quantities of cleavage.

His sudden enthusiasm for the corset project was startling. "What about stockings?" he asked. "You know I'm a stickler for historical accuracy."

Historical accuracy, I was learning, doesn't come cheap. Whereas even custom-made Regency gowns could be had for perhaps $150, made-to-measure corsets ran $200 or more. And which company should I order from? One website seemed on the less expensive side, but could I bear to patronize a merchant who spelled Jane Austen's last name with an "i"? I could splurge on a $375 corset, but that site featured a testimonial from Madonna's stylist, which seemed way out of my league. I wasn't planning to wear *just* the corset, after all.

With five months to go until the ball, I had to make up my mind. Until I had the underwear, I couldn't get the gown, since achieving the Regency shelf look would change my measurements. One day in May, I took a deep breath and ordered the "1815 corset" from an online company called the Very Merry Seamstress. It cost $260, plus another $20 for the shipping. I hadn't spent this much on a dress since my wedding, and this wasn't even the dress.

In October 1997, Baronda Bradley was a graduate student in English who needed academic credentials to fatten her résumé. She prepared a presentation on Jane Austen and the British landscape painter J.M.W. Turner and headed off to JASNA's AGM in San Francisco. She'd heard that people sometimes dressed in costume, so she rented a beige satin gown for the ball and spent the evening dancing with an acquaintance. Neither of them knew much about English country dancing; they would barely master the steps for one dance before it was time to start another. That weekend, Baronda noticed a couple who dressed up throughout the conference, in both day- and eveningwear. "I thought it was elegant and graceful, and I admired that there were these people who didn't care that they were doing something different, because I was already of that mindset anyway," she says. "And so I just thought, 'Well, that looks kind of fun. Maybe next year I'll have a couple of pieces.'"

But it would be four years before she went to another AGM. In the interim, she and her husband moved back to Fort Worth and had two sons. Baronda worked for a while, stayed home with her kids for a while, and went back to school, thinking she might pursue a doctorate in English.

When she finally had time for another JASNA conference, she turned to the Internet, finding a seamstress in Colorado who produced three new dresses for the 2001 Seattle AGM: a red-and-white day dress with a matching spencer, an ice-blue satin afternoon gown, and an elegant green silk. Slender and well-proportioned, with long blond hair that held a curl, Baronda looked every inch the Regency belle, and she drew compliments wherever she went. After a lifetime as the smart girl, she was suddenly the beautiful girl. "It was like I was Cinderella," she says. "It was like I was the homecoming queen, and they had me leading the ball." The next year, she decided, she would have to wear something even more spectacular.

Gradually, preparing for the upcoming AGM became a year-round project. Baronda acquired a shelf of books with titles like *Let There Be Clothes: 40,000 Years of Fashion* and *Support and Seduction: A History of Corsets and Bras.* She trolled resale stores and eBay, looking for vintage accessories and period-appropriate dancing shoes. She took classes on hat making and antique-lace restoration, commissioned at least one new Regency dress a year from her devoted seamstress, spent several hundred dollars annually on costumes and accessories, and kept careful track of which outfits she

had worn to which AGMs, rotating older gowns on a predeter-
mined schedule. She perfected useful tricks for ensuring that her
wardrobe arrived intact at each new host city, swathing easily wrin-
kled dresses in dry-cleaning bags and packing fragile feathers in the
lightweight tins that shortbread cookies come in.

She began to see each year's outfits as both performance and
research project, and though she wasn't as exacting as some devotees of historical costume — she was willing to compromise on a
polyester that looked like silk, to avoid the hassle of caring for the
real thing — she carefully considered each decision. "I want to be
thorough, and I want the choices I make to be choices, not just
things I do because I don't know any better," she says. As she reread Austen's novels and letters, she watched for details about hats
and dresses. To add authenticity to her performance, she filled the
drawstring reticules she carried during the conference with period
coins and playing cards, and she tried to avoid using her cell phone
in public because the modern technology would shatter the illusion
she was trying to create. She felt a responsibility to the people she
knew were looking for her each year.

Her husband never accompanied her to a JASNA AGM. For Baronda, dressing up for JASNA had become a mode of self-expres-
sion, a way to feel admired, valued, and beautiful after a lifetime
of feeling quite otherwise. But her husband saw JASNA gatherings
as the literary equivalent of *Star Trek* conventions filled with geeks
in pointy Spock ears. "I wanted him to see how respected I was. I
wanted him to experience that," Baronda says. "He never did."

Back home in Texas, a research project on the disheartening job
market for English Ph.D.'s persuaded Baronda to reconsider her career path. "I just didn't feel that strongly about literary criticism,"
she says. "It was just somebody else's opinion, and then they try
to find things where they back it up and ignore other things, and

killing a lot of trees." She switched to a business degree. By then, she had three children under the age of seven, and her days became grueling rounds of classes, child care, and late-night studying, all on five hours of sleep. Her marriage, which had been difficult for years, was falling apart, and by the time she got her MBA, she and her husband had separated. Baronda took a job in logistics for a yogurt company and began dating a city planner named Eric, whom she had met on the Internet. In 2009, they had been together less than a year when the Philadelphia AGM rolled around. Eric came along and gamely joined in the dancing, wearing rented knee breeches and a cutaway coat. Baronda, who graced the ball in a breathtaking red-and-gold dress modeled on an Indian sari — in tribute to Jane Austen's Aunt Philadelphia, who had traveled to India in search of a husband — spent the conference teasingly introducing Eric as her "accessory."

When I visited in mid-2011, Baronda was hard at work on the upcoming AGM, which was to be held right there in Fort Worth. She was organizing the ball and planning her talk on creating a Regency wardrobe: "Managing Muslins in the Modern Millennium." (When the title was announced, one clueless JASNA member contacted conference organizers to express outrage at their anti-Islamic bias. Managing Muslims? How bigoted could you get?) With her fortieth birthday a few years behind her, Baronda was beginning to wonder how much longer she could keep up her costume obsession. Soon she would be too old to wear the cleavage-baring gowns appropriate for young women of the Regency. But for her hometown AGM, she was planning to have some fun. Attendees could sign up for a Friday night jaunt to a honky-tonk with a mechanical bull, and Baronda was going to attend in pink cowboy boots and an Empire-waist gown made of denim.

Her JASNA work, I suspected, was providing a useful distraction from the grimmer realities of her life. Three months earlier, in the midst of the economic downturn, the yogurt company had laid her off. Baronda insisted that the layoff had come as a relief, an escape from an increasingly unsatisfactory job. She had spent her downtime tending her garden, and she had a promising lead on a new position. Still, from time to time I thought I heard a note of insecurity jangling under the tireless hum of her hard-won self-confidence. "I have a good network. I'll find something," she said. "I always land on my feet." As we said goodbye, promising to meet again at the AGM, I wondered if she was trying to convince herself.

My adventures in corsetry were behind me; the next order of business was buying a dress. (Just *one* dress, thank you; I was no Baronda.) My abortive investigations on eBay had made clear that buying an off-the-rack Regency gown would be problematic; some of the pictures looked pretty enough, but I had little idea of which size I would wear once I put on the corset. Buying a made-to-measure gown seemed like a better approach, and from a JASNA e-mail, I had learned of Maureen O'Connor, who lived in nearby New York City and had volunteered to sew $150 gowns for JASNA members and donate her profits to the 2012 AGM, which was to be held in Brooklyn. I could buy a ball gown and feel philanthropic, all at the same time!

Maureen, it turned out, was a retired Goldman Sachs vice president who had begun sewing at eighteen, when she graduated from high school, went to work as a secretary, and needed something affordable to wear besides her Catholic school uniforms. She had sewed everything from a goddaughter's christening gown to a niece's Marie Antoinette–style wedding dress, as well as Halloween costumes running the considerable gamut from Catwoman to Cleopatra. Regency gowns were a recent addition to her repertoire, however. Maureen's husband of nearly forty years was dying of a rare blood cancer when she read Laurie Viera Rigler's time-travel novels about a Regency woman who switches bodies, and centuries, with a contemporary Californian. Rigler's author biography mentioned JASNA, and Maureen, who had read *Pride and Prejudice* in high school, joined the local chapter and volunteered to use her sewing skills to raise money for the AGM. Eventually, she read most of Austen's other novels too, but it seemed to me that the books hadn't really been the point. "Over the last sixteen months, it's been a great diversion," Maureen said, when we finally spoke in late June 2011, three and a half months before the JASNA ball and seven weeks after her husband's death. "All that we went through, and have been going through — a godsend, really."

We spoke about fabrics, colors, and styles — *I am conferring with my dressmaker!* I thought in amazement — and Maureen e-mailed me pictures of patterns she might use. I was drawn to one in particular, an elegant gown with puffed sleeves, worn with a sleeveless overdress that cinched under the bust. Briefly, I imagined myself in this outfit, perhaps looking a bit like a brunette version of Gwyneth Paltrow in the Miramax *Emma*. Then I reminded myself that I was seven years older, five inches shorter, and God knows how many pounds heavier than Gwyneth Paltrow. But this was the gown I wanted.

The two-dresses-in-one outfit would take far more work and cost an extra $100, Maureen cautioned me. But the Regency-dress-up Janeite aliens had long since eaten my brain, so I accepted the price without a moment's hesitation. Hey, I was going to a ball!

Two weeks later, a package arrived from the Very Merry Seamstress. Out came a peculiar girdle-thing with ribbons that tied on top of the shoulders and a back panel that laced up like a giant tennis shoe. My husband laced me up, and I instantly felt a posture-enhancing back support that pulled my spine up straight, just the way the ballet teacher had demanded when I was five. Clearly, it wouldn't be physically possible to slouch in this garment. But would the corset provide enough support without those reliable elasticized bra straps and accompanying underwire? A prickle of panic. Falling out of the dress in the middle of the JASNA ball would be very embarrassing.

I packed the corset away at the top of my closet. I had no time to worry because I was about to take the next step on my Janeite journey. I was leaving for a tour of Jane Austen's England.

CHAPTER 2

WALKING WHERE
JANE WALKED

I ALWAYS MEANT TO GO back to Chawton cottage, but somehow I never did. Maybe a part of me feared dispelling the enchantment that still clung to my memories of that first visit to Jane Austen's house, when I was sixteen and living most of my life in books. But if the demands of Janeite research were enough to get me into a corset, they could surely overcome any unconscious resistance to a fabulous English vacation doubling as a tax-deductible business expense. One spring day, I charged a frighteningly large sum to my credit card, and voilà — I had officially joined the Jane Austen Society of North America's upcoming summer tour of Jane Austen's England, the ninth in fifteen years.

Today, Jane Austen is public property, her abortive romances dramatized on screen, her personal correspondence available in bookstores. But in her own time, she lived a low-key, essentially private life. The daughter of an Anglican clergyman, she never married or bore children — her most important relationship was with her only sister, Cassandra — and she never traveled more than a couple of hundred miles from her birthplace in the English countryside. She published anonymously, as "A Lady," perhaps to avoid the notoriety that might attach to someone, especially a woman, working in the then-disparaged genre of the novel. Although her books sold fairly well in her lifetime, and some prominent contemporaries admired her work, she was never a literary celebrity, lionized at London dinner parties or courted by patrons of the arts. The obsessive love and extravagant commercialization that, in our time, have made her an international phenomenon — a brand name worth building a tour around — find no echoes in her own era.

That's not to say that her life was easy, untroubled, or devoid of incident. A cousin's husband was guillotined during the French Revolution, and for much of Austen's life England was at war with Napoleon's France. Two of her six brothers joined the British navy and spent years abroad on dangerous, uncertain voyages; during her lifetime, childbirth killed two of her sisters-in-law. She grieved the deaths of a dear friend and a beloved father, rejected a marriage proposal from a wealthy man she didn't love, endured professional setbacks, and worried about money. She was never destitute or abandoned, but she knew what it was to struggle. And she died young, snuffed out at forty-one by a still-mysterious illness.

Nevertheless, it's more than a little incongruous that such a short, unglamorous life should have brought a group of strangers together this morning in the lobby of an airport hotel. Jet-lagged but excited, we are preparing to embark on our ten-day, JASNA-sponsored Austen tour. Outwardly, the thirty-two of us are a homogeneous lot: all white, all American, most female, most middle-aged. Many of us are professionals, active or retired — three schoolteachers, three librarians, two accountants, two college professors, even a Freudian psychoanalyst. Our oldest member is an intrepid eighty-six-year-old who, a year earlier, trekked to Rwanda to see mountain gorillas; our youngest member is her seventeen-year-old grand-daughter, who packed nine pairs of shoes for this trip and has never read a word of Austen.

She's not the only fish out of water. Four men are loyally escorting their Janeite partners. One of them is Ernie Torok, a Vietnam veteran from Kansas who worked for the Department of Defense after leaving the army and still sports the military-style haircut to prove it. His wife, Dolores, made him read *Sense and Sensibility* in preparation for our trip, which commemorates the novel's publication two hundred years earlier. Behind his hand, he confides to me his heretical reaction to Austen's first great masterpiece: "Will it never end?"

The rest of us vary in our level of Janeite obsessiveness. Roxanne Milton, fifty-six, a golden-haired, unfailingly sunny Texan who works as a rehabilitation counselor, read so many nineteenth-century novels as a teenager that she sometimes talked like one. She still has those hand-me-down paperbacks. "One of the most exciting moments of my life was reading the scene where Darcy proposes to Elizabeth," she says.

Debra Call, a fiftyish high school English teacher from New Mexico with chin-length brown hair, is writing a graduate thesis on *Northanger Abbey* and listens, bemused, to conversations that seem to blur the line between fiction and reality. ("People were talking about Jane Austen's characters like they were people," she will say to me in exasperation one day. "I wanted to say, 'These are characters in books!'") But even she has her moments, it seems. One of her students watched her gazing at the screen during a classroom showing of the Firth *Pride and Prejudice* and said, "Ms. Call, you're just waiting for someone like Darcy, aren't you?"

Sue Forgue, an accountant from Chicago, has spent untold hours compiling an online encyclopedia of Regency culture where devotees can find everything from period fashion plates to maps of the places mentioned in Austen's novels. She launched the site to help the writers of Austen spinoff fiction find accurate information about the Regency and avoid the elementary factual errors that often cropped up in their stories — stories in which, for example, characters with no mode of transportation speedier than a horse-drawn carriage traveled from the Bennet home in Hertfordshire to the Darcy mansion in Derbyshire, a distance of perhaps 138 miles, in an afternoon. "You can barely do that today, with superhighways and fast cars," Forgue will tell me later. "There's no way you can do that in a carriage."

Debbie McNeil — whose round face, sweetly tentative smile, and fringe of bangs suggest a dark-haired Raggedy Ann doll — is the kind of Janeite you would expect to meet on a trip like this. Debbie McNeil keeps bars of Elizabeth and Darcy soap in her guest bathroom. In 2010, she drove six hours from her home in northern California to watch Colin Firth accept an acting award, waiting in a crowd of other fans for the chance to shake his hand. When the Morgan Library & Museum staged a major exhibition of Jane Austen letters and manuscripts, she flew to New York City for the occasion and spent a full day and more in the museum, puzzling out each line of Austen's small, neat handwriting, even though every letter is easily available in print. "I wanted to read it like I was the recipient of that letter," she says, to experience "what it was like to get a letter from Jane." As she read, she noted especially striking phrases in her journal, the one with a *Mansfield Park* quote on the cover.

Debbie McNeil's Janeite journey, I will learn, is most remarkable for the speed with which she progressed from ignorance to all-consuming enthusiasm. Just six years before she and her wryly tolerant husband, Skip, joined JASNA's 2011 trip, Debbie had barely heard of Jane Austen. Debbie was a middle-aged wife and mother who had spent nineteen years at home with her sons, chauffeuring them to their activities and volunteering at their schools, the kind of person who read magazines and newspapers but only occasionally picked up a book. At the movies, Debbie saw a trailer for a soon-to-open new film starring the British actress Keira Knightley and decided she should read the novel on which it was based—*Pride and Prejudice.*

That summer, the family vacationed on Catalina Island, and Debbie brought *Pride and Prejudice* along. Her fiftieth birthday was a day or two away, and she was in a reflective mood, mulling over her half-century of life and wondering how to make herself a better person, a better friend, wife, and mother, in the years ahead. Her two sons were nearly grown, and she was studying accounting at the local junior college, preparing to take on new responsibilities in the family's thriving insurance business. As their happy marriage entered a new chapter, she and Skip were talking about how to recommit themselves to their relationship.

She was at a crossroads in her life; perhaps, unconsciously, she was looking for something new to fill the space that motherhood had occupied. In any event, Debbie fell suddenly, passionately in love with Jane Austen. She devoured *Pride and Prejudice,* reading with a flashlight under the covers to avoid waking her sleeping family. "She is so modern," she whispered to herself, marveling at Elizabeth Bennet's courage and independence.

"I read it, not being a great reader. I read it in four days, and it was not modern English," Debbie says. "I couldn't put it down."

And then, suddenly, the book was over, and Debbie was bereft. She hadn't wanted the story to end. She wanted to know how Darcy and Elizabeth would navigate their married life.

Back home, Debbie mentioned her new discovery to a friend, who promptly lent her the Colin Firth film. Debbie had missed the whole wet-shirt moment a decade earlier, but she quickly made up for lost time, renting Firth's other movies and trolling fan sites for information. "I don't want to use the word 'obsession.' I just was interested," she says. "'Obsession' sounds really weird." (Skip, laconic and relaxed, was unfazed by his wife's new — um — interest. "If Colin starts calling, then I might worry about it," he says.)

Surprised by her own sudden intensity, Debbie threw herself into her passion for Austen. She read and reread all the novels, bought Austen biographies and books about life in Regency England, and devoured the *Pride and Prejudice*-inspired fan fiction she found online. She bought a lifetime membership in JASNA and attended her first Annual General Meeting, in Chicago, in 2008. At the welcome desk, she saw a young woman in head-to-foot Regency garb, complete with a muff, registering for the conference. (Naturally, this turned out to be Baronda Bradley.) "Checking in! It wasn't the ball!" Debbie says. "I thought, 'OK, these guys are hardcore.'"

But Debbie was becoming pretty hardcore herself. By 2011, her collection of Austen-related books and pamphlets had ballooned to four hundred items. She stored her favorite unpublished fan fiction — 140 stories, whittled down from more than 200 — in twenty-five loose-leaf binders, which she kept in a closet. She owned three limited-edition Austen-inspired Madame Alexander dolls, a dozen original Regency fashion plates, and nearly nine years' worth of copies of *Jane Austen's Regency World*, the official magazine of the Jane Austen Centre in Bath, England. For $900, Skip had even bought her a first edition of *Camilla*, a novel by Austen's much-admired older contemporary Fanny Burney, because the list of sub-scribers included "Miss J. Austen, Steventon" — the first time Austen's name appeared in print.

Fittingly, Steventon — the rural village in the southern English county of Hampshire where Austen was born on December 16, 1775 — is the first stop on our JASNA tour. As our bus drives through impossibly green fields sliced by hedgerows and spangled with wildflowers, our British guide, Anthea Bryant, serves up tidbits about English traffic, thatched roofs, and the history of umbrellas, in fluting, rounded tones. Steventon has its challenges for the Janeite pilgrim: Austen's family home was razed in the nineteenth century, none of her possessions are on display in the village, and her grave is located somewhere else entirely. Still, this is the place where, at age eleven or twelve, Austen first became a writer, beginning with comic vignettes mocking the literary conventions of her day and then moving on to increasingly sophisticated novellas and epistolary novels. And as we negotiate lanes so narrow that branches brush the bus windows and, after a short walk down an unpaved path, stand in the small whitewashed medieval church where Austen's father served as rector, we begin to grasp how deep was the rural isolation that shaped the first twenty-five years of her life. Steventon today has a population of two hundred, the retired rector tells us, and in Austen's time it was probably no larger. The Austen connection furnishes Steventon with its sole tourist attraction, and outside, a few volunteers are selling key chains and postcards from a table set up for our visit. Amid the moss- and lichen-covered tombstones in the churchyard, no sounds but our own pierce the silence.

Back on the bus, we compare notes about our walk down the church lane, which Jane Austen herself must have known well.

"We walked in the same place she walked," Sonya Samuels, a red-haired retired accountant from Los Angeles, says contentedly.

"The only thing I wished was that it had been muddy, and I had been wearing my dress," says Debra Call, the high school teacher from New Mexico. "Then I could pretend like Darcy was down at the bottom of the lane."

"Six inches deep in mud!" chimes in a voice — or perhaps several voices. Nobody in this crowd needs to be reminded that such is the condition of Elizabeth Bennet's petticoat after a vigorous country walk early in *Pride and Prejudice*.

We are spending the night in Winchester, the ancient cathedral city where the ailing Jane Austen passed her last months in rented rooms, searching in vain for medical care that could save her life. At dinner, the talk turns to the relative merits of various Darcys — Colin Firth is our favorite, but Laurence Olivier has his backers — and to sex in Jane Austen's novels (offstage, implicit) and in Jane Austen fan fiction (plentiful, explicit). "The most erotic moment in *Pride and Prejudice* is when Darcy says, 'Dearest, loveliest Elizabeth,'" says Sue Forgue, the proprietor of the Regency Encyclopedia website. "That's cold-shower time."

In the evening, we hurry to the cathedral to hear a men's choir sing the compline service by candlelight. Afterward, we are introduced to the cathedral's dean, who seems mildly disappointed that none of us have come in Regency costume. If only Baronda was here.

The next day, as Anthea Bryant discusses brick making in Roman and Anglo-Saxon times, we drive through fields studded with cows, heading for Ibthorpe House, where the young Austen sometimes stayed with her close friend Martha Lloyd. The house's present owners, who generously open their home to visiting Janeites, seem drawn from a Central Casting version of Brits-as-Americans-imagine-them: their surname is ffrench Blake, the husband used to work for Prince Charles, and they attended both Princess Diana's funeral and Prince William's wedding. The house is exquisitely tasteful but unpretentious, with clocks, candlesticks, family pictures, and signed photos of the royal family mingling on tables and mantels. Sabina ffrench Blake, a blond in flowery pastels, takes us to the eggshell-blue guest bedroom on the second floor, where Jane Austen slept when she visited. "It's just lovely to think that when she was here, she was happy: writing, having a great social life," ffrench Blake says. "All her life ahead of her, or so she thought."

Back on the bus, Elizabeth Richmond and Joann Graham, retirees who met on last year's tour, are discussing the likely futures of the married couples in Jane Austen's novels. Liz thinks that Anne Elliot, the heroine of *Persuasion,* will be happy in her marriage to the dashing naval captain Frederick Wentworth.

"But her husband's going to be away so much," says Martha-Grace Duncan, a writer and law professor from Georgia who has just bought a silhouette of Austen to hang above her desk, for inspiration.

Liz: "I wonder about Edmund and Fanny."

Martha-Grace: "I still wonder about Anne Elliot, because it's so dark."

Joann: "What about Wickham and Lydia?"

Liz: "I really hate Wickham!"

And Liz and Joann settle in, trading favorite examples of the atrocious behavior of *Pride and Prejudice*'s thoughtless Lydia Bennet, their voices and laughter overlapping merrily: "Showing her ring!" "And she didn't even seem to care!"

· · ·

It is raining as we pass Stonehenge. We are traveling to Bath, but on the way we stop at Lacock, a perfectly preserved medieval village in Wiltshire, where the 1995 *Pride and Prejudice* and the 1996 *Emma* were filmed, along with a seemingly endless number of other period adaptations of works by the likes of Hardy, Defoe, and Elizabeth Gaskell. Lacock is a peculiar Potemkin Village sort of place, whose residents rent their quaint homes of wood and stone from Britain's historic-preservation charity, the National Trust, which in turn rents out the public spaces to film crews trying to avoid such bothersome anachronisms as modern street signs and television aerials. If it was up to me, I've already decided, I would skip Lacock in exchange for a few more hours in Bath, a premier tourist destination in both Austen's time and our own.

But on further reflection, perhaps it's appropriate that our tour should stop here; our itinerary, which includes places where Austen lived, places she mentioned in her novels, and places used in filmed adaptations of her work, is a similar mélange of the real and the fictional, the historical and the invented. As we near the town, JASNA's president, Iris Lutz, a technology marketer from Arizona, reads off a list of Austen-adaptation-related locations we may want to seek out: the Red Lion, the Carpenter's Arms, the white cottage with the blue door . . .

I decide to skip the ersatz Austen and instead go off to see Lacock Abbey. I figure my kids might like a picture of the cloisters, which stood in for Hogwarts in a Harry Potter movie.

That afternoon, we are touring Bath, where Austen's father retired in 1801, taking along his wife and their two unmarried daughters. Despite her early promise, Austen had published nothing by the time she moved here, at age twenty-five. One publisher rejected an early version of *Pride and Prejudice,* sight unseen, when Austen's father wrote to offer it; another — in the episode that, more than two centuries later, would so anger the New Jersey Janeite Mary Previte — agreed to publish the book that would eventually become *Northanger Abbey,* only to sit on the manuscript for thirteen years, until Austen finally mustered the funds to buy it back. As we wander through elegant crescents lined with beautifully preserved Georgian houses of honey-colored stone, our tour guide tells the grim story of the Austen women's inexorable descent: from the respectable lodgings they rented on first arriving in the city to the damp, unpleasant places they were forced into after 1805, when Austen's father died, money ran low, and his survivors could barely make ends meet on old legacies and contributions from the Austen sons. According to Janeite conventional wisdom, Jane Austen disliked bright, noisy Bath — she wrote very little while she lived here — but our tour guide takes a more benign view.

"I think she did enjoy Bath, but it wasn't her favorite place, because she was a country girl," the guide says. "I'm really happy she came to Bath, because we can cash in."

Cashing in on Austen is a citywide sport, it appears. Out shopping, my tour-mate Sonya Samuels stumbles across some surprising news: for about $25 a head, Mr. Darcy will host your bachelorette party. The package includes champagne, chocolate, strawberries — and a glass-blowing demonstration.

Mr. Darcy, it turns out, is a glass blower.

"They do have to pay extra for me to have a bucket of water thrown over me, to have the wet-shirt experience," jokes Mr. Darcy, aka Adrian Dolan, when I reach him by phone as he is starch-ironing the shirt and collar he wears when entertaining British brides-to-be.

Dolan is a fifty-three-year-old retired teacher who sells handmade glass bowls, jewelry, and sculptures out of the shop he owns with his wife, in the center of Bath. But on Saturday afternoons, he puts on a royal-blue tailcoat, knee-high boots, and a cravat to make some extra cash presiding over what the British call "hen parties." Guests have been known to wear bonnets.

Glass blowing in full Regency regalia is hot and sweaty work, and at one hen party early in his career as Darcy, Dolan began unwinding his cravat to get some air. The bride-to-be looked daggers at the friend who had organized the occasion, and Dolan suddenly realized why: *She thinks I'm a stripper.* Quickly, he reassured his audience that *only* the cravat was coming off. "Darcy doesn't get involved in any shenanigans on that front," he tells me.

Dolan isn't the only entrepreneur who has capitalized on Bath's Austen connections in the wake of Firth-driven Austenmania. The Jane Austen Centre (motto: "Celebrating Bath's most famous resident") opened in 1999, and after some financially rocky years, it now attracts sixty thousand visitors annually to its mix of historical exhibits, movie tie-ins, and Austen family lore, all presided over by staff in Regency costumes. The Jane Austen Festival, which the Centre launched in 2000 and which Mary and Alice Previte so enjoyed nine years later, draws hundreds of people from around the world for more than a week of costumed balls, historical lectures, and dramatic performances.

The Centre's founder, David Baldock, was the principal of a school for troubled teenagers when he realized that Bath had an empty Austen niche he could fill. At the time, he had read no Austen; apparently, actual acquaintance with her works is not a prerequisite for Austen-related entrepreneurship in Britain any more than in America. He has read her books by now, of course. "Once I started, I thought I had to," he explains. "Because I was dealing with people that immediately assumed that I had this extensive knowledge, so I needed to acquire some."

On the door to the Centre's ladies' room hangs a painting of "Elizabeth Bennet"—a painting bearing a striking resemblance to the actress Jennifer Ehle, who played the role in the famed 1995 BBC *Pride and Prejudice*. Mounted on the door to the men's room, of course, is the smoldering visage of a Firth-like "Mr. Darcy." Another Firth-as-Darcy image hangs inside the ladies' room, the intense dark eyes regarding you gravely as you wash your hands. Overcome by curiosity, Sonya Samuels and I peek into the men's room, but the wall is bare. No Ehle-as-Elizabeth supervises the hand-washing there.

On the doorstep of the Jane Austen Centre, next to a bonneted mannequin named Lizzie, twenty-five-year-old Howard Whiteside greets visitors. Whiteside majored in performing arts, but his acting career seems to be on hold; two days a week he stands on the Centre's doorstep, wearing a brocade waistcoat, a top hat, and a navy-blue cutaway coat with brass buttons. From time to time, he tells me, passing teenage boys shout insults that Whiteside won't repeat— "You do have to have quite a tough hide" —but the women are kinder. Although he says he's "not a massive fan," he has read and enjoyed four of Austen's novels. *Pride and Prejudice and Zombies*—now, that one he does recommend. He breaks off our conversation as a young Asian woman in shorts pauses to take her picture with him.

After our visit to the Jane Austen Centre, the tour members scatter, some to track down the many addresses where Jane Austen lived during her Bath years, others to visit the city's historic sites. I have a different agenda. Armed with a tourist map, I find my way to Union Street, where Anne Elliot and Captain Wentworth reunite—yes, Jane Austen certainly had that pun in mind

—in the closing pages of *Persuasion*. "Soon words enough had passed between them to decide their direction towards the comparatively quiet and retired gravel-walk," Austen tells us, and I bend my steps in the same direction, toward a tree-lined path off one of Bath's most famous Georgian crescents. "There, as they slowly paced the gradual ascent, heedless of every group around them . . ." As I walk along, reading the words I know so well, brushing raindrops off my Kindle, the path ascends gradually under my feet too.

I wish fewer people liked Jane Austen, I think crossly, as I thread my way among the other tourists crowding the low-ceilinged rooms of Chawton cottage, now officially known as Jane Austen's House Museum.

Nearly thirty years after my first visit, Chawton remains a key stop for the Janeite pilgrim, the place where Austen, her mother, and her sister finally settled in 1809, after a precarious four years living at those increasingly downmarket addresses in Bath and sharing a house in Southampton with one brother's family. The cottage back home in rural Hampshire, not far from much-loved Steventon, belonged to the estate of the Austens' third-oldest son, Edward, who had been adopted by rich cousins and would eventually take their surname, Knight. During the extraordinarily productive eight years Austen spent here, she finally began publishing her work — revising earlier versions of *Sense and Sensibility* and *Pride and Prejudice,* writing *Mansfield Park* and *Emma,* and leaving behind manuscripts of *Northanger Abbey* and *Persuasion,* both of which her family published months after her death.

In the rose-tinted memories of my first Chawton visit, I wander around virtually alone, free to read the exhibit cards and soak up the atmosphere in the house that birthed so many works of

genius. But today the cottage seems crowded, even though its attendance figure of roughly thirty-eight thousand visitors a year is well
below the peak reached during the first flush of mid-1990s Austenmania. Every Janeite wants to see the few remaining relics of our
saint: the lock of hair ("faded from its original auburn brown"); the
topaz cross that her sailor brother Charles bought her on one of his
voyages; the impossibly small pedestal table, more lamp stand than
desk, on which Austen wrote her books. Amid these genuine articles are items whose connection to Austen is more questionable:
a period piano that "may be similar" to the one Austen owned, a
bonnet with green ribbons that Kate Winslet wore when she played
Marianne Dashwood in the 1995 film of *Sense and Sensibility*. The
gift shop offers more evidence of Austen's continued standing as
an international profit center. Alongside handsome editions of the
novels, Jane Austen tea towels, aprons, tote bags, calendars, and
thimbles crowd the shelves, and the face of Firth/Darcy smolders
alluringly from mugs, coasters, key chains, fridge magnets, and
notepads. The Chawton gift shop seems to crystallize the tensions
implicit in the whole project of our tour, which at times seems like a
wrestling match between the real Austen and her fabricated every-
thing-for-sale brand.

Still, if Chawton hasn't quite lived up to my teenage memories
—you can never go home again, even when it's someone else's
home you're going to—the drawbacks of popularity and commercialization can't entirely eclipse the magic of this place, of the
work that was created here and the love it still inspires. Bolted to
the house front is a plaque erected in the early twentieth century
by British and American admirers. JANE AUSTEN LIVED HERE
FROM 1809–1817 AND HENCE ALL HER WORKS WERE
SENT INTO THE WORLD, read the engraved words. SUCH ART

AS HERS CAN NEVER GROW OLD. I feel an unexpected lump rise in my throat.

"I'm not sure how I feel about this putting flowers on Jane Austen's grave," says Beverly Francis, a sixty-one-year-old New Jersey school librarian who wears her graying waist-length hair in a bun and moonlights as a well-known country-dance caller. "But I'll do it. I'm a team player."

It is morning in Winchester, and we are walking from our hotel to the cathedral, under whose stone floor Jane Austen was buried soon after her death on July 18, 1817. How the little-known daughter of a country clergyman won the right to lie for all eternity in one of England's grandest sacred spaces is a small mystery; one plausible theory suggests that her brilliant, charming brother Henry, whose peregrination through a variety of careers finally landed him in the church, pulled strings with fellow clergymen. Since the first JASNA tour in 1997, every group has visited Winchester, and today we too gather around the flat black gravestone, whose engraved epitaph praises Austen's sweet temper and Christian faith but says nothing about her accomplishments as a writer. Unlike Beverly, I've been looking forward to this moment, which surely will encapsulate everything good about Janeites — our deep love for our author, our respect for her accomplishments, our sense of quasi-spiritual kinship with her.

A white-haired Anglican priest in a floor-length black cassock leads a short ceremony. "It's amazing what films and other things have done to bring her to the public attention," he says. "And some of the films extremely good, I think." He offers a brief prayer of thanksgiving for Austen's life and works and then leads us in the Lord's Prayer. We each take a thornless pink rose from JASNA president Iris Lutz and place it in a vase on the wall nearby. I want to be moved—I *expect* to be moved!—but once again, it's too crowded for reflection. "This is a club?" asks a passing American tourist in a leopard-print coat. "Or what are you guys?"

Outside, rain pours down, but Beverly and I are determined to see the house where Jane Austen died in her sister Cassandra's arms. By the time we arrive at the three-story yellow building at 8 College Street, my map is a sodden lump. A plaque over the door notes the significance of the spot, but Janeite pilgrims cannot enter —although, apparently, many have tried. In the corner of one window, an index card hand-printed in blue ink states tartly, "This is a private house and not open to the public."

A few hours later, we are back at Chawton—not the cottage, this time, but Chawton House, the stately home just down the road, where Austen's wealthy brother Edward sometimes lived and where the British Jane Austen Society is holding its annual meeting under a white tent on the grounds. The JAS was founded during World War II to acquire and restore Chawton cottage, which had been divided into laborers' flats nearly a century earlier, long before Austen seemed like the kind of writer whose home deserved museum status.

Her posthumous reputation grew slowly. After her death, her novels fell out of print for a few years, but they were republished in the 1830s and sold modestly until 1870, when her nephew, James Edward Austen-Leigh, age eighteen when she died, collected family reminiscences into a memoir of her life. Austen-Leigh was a solid, respectable Victorian clergyman, and his memoir portrayed Aunt Jane as the type of woman writer the Victorians could admire, a kindly maiden aunt whose charming, lighthearted novels were of a piece with her other ladylike domestic accomplishments—the prose equivalent of a needlepoint sampler. However out of sync this picture might seem with the sharp, satirical Austen whom many readers find in her pages, it was an immediate hit with the public, inaugurating a popularity that has never waned. Just twenty-four years later, when the critic George Saintsbury christened them "Janeites," her adoring fans were already a prominent, identifiable group.

The Janeites are out in force today, albeit in a decorous British fashion. Although JASNA officials sometimes refer to Britain's JAS as "the mother ship," with fifteen hundred members it is far smaller than its North American cousin, and its yearly meeting is more sub-dued than JASNA's extravagant party. Mingling in today's crowd are prominent Austen scholars, the retired clergyman who showed us around the church at Steventon, an actress who performed a one-woman Austen show at a JASNA AGM the year before, and a handful of Austen relatives. (Although Jane Austen had no children of her own, her collateral descendants seem to pop up everywhere; four of her brothers produced a startling total of thirty-three sons and daughters, most of whom survived to adulthood.) A parade of speakers report on the society's business affairs with a bracing lack of sentimentality — "our finances are sound; not particularly bril-liant, but OK at the moment" — and offer tributes to recently de-ceased Austen luminaries. The editor of an important edition of Austen's works gives a talk on the transformation of Mr. Darcy from fictional character to female fantasy object. She makes a couple of wet-shirt jokes. Her talk concluded, the audience begins streaming out of the tent to line up for tea and scones. I overhear a woman tell-ing her companion, "I gave a talk once — I didn't believe in Darcy — and nearly caused a riot."

After dinner that night, we meet some British Janeites at our ho-tel for what is billed as "informal discussions about Jane Austen."

Like us, most of the British Janeites are white women no younger than middle age. The ice is soon broken, and we chat happily, jumping indiscriminately from talking about Jane Austen's life — her abortive romance with the young lawyer Tom Lefroy ("Clever people sometimes do not want clever wives," suggests a British Janeite descended from one of Austen's nieces), the protocol for burial in Winchester Cathedral — to talking about her characters' lives: the fate of Marianne Dashwood, the most despicable men in the six novels, the prospects for the marriage of Emma Woodhouse to the older, wiser Mr. Knightley. "I think he liked to be always right," an elderly woman declaims in razor-edged tones. "I think men *do*. And I think if you can make your husband feel that he's right, that's a very good thing."

Our tour guide in Lyme Regis is wearing a high-waisted green dress, a bonnet with purple ribbons, a long olive-green coat (in Regency-speak, a pelisse), and a star-shaped stud in her left nostril. Her name is Natalie Manifold, and she is holding a sign that reads, LITERARY LYME: THE JANE AUSTEN TOUR. Like a flock of baby ducks, we follow in her wake as she leads us toward the Cobb, Lyme's famous stone seawall, which Austen visited during a family vacation and on which the vivacious Louisa Musgrove falls during a crucial episode in *Persuasion*. I have wanted to see the Cobb for as long as I can remember.

Manifold walks us out onto the lower of the Cobb's two levels and shows us the stairs up to the top — Granny's Teeth, the forbiddingly steep and narrow steps that I have always heard described as the ones on which Louisa falls. But Manifold tells us that these are not the steps Jane Austen had in mind; Austen placed Louisa's accident on a newer section of the Cobb, where the steps are less forbidding. Still, a moment later, when I clamber up, I find them steep enough, and the top of the Cobb is genuinely unnerving: the wind is strong, the moss-covered edge has no railing, and the surface slopes down toward the sea.

"It's a little intimidating, actually," says Debra Call, who used to go rock climbing in the Rocky Mountains.

"But you know what?" says Debbie McNeil. "You're walking where Jane walked."

Lyme is a charming seaside town, all twisty streets and lampposts shaped like ammonites, the spiral fossils that strew Lyme's beaches. But we have little time to wander; we are due at the town's Guild Hall to hear an ancient Austen descendant lecture on her famous ancestor's limited romantic life. We settle into our seats, and a white-haired old lady in a straw bonnet begins her talk. It is rambling and disconnected, a farrago of well-known Austeniana, out-of-context misquotations, and anecdotes of dubious provenance — at least one, Google informs me later, lifted from a fictionalized play about Jane Austen's life — all delivered in a British-accented mumble and punctuated with occasional tiny chuckles. It goes on and on. Past JASNA tour groups have attended lectures by the same speaker, and from hints dropped earlier in the day, I have already gathered that those occasions were similarly . . . unsatisfactory. Nevertheless, JASNA has sent us here again, presumably motivated by some mixture of deference to the Austen gene pool, unwillingness to hurt the feelings of a well-meaning elder, and a perceived need to keep the peace between British and American Janeites.

No doubt this combination of family feeling, genuine kindness, and hardheaded calculation is appropriately Austenesque, but right now, I can't quite see it that way. For *this*, I think resentfully, we were yanked away from the lovely town outside? My mind begins to wander, but through the fog, I hear our speaker begin discussing, bizarrely, Jane Austen and astrology. "Jane Austen was a Libran," she says.

Jane Austen was born in December. She was not a Libran. I seethe quietly.

Halfway through our tour, we have left most of the genuine Austen sites behind, exchanging literary history for the silver-screen edition. Austen movies, fictionalized versions of fictions, are twice removed from reality and yet simultaneously far more concrete than anything on the page, where Austen usually offers few details about eye color and hair color, chairs and tables and wallpaper. As we're discovering, no matter how much we love the books, concrete objects have their own seductive power. Today we are visiting Saltram House, a spectacular Georgian mansion near Plymouth, but the scene before me recalls Filene's Basement more than *Debrett's Peerage*. All around, giddy JASNA tour members with bra straps slipping off their shoulders are pulling Regency gowns over their heads, stepping out of jeans and shoes, hunting for matching reticules and turbans. Saltram is run by the National Trust, and the staff have offered us the chance to dress up in period costumes sewn by volunteers and have our photos taken against the backdrop of the magnificent Robert Adam interiors. Many of us can barely contain our excitement. (Though not me, of course. Research may require a corset and gown for the Saturday night of the JASNA AGM, but I have no desire to star in Regency Halloween any other day of the year. I stand back and take pictures of everyone else.) When his turn comes, Skip McNeil, racking up the Good Sport points, dons a jacket, breeches, waistcoat, and cravat, along with his socks and sneakers. "Now I am your Mr. Darcy," he tells Debbie.

Our visit to Saltram House is further evidence of how far the lines have blurred between Jane Austen the novelist and Jane Austen the international brand. The Countess of Morley, who lived at Saltram, was an Austen enthusiast, and the novelist sent her an early copy of *Emma*. But let's be honest: that's not why our JASNA tour has come here. Nor are we really here for the Adam ceilings, the Reynolds portraits, or the Chippendale furniture. We are here because Saltram House stood in for Norland House, the lost family home of the downwardly mobile Dashwood sisters, in the 1995 film of *Sense and Sensibility*. Emma Thompson ate in that dining room! Hugh Grant walked down that staircase!

In the Morning Room, our guide tells the story of Saltram's handsome, arrogant earl, mentioning the three illegitimate children he fathered with a married mistress. "All very un-Darcy-like, you must admit," she says.

"Well—maybe," Sue Forgue mutters under her breath.

What heresy is this? "I'm not of the opinion that he is pure when he marries Elizabeth Bennet," Sue tells me as we proceed into the Velvet Drawing Room. "He is a man of his class."

Some hours later, we are on our way to another film set—the fifteenth-century church in the hamlet of Berry Pomeroy, where Marianne Dashwood marries Colonel Brandon at the end of the 1995 *Sense and Sensibility*. Alas, Alan Rickman, who played the movie's sexy, tortured Brandon, is not here to greet us.

We make do instead with three hospitable residents of Berry Pomeroy, who regale us with charming stories about the three days the film crew spent in the village—which movie stars were friendly and which standoffish, what happened when a passing van ruined one take, how the children reacted to their cameo appearance in the finished film ("absolute mayhem").

"Did it continue with an interest in reading Jane?" Anthea Bryant, our guide, asks hopefully.

"I would say not," the retired school principal says.

Afterward, we drink tea and eat homemade scones, with jam that one of our hosts, Nichola Boughton, made from the strawberries in her garden. In the Steventon of Jane Austen's day, the Church of England was the center of communal life, but now, though Berry Pomeroy's parish has six hundred residents, only twenty or thirty show up for Sunday services each week, and the vicar divides his time among eight small rural churches. Jane Austen's sharp, ironic voice rings with so modern a sound that it's easy to forget how much the culture has changed over two centuries, how much of what she took for granted seems unimaginably foreign to us, and almost impossible to recapture.

Still, our hosts in Berry Pomeroy remain unbowed. "We're surviving," Boughton says cheerfully.

Our tour of Austen Movieland continues at Mompesson House, in the cathedral city of Salisbury, which played the Dashwood sisters' London residence in the 1995 *Sense and Sensibility*. We will meet the property manager who oversaw the filming, Anthea Bryant tells us. "She was definitely — and I'm in full agreement with her — an Alan Rickman fan," Bryant says. "So be careful of any anti–Alan Rickman remarks, ladies." (Perish the thought. I love Alan Rickman.)

The Rickman enthusiast, sixty-one-year-old Karen Rudd, is a forthright blond who offers entertaining anecdotes about the travails of setting a modern film crew loose in an eighteenth-century house filled with priceless antiques. One night, a parrot that has a brief cameo in the movie escaped from its handlers. "It wasn't a laughing matter at the time," Rudd says, as we laugh. "If it had perched on the plasterwork and decided to poop, we would have had big problems. I was tempted to nail it to the perch."

After a week of touring historic homes, all the exquisite ceilings, antique glassware, and highly polished furnishings are beginning to pall on me, but I dutifully make my way through the house. Up-stairs, a young docent directs us to the highlights: "The bedroom where Marianne cries her heart out is there," she says, pointing the way.

However tenuous, the Jane Austen connection has helped raise the profile of Mompesson House, Rudd says, attracting visitors who might not otherwise find their way there. Rudd herself, it turns out, has been something of a Janeite since her school days. "People don't realize what an ardent feminist she was," Rudd says. "She railed against the whole ridiculous nonsense of primogeniture. And that's what she's writing about. It's not nibbling a biscuit with a cup of tea with other ladies whilst talking about the weather."

Like so many of us, she seems to forget for a moment that Austen's characters are, well, fictional. "Mr. Knightley — I'm still wait-ing to meet him," she says. "Mr. Knightley was always my idea of the perfect gentleman, and I'm sure he's terribly good-looking, as well. Otherwise, Emma wouldn't have touched him with a barge-pole."

Female lust is hinted at only discreetly in Austen's novels, which pack a world of meaning into lines like "his tall, firm, upright fig-ure, among the bulky forms and stooping shoulders of the elderly men, was such as Emma felt must draw every body's eyes." Post–sexual revolution, post-feminism, and post-Firth, Janeites feel less need for restraint. In cyberspace, Austen blogs and YouTube mash-ups fairly pant with appreciation for the many fetching actors who have portrayed Austen's heroes, and as our bus heads for London, I giggle as Anthea describes "Undressing Mr. Darcy," a presentation on historical costuming she saw with the Kent chapter of the Jane Austen Society. The protagonist began fully dressed in Regency costume, she tells us, with a many-caped greatcoat and a silver-topped cane, a magnificent specimen of manhood. But, she explains, clothes really had made the man: as he removed each layer, his magnificence diminished, until "at the end, we were left with a fairly ordinary-looking man in his underdrawers."

"I can't tell you how fascinating this was," Anthea says. "The intellectual content was so high. Let alone anything else."

In my London hotel room, Colin Firth is waiting — his hairline receding a bit farther than in his Darcy days, his chin more stubbled, but still with those same beautiful eyes . . .

All right, he's on the cover of a magazine called *Pomp*. A girl can dream, can't she?

And Firth can live with my dreams, at least according to the author of the magazine story: "He seems to have come to terms with the fact that most women of childbearing age at some stage seem to have fantasized about him walking towards them, soaked to the skin, in an oversized white shirt and breeches, holding a riding crop." I save the magazine for Debbie McNeil.

We are in London to see Jane Austen's portable mahogany writing desk, which yet another Austen descendant, a Canadian who cofounded JASNA, donated to the British Library in 1999. A portable desk was the Georgian equivalent of a laptop computer, and Austen's father gave her one, perhaps as a nineteenth-birthday present, three years before he tried unsuccessfully to get an early version of *Pride and Prejudice* published. As I stand in the British Library's exhibit hall, where the Austen desk is on display not far from Shakespeare's First Folio and Paul McCartney's handwritten lyrics to "I Wanna Hold Your Hand," I feel a sudden rush of affection for the Reverend George Austen, who could have told his brilliant daughter to stop scribbling and get married, but who chose instead to encourage and support her. The manuscripts, Skip McNeil says later, have given him a new sense of the contingency of great art. "It makes you realize someone had to sit there and write every single word by hand," Skip says. "And there was a point where that sentence never existed before, and now it exists."

If *Pride and Prejudice* and *Emma* and *Persuasion* had never existed, we would have no Colin Firth key chains and Jane Austen tea towels and I ♥ MR. DARCY tote bags, no special reason to gawk at those stately homes that stand in for Norland and Pemberley in movies and miniseries. We would not compare our disagreeable relatives to Anne Elliot's whiny sister Mary Musgrove or look for a kind, sensible Mr. Knightley to sweep us off our feet. We wouldn't be Janeites, bonding over our love for witty Elizabeth Bennet and our disdain for glib, selfish Mr. Wickham.

Ultimately, although we've done our share of shopping and gawking, this trip has been about those bonds. Solitary fandom has its compensations; I preferred Chawton cottage when I could tour it alone, feeling like the only Janeite in the world. But given a choice, I decide, I opt for community — the company of clever, well-informed people, who have a great deal of conversation.

That's a quote from *Persuasion*. You'll know that if you're a Janeite.

On the last night of our tour, we gather at a bistro in Covent Garden, not far from a house where Jane Austen stayed when visiting her brother Henry. Debbie McNeil has been telling Sonya Samuels about one of her favorite Austen spinoffs, which rewrites *Pride and Prejudice* so that the Darcy-Elizabeth romance begins aboard a ship bound for America. Sonya, who has never read fan fiction, is beginning to think she'll try some. "Debbie, you've changed me," she says.

As we sit down to dinner, JASNA president Iris Lutz leads us in a toast "to the woman who brought us all together, the woman whose brilliant observations and sheer genius with quill and ink made us all fall in love with her — to Jane." We talk about the highlights of the trip, the new insights we've gained by walking in Austen's footsteps, the mystery of artistic creation. Skip McNeil wonders if any of us would be here if Jane Austen's books had never been adapted for the screen. Those of us who loved Jane Austen long before the wet-shirt scene insist we would have been.

"I was a Jane Austen fanatic before Jane Austen was cool," Roxanne Milton says, in her Texas drawl.

Most likely, Skip is just teasing the Janeites. "I had such a good time on this trip," he says, "I might actually read Jane Austen."

CHAPTER 3

———

SANDY'S PEMBERLEY

WHILE JANE AUSTEN SAT at her tiny desk in Chawton cottage, penning immortal masterpieces, her older brother Edward lived with his family in Chawton House, the Elizabethan mansion down the road—at least when he wasn't staying at his *other* mansion, a hundred miles away in Kent. Edward was lucky; as a twelve-year-old, he so delighted a pair of older, childless cousins that they eventually bequeathed him their considerable fortune and their surname, Knight. And because Edward was lucky, so were we: along with his houses and his lands came Chawton cottage, the place where his little sister finally found the peace and security she needed to write. Her cottage didn't have the accoutrements of Chawton House—the Great Hall, the elegant paneled dining parlor, the Oak Room with a window alcove where, legend has it, she sometimes liked to sit—but it had enough.

By the late twentieth century, Chawton cottage was a flourishing tourist attraction. Chawton House was a different story, a decaying hulk trembling on the brink of disintegration.

Then someone rescued it. She was a Janeite—a Janeite with a great deal of money.

"Are you a Janeite, or are you normal?"

The speaker, seated behind a table stacked with copies of her new *Pride and Prejudice* sequel, is a striking fifty-six-year-old with a sheet of long hair in a shade located somewhere east of auburn and north of magenta. She is wearing skinny purple pants, a sleeveless faux-fur jacket over a silky purple blouse, and sneakers with two-inch wedge heels. The fountain pen poised above the book she is preparing to sign is decorated with cartoonish depictions of cats. For customers willing to admit to extreme Austen-love—"It has to be out of control," she explains to one woman who isn't sure she qualifies—she signs on the page carrying the book's dedication: "To those most constant and DEVOTED JANEITES."

Sandy Lerner—computer nerd, organic farmer, cat lover—has spent half her life as a constant and devoted Janeite. She's read every bit of Austen's writing, from teenage burlesques to unfinished novels. She's stitched Empire-waist gowns and worn them to Regency balls. She's passed countless hours researching the history, geography, technology, and inheritance laws of the early nineteenth century. She refers to her author as "Jane." All the usual stuff.

What sets Sandy Lerner's Janeite devotion apart is, oh, roughly $20 million. That's about how much Lerner has spent since 1992 to lease Chawton House, restore it to its former glory, and operate it as a research library for the study of early English writing by women. Lerner, an Internet pioneer who made money the old-fashioned way—by taking her company public—is that rare Janeite who can put serious purchasing power where her heart is, collecting first editions the way the Debbie McNeils of this world collect Elizabeth and Darcy soap. She's a case study in what Janeite obsession can lead to if the usual constraints — time, money, family obligations — are truly no object. "Jane Austen is my drug of choice," Lerner says.

Lerner has been doing offbeat things for so long now that spending a fortune on feminist literary history barely registers as odd. She started kindergarten at three, declared herself a socialist at twelve, posed nude astride a horse on the cover of *Forbes* magazine at forty-one, started a cosmetics company that sold nail polish in a shade called Asphyxia, and has pursued hobbies ranging from cigar smoking to jousting. She likes to say that she quit watching television when *The Addams Family* was canceled, in 1966. During the bitter battles surrounding her ouster from Cisco Systems, the legendary technology company she cofounded, detractors called her bossy, unreasonable, and brutally critical, but when I met her, more than twenty years later, she was gracious and kind. Still, it was clear that her unvarnished conversational style made no concessions to conventional notions of girly talk. ("Negative," she sometimes barked, when answering a yes-or-no question.)

"Do you think you're a bit eccentric?" the newscaster Chris Wallace once asked her.

"I am now that I'm rich," Lerner replied. "I used to just be weird."

Sandy Lerner, restless rebel, was born in Arizona on Bastille Day, 1955. Her parents — her father an artist, her mother a salesgirl — had no money. By three, little Sandy was already reading, and her father enrolled her in kindergarten. A year later, her parents split up; her father moved to New York, her mother took her baby brother and moved to Los Angeles, and five-year-old Sandy was sent to a hundred-acre ranch in Clipper Gap, California, northeast of Sacramento, to live with an aunt and uncle who ran a heating-oil business. Her mother couldn't support two children on a dress-shop salary, and Sandy had clashed with her even as a toddler. "I was named after my father. I was Daddy's girl," Lerner says. "It was just a better thing that I wasn't there."

To an outsider, much about her childhood sounds sad. After her parents' split, she saw her mother occasionally and her father even less, and her relationship with her aunt was difficult. As the only child on the ranch, she led a lonely life, envying her classmates their normal lives and feeling awkward about her own, with its missing parents, early-morning chores, and long bus ride through the mountains to school. She was a reader — "I read like most people breathe," she says — in a house with few books. She bought ninety-eight-cent paperbacks through a school reading program and learned to read upside-down so it would take longer to finish them.

But Lerner focuses resolutely on what she had to be grateful for: kind relatives who were willing to take her in, give her food to eat and a roof over her head, and teach her the value of work. "I was the luckiest little girl on the planet," she says. "For somebody with my energy, it was just a wonderful place to be. I didn't know that at the time, but I know it now." So she worked. In the venerable 4-H program for rural youth, she learned to sew and to speak in public. She raised animals and sold them for a profit. She rose at 6 A.M. to feed the cows, never missed a day of school, and graduated at fifteen, still two years ahead of her peers. No one in her family had ever gone to college.

The 1960s were happening all around her, and Lerner was deeply affected by what she read in the newspapers. In fifth grade, she stopped saying the Pledge of Allegiance, partly because she was a budding atheist who resented the phrase "under God" and partly because she did not want to swear allegiance to a country dominated by corporations, escalating its war in Vietnam, and oppressing its black citizens. The summer she was eleven, she lay on the floor, wondering what it would feel like to be incinerated in a nuclear war. At thirteen, she saw *Hair*, marched in a Vietnam War protest, and was detained by the police. From *The Addams Family*, she learned that difference was to be embraced, not hated. "I was an old kid," she says. "In California, if you were bright and you were reasonably sensitive and you thought about things, it was a very aware time."

After high school, Lerner's uncle got her a job as a teller at a local bank, but after a year of sexist condescension from the bank manager, she was ready for college. She went to California State University at Chico, where tuition was an affordable ninety dollars a semester, and commuted back to the ranch on weekends to look after the animals. She majored in political science, focusing on comparative communist theory; skipped the beer drinking and the parties; and finished in two years. Soon after, she discovered computers, and mastering their intricacies looked like a good way to make money. "It was not my intention to get rich," she told an interviewer years later. "My intention was to not be poor."

In her Stanford University graduate program in statistics and computer science, she was a rare woman in a field dominated by men, many of them unregenerate nerds with limited social skills. The exception was Leonard Bosack, a fellow graduate student three years older than she was. "Len actually knew how to bathe and eat with silverware, and I was absolutely enchanted," Lerner told an author years later. "He used to take Wisk and wash his collar and cuffs, which was way more than I ever did, and I just didn't think that a more perfect man could exist." They married in 1980, less than a month after her twenty-fifth birthday.

Unlike Lerner, Bosack hadn't abandoned television after *The Addams Family*, and that fall, he persuaded her to keep him company while he watched something he thought she'd like, a new BBC version of *Pride and Prejudice*. Later generations of Janeites, addicted to the melting vulnerability in Colin Firth's brown eyes, would sometimes complain about the 1980 production, with the actor David Rintoul playing a repressed, formal Mr. Darcy. But Lerner was entranced. How soon did she buy the book? "I'm not sure that the first episode was over," she says. And during the next few years, Lerner read and reread Austen—her novels, her letters, "every scrap of doggerel, syllables, exclamation point, period, bent paper that I could find." Eventually, she would read her favorites, especially *Persuasion,* scores of times.

In Austen's pages, Lerner found something that was missing from her own life: a feeling of complete self-confidence. Austen, she was sure, had believed herself to be living in the best of all possible countries at the best of all possible moments in history, and had felt secure enough to laugh at the people she saw around her. "I just found that very—addicting," Lerner says. Austen's serenity contrasted strikingly with the feelings Lerner had lived with for so long as a child of the Vietnam era, the sense of being "a square peg in a round hole, and I was wrong, and everything around me was wrong." She was deeply attached to the kind, kooky goths of *The Addams Family,* and Austen's characters, with their bonnets and waistcoats and precise, witty speeches, seemed just as alien to her world, and just as appealing. "They were the people I wanted to be," Lerner says. "I'm from an *Addams Family* world, and the good people were people that were a little strange. I just wanted to be an unusual good person."

Lerner was still at Stanford—after finishing their master's degrees in 1981, both she and Bosack had taken jobs at the university as directors of computer services, he for the computer science department and she for the business school. On campus, she found kindred Janeite spirits, and in 1984, some thirty women banded to-gether to form the Stanford Jane Austen Society, unaffiliated with the five-year-old Jane Austen Society of North America. JASNA had a branch nearby in San Francisco, but to Lerner, its members seemed more interested in tea parties than in serious academic study of Austen's life and works. Together, the Stanford Janeites read their way through the novels and, six months after starting, reached the inevitable denouement. "We had all read everything. There was nothing more," Lerner remembers. "You could have cut that atmosphere in that room that day with a knife. We were all sit-ting around with these long fish faces. And I said, 'Well, you know, we could write one. It won't be that good, but at least we'll have something to read.'"

Lerner loved *Pride and Prejudice,* but some elements of its end-ing disturbed her. Why did Jane Austen leave Elizabeth Bennet's pedantic sister, Mary, unmarried, when clearly she was meant for foolish, sycophantic Mr. Collins? And how could Darcy's over-bearing aunt, Lady Catherine de Bourgh, be permitted to insult Elizabeth for all eternity? A homegrown sequel could solve these problems and put Austen's characters where, surely, Austen had meant them to be. Lerner sketched a chapter outline for her book, gave it a title — *Two Sisters* — and began filling in the chapters. She hadn't gotten far before Internet history intervened.

In later years, legend would have it that Bosack and Lerner, mar-ried lovebirds working in different Stanford offices, had invented a key component of the modern world because they were frustrated that their university computers couldn't exchange e-mail messages. In fact, however, linking Stanford's computers into a serviceable network was a longstanding project that involved engineers and re-searchers across the campus, not just Bosack and Lerner. The ad hoc team pulled wires through disused sewer pipes to connect far-flung corners of the university and tweaked the software for an already-existing invention, a box known as the multiprotocol router, which allowed disparate computer systems to talk to each other and connect to the era's fledgling Internet.

The router's commercial possibilities were apparent, at least to Lerner and Bosack, but Stanford wasn't interested in pursuing them or in allowing its employees to do so. Lerner and Bosack went ahead anyway. In December 1984, they registered their new company, which they named Cisco Systems, after the Bay Area's biggest city. Lerner designed a logo that incorporated the iconic Golden Gate Bridge, and the couple started building routers in their living room. For three years, they worked hundred-hour weeks without compensation, financing the project with credit cards and outside work and eventually parting ways with Stanford. Lerner's Jane Austen sequel slipped to the back burner.

Cisco shipped its first product in March 1986, and less than three years later, with the help of a cash infusion from a venture capitalist, its monthly sales totaled $3.5 million. In February 1990, when Cisco went public, the stock market set the company's value at $288 million. Lerner and Bosack were suddenly spectacularly wealthy, their Cisco shares worth $40 million each. When the first check hit the bank, Lerner had only two items on her shopping list: a black Jaguar and a set of Jane Austen first editions.

Behind the scenes, however, the picture was darker, both personally and professionally. The long hours that Lerner and Bosack had devoted to building Cisco had undermined their marriage, and in 1988, they had separated amicably. Meanwhile, at work, tensions were building between Cisco's founders and the outside managers hired by their chief investor. Six months after the initial public offering, seven company vice presidents issued an ultimatum: either Lerner was out, or they were. They said she was demanding, confrontational, given to publicly eviscerating anyone who displeased her. "Sandy was born a barracuda," one early Cisco executive told an interviewer. She was fired on August 28, 1990, and Bosack soon quit in solidarity. By year's end, they had sold their third of the company for $170 million. Still close friends, they used a sizable chunk of their Cisco money to launch a foundation, named for his father and her mother, as a vehicle for supporting the causes they believed in. Bosack funded what Lerner called "weird science," like the search for extraterrestrial intelligence. Lerner supported animal welfare causes.

And she continued to reread Jane Austen. After discussing Austen's novels, the Stanford Jane Austen Society had moved on to exploring her historical context, and someone—perhaps Lerner herself—suggested they read a new book, *Mothers of the Novel,* by the Australian feminist and academic Dale Spender. The book identified nearly six hundred novels by more than a hundred women writing from the late seventeenth through the early nineteenth century, setting Austen's achievement in the context of a female literary tradition that, Spender argued, had been deliberately excluded from the conventional story of the novel's development. Suddenly, Austen wasn't a lone genius flowering in a vacuum; she was a link in a long chain of woman writers. For Lerner, the new context gave the lie to images of Austen as an unhappy, repressed spinster, or as a proto-Victorian maiden aunt too shy and retiring to crave money and fame. "I was so happy she had company," Lerner says. "I was so happy that she was not ashamed of her writing, and that she was writing for money, and that there were a lot of women writing for money, and that she didn't feel like a weirdo and persecuted."

With her Cisco fortune, Lerner began collecting the early, forgotten women's novels Spender had identified, and before long she found the perfect home for them. In October 1992, JASNA held its annual conference in Santa Monica, California, and Lerner was in the audience for Sunday morning's lecture by the British man of letters Nigel Nicolson, who had written a coffee-table book about the houses Jane Austen had lived in and visited. In passing, he mentioned that one of those houses, Edward Austen Knight's Chawton House, was on the market. One group of enthusiasts hoped to turn Chawton House into a Jane Austen center, Nicolson said, but he was spearheading a competing effort to place such a center in a house in Bath where Austen had once lived. " 'If you're really smart, you'll like my proposal,'" Lerner remembers Nicolson saying. " 'And if you like this other proposal, you're a stupid old cow.' And then he said, 'If you believe that my brilliant idea is wrong because it's in Bath and Jane Austen didn't like Bath, then you're a silly, *superstitious* old cow.' And he kept on like this for forty-five minutes."

To Lerner, Nicolson's casual upper-class British misogyny sounded like egregious disrespect for his audience, with its preponderance of smart, well-educated older women. She was deeply offended, and nearly two years after cashing in her Cisco chips, she had the money to get even. She picked up the telephone and told her secretary to buy Chawton House.

The property had first gone on the market three years earlier, after the latest of Edward Knight's descendants, Richard Knight, had inherited a crushing estate-tax bill and a sixteenth-century house in need of a million British pounds' worth of emergency repairs. When fundraising for the proposed Jane Austen center fell short, Knight accepted a developer's offer to turn the house and grounds into a fifty-one-room hotel with a golf course. But by the fall of 1992, the hotel project had collapsed into receivership, clearing the way for Lerner. She envisaged turning Chawton House into a residential study center where scholars consulting her rare-book collection could live under nineteenth-century conditions, gaining a visceral sense of the historical moment that produced those books. They would wake up to frost on the windows, grates without fires, and nothing but cold water to wash in. It took eighteen months to unwind the complicated financial entanglements and to evict a troublesome tenant, but by mid-1994, Lerner and Bosack's foundation had paid about $1.6 million for a 125-year lease on Chawton House and its 275-acre grounds; another $225,000 had bought the stable block outright. Lerner had yet to lay eyes on any of it.

She had heard, of course, that her new house was in bad shape. She just didn't understand *how* bad. "I don't think that an American can really conceptualize four centuries of decay," she says. In late 1994, she finally came for a visit and decided that she had bought the ugliest house in Great Britain, a brick mansion ravaged by four hundred years of bad taste and the declining postwar fortunes of its once-wealthy owners. As she walked through the many rooms, she saw the damage that the newspapers had been reporting for years. Part of the roof was missing. A cinder-block billiards wing added in Victorian times had pulled so far away from the rest of the house that daylight was visible in the gap. Upstairs flats had been rented to hippie tenants who had painted the walls hot pink and lime green. Deathwatch beetles were eating away the wooden beams. At the top of one stairway, Lerner's cowboy boot went through the floor. "At that point, I was numb," Lerner says. "It was beginning to dawn on me what I had done."

In the village of Chawton, meanwhile, rumors were spreading — abetted, Lerner says, by a disappointed investor in the golf course project. The rich American would turn Chawton House into a Euro Disney–style theme park. The library of women's writing that she claimed to be planning was a front for a lesbian commune. Her erstwhile husband, the computer expert, would be testing missile guidance systems for the defense ministry. To the villagers, Lerner soon realized, everything about her seemed *wrong:* her American accent, her computer background, her gender, her purple hair. The culture clash was total. Lerner attended a village meeting to answer questions about her project, and a man in the audience asked, "What are your feelings about field sports?" Lerner had never heard the term before; she thought he must mean cricket. She was starting to tell him how much she approved of sports when the gracious British matron next to her leaned over and explained quietly, "Here, 'field sports' means hunting." Apparently, the impoverished Chawton estate recently purchased by the American animal-rights activist had had been selling its hunting rights for years.

The local resentment blindsided Lerner. She was rescuing a dilapidated historic home, returning important works of British literary history to their homeland, and celebrating the milieu that produced one of England's greatest writers. How could anyone be against that? "It never entered my consciousness at any appropriate time that making this library was not just an inherent good," she says. "Like rescuing little birds. Helping a little old lady across the street." Fiercely logical herself, she was disconcerted by the illogic of her adversaries, who apparently wanted her to spend millions renovating their decaying local landmark and then do nothing with the building. Even after the library filed for planning permission with an application that mentioned bookshelves, not missile silos, the opposition continued. Most of 1997 was eaten up by a dispute over a twentieth-century swimming pool, which Lerner wanted to remove as part of her restoration; animal-rights supporters claimed the pool was a badger habitat, and under the UK's Protection of Badgers Act, it is illegal to destroy a badger habitat. It took months to establish that, in fact, no badgers lived under the swimming pool. "I'm just so fucking sick of it right now," Lerner told a reporter late that year. "I just wish it would all just kind of go away."

As the Chawton House project dragged on, Lerner kept busy. She paid $7 million for an eight-hundred-acre spread, Ayrshire Farm, in the pastoral horse country of northern Virginia, where she planned to raise heritage animal breeds under humane, organic conditions, to prove that socially responsible farming could be economically viable. She launched a cosmetics company dedicated to women who shared her *Addams Family* fashion sense, with an edgy name — Urban Decay — a no-animal-testing policy, and an in-your-face advertising slogan ("Does Pink Make You Puke?"). The product line came in bold, extreme colors with deliberately unsettling names like Gash, Acid Rain, and Oil Slick. By the time she sold the company to an international luxury conglomerate five years later, doubling her investment, mainline cosmetics companies had caught on to the existence of women like her, who disdained the industry's pretty-pretty ethos. Those big companies had begun catering to the market niche she had identified. And, once that happened, Lerner wasn't interested anymore. It was like her penchant for Cuban cigars, a hobby she abandoned once its edginess evaporated. Cigar smoking "became — *commonplace* isn't the right word — middle of the road," she says. "It was kind of fun, and then everybody else started doing it, and it wasn't fun anymore. I just keep getting mainstream, and I hate it, and I have to go do something else."

In 1998, more than five years after Nigel Nicolson's incendiary speech to JASNA, full-scale restoration of Chawton House finally began. Lerner's original vision of a residential center for scholars eager to taste life without modern conveniences had fallen by the wayside; meeting fireproofing standards would have wreaked havoc on the historic building, not to mention increased renovation costs. Over the next five years, Lerner's team of builders, architects, and historical consultants gradually brought Chawton House back to life, demolishing the problematic Victorian wing, rebuilding the roof with twenty-two thousand square feet of hand-carved oak timbers, and replanting lawns and flower beds. When the copse behind the church was cleared, the Knight family's pet cemetery emerged from the underbrush; in the archive room, a secret cupboard hidden behind a panel turned out to hold a seventeenth-century telescope. Lerner's seven thousand rare books, which had been stored for years in California and Washington State, finally moved in. The price tag for the restoration came to $10 million.

Chawton House Library, dedicated to the study of women's writing in English from 1600 to 1830, opened on July 10, 2003. The barricades and hard hats and four-story scaffolding were gone; ladies in white dresses strolled in and out of the once-derelict house, carrying tiny pocketbooks. Soon, scholars would begin gathering at Chawton for conferences and planning their research trips around its growing collection. "That day was very surreal," Lerner says. Everyone kept telling her she must feel wonderful, but after the long, traumatic ordeal, she just felt numb. And the expense of the project hadn't ended with the restoration. Operating Chawton House Library cost Bosack and Lerner's foundation $1 million a year, and even for someone with Lerner's fortune, that was real money. Perhaps, she began to think, she could earn the library a nest egg by finishing her *Pride and Prejudice* sequel.

In the years since Lerner had begun her book, Jane Austen fan fiction, some of it so sexually explicit that it verged on soft-core pornography, had become its own genre, proliferating both on the shelves of bricks-and-mortar bookstores and in the archives of online fan sites. But although Lerner was one of the world's richest and most famous Janeites, she remained disconnected from much of Austen fandom; she had never joined online discussion forums, never read any of the sequels and spinoffs, never even seen the Colin Firth *Pride and Prejudice*. The wet-shirt scene — she had seen *that* clip — turned her off because it wasn't in Austen's novel. "I'm a hardliner — what can I tell you?" she says. Even the covers of the spinoff books repelled her, let alone whatever might lie between them. "It would be like a Christian fundamentalist reading the autobiography of Timothy Leary," she says. "I just don't think I can do that."

The book she wanted to write would be something different, a historically accurate follow-up set a decade after the end of Austen's novel. Over the years, Lerner had evolved what she liked to call "Lerner's Theory of Austen": every time Austen gives a concrete detail — specifying, for example, that characters ride in a barouche, a landaulet, or a gig, rather than merely a generic horse-drawn carriage — she is conveying crucial information that modern readers miss because they know too little about Austen's historical context. Lerner's book would insist on that context. Her characters would visit places popular with nineteenth-century tourists, marvel at the technology of the early industrial revolution, and speak only words that were in use in Austen's era. They would hold the sometimes xenophobic social attitudes of their time, not the politically correct views of twenty-first-century Americans, and they would have exactly as much onstage sex as Austen's characters do — which is to say, none.

Lerner read everything she could find that might help her recreate Austen's world. "My MO is work so much harder for so much longer than anybody else is willing to do that you win just for that reason," she says. She spread out nineteenth-century maps on the floor and crawled over them with a magnifying glass, collected more than a hundred period guidebooks, and read Sir William Blackstone's famed eighteenth-century commentaries on English common law. She checked and double-checked her vocabulary against Samuel Johnson's 1755 dictionary (she owned a first edition) and the scholarly *Oxford English Dictionary*. She took a hellish two-week trip over the Alps in a mail coach drawn by five horses. The title of her book, she joked, should be *Plot and Plausibility*.

Lerner's busy life often left her little room for novel writing, and the project proceeded by fits and starts. By the time she finished the book, twenty-six years after beginning it, the world of publishing had changed completely, largely because of the Internet revolution that Lerner's company had helped kick-start. By now, aspiring writers who couldn't get a contract from a traditional publisher, or who didn't want to give up control of their work, could self-publish and sell their books online. Lerner figured it could take years to land a traditional publisher, so instead she set up a website and printed five thousand hardback copies of her book, now titled *Second Impressions*, an inside-baseball reference to *First Impressions*, Austen's original title for *Pride and Prejudice*. The profits were going to Chawton House Library, and Lerner was hoping a movie sale would eventually follow. The book was designed to look as much as possible like a novel of Austen's era, with a dust jacket that resembled a leather binding and two separately numbered, two-hundred-page volumes contained within the covers of a single book. Lerner's name did not appear on the title page; like Jane Austen herself, she had decided to publish under a pseudonym. She called herself "Ava Farmer," a rebus that the alert could deconstruct into "A Virginia Farmer." Though Ava Farmer's true identity was no secret — Lerner promoted the book to JASNA groups, and a picture of her surrounded by Ayrshire Farm turkeys appeared above the author's biography on the jacket flap — she didn't want anyone who recognized the name of a former computer mogul to dismiss her book without giving it a chance.

When the first copy of *Pride and Prejudice* arrived at Chawton cottage in 1813, Jane Austen wrote to her sister, "I have got my own darling Child from London." Over onion soup one afternoon a month or so after her book's publication, Lerner sounded almost as delighted. She had written the book she wanted to write — funny, well paced, and true to its time.

"There's two sex scenes in the book," she said. "Nobody's found them."

Around the time she turned forty, Sandy Lerner stopped feeling like a square peg in a round hole. She came to terms with the difficult but loving people who had raised her and took pride in what she'd accomplished at Cisco, despite the bitterness with which it had ended. "I finally made peace with who I was and what I was," she says. "I finally got happy." In middle age, she had achieved the confidence and security that she had glimpsed in Jane Austen all those years before, and her creation of the Chawton House Library had made her a Janeite heroine.

Most Janeites don't have Lerner's vast financial resources, of course. Most of us can't expand the horizons of scholarship, or collect rare books and historic homes. We limit our Janeite community service to modest local efforts and satisfy our acquisitive urges with coffee mugs and tote bags. Usually, that's good enough for me. What would I do with an Elizabethan manor house anyway? Every so often, though, I too feel that craving to own something that could bridge the centuries separating me from Jane Austen. Perhaps all Janeites do. For sale: a turquoise ring that Austen once wore; a first edition of *Emma* that she presented to a dear friend. If we had money to burn — that ring eventually sold at auction for $236,000, and that first edition went for $350,000 — would we spend it this way, trying to draw closer to her elusive genius? Would we Janeites all become Sandy Lerner, if only we could afford it?

By the early twenty-first century, Lerner's English neighbors no longer viewed her with hostility and mistrust. The careful renovation of Chawton House had won over the village, and by 2009, one resident would tell the London *Sunday Times,* "I don't think there's anyone who's not on her side." In the tower of St. Nicholas Church at Chawton, in whose cemetery Austen's mother and sister are buried, hung a bell that Lerner had donated. She had asked that it be inscribed TO THOSE WHO WENT BEFORE US.

Back home in Virginia, Ayrshire Farm won certification for both its organic farming and its humane treatment of the animals raised there, though the money-losing operation had not yet proved Lerner's point about the financial viability of organic agriculture. Lerner opened a small store to sell the farm's meat and launched a line of raw organic pet foods. She gave a commencement address at nearby Shenandoah University and accepted an honorary doctorate in return.

When she signed her new novel at an independent bookshop in the nearby town of Winchester, dozens of locals — friends, employees, strangers who had read about her in the previous day's newspaper — streamed in to get their copies, chat about their cats, or thank her for hosting a benefit for the local wildlife rescue organization.

"How does a feminist fall in love with Jane Austen?" asked one middle-aged woman with tastefully gray hair, as she presented her copy of *Second Impressions.*

"Jane Austen was a feminist," Lerner said. "If you describe feminism as a female class consciousness, she definitely had a class consciousness. She was very aware of women as a separate class within the society. She definitely wrote from a woman's point of view."

If some of the afternoon's customers were there for the Austen connection, others were clearly drawn by Lerner's Cisco-era fame.

"Do you ever lie awake at night thinking about what you've done," began a man in a red hat, with wonderment in his voice, "how you've helped revolutionize—"

"No," Lerner said. She missed nothing about Cisco except the doughnuts and the Chinese takeout, she told him.

"You're living in an era that you've made tremendous change," he pursued.

"I'm not responsible," she said quickly.

She didn't seem to be modestly insisting that the Internet was a group effort. She seemed to be denying culpability for our distastefully Twittering, be-Friending world, for the e-mail inboxes overflowing with pornographic spam. She had done as much as anyone to create the networked lives everyone took for granted, but sometimes it sounded as if she'd rather live in a world where the sex scenes stayed offstage.

Jane Austen moved to Chawton cottage on July 7, 1809. Two hundred years later, Sandy Lerner threw a $5,000-a-head Regency ball at Chawton House to mark the anniversary and to raise money for the library. Elizabeth Garvie and David Rintoul, the actors who had played the leads in the long-ago BBC *Pride and Prejudice* that had turned Lerner into a Janeite, hosted the ball in character, as "Mr. and Mrs. Darcy." Guests came in Regency costume—Lerner, calling herself "Lady Ayrshire" for the occasion, wore a low-cut, pale-blue ball gown and an elaborate overdress—and the house was decorated with ostrich feathers and lit by candles. A prominent chef had pored over the library's period cookbooks to produce such Austen-era delicacies as nettle and potato soup, pickled ox tongue, and sweetmeats, and liveried staff served the meal on Edward Knight's mahogany dining table. In the Great Hall, live music played, and Sandy Lerner danced the Congress of Vienna Waltz with her favorite Mr. Darcy.

The next day, Lerner and Rintoul went horseback riding in the countryside near Chawton. Her quarter-century love affair with Jane Austen had come to this: a scene right out of a Jane Austen novel, or at least a movie of a Jane Austen novel. The ridiculous perfection of the moment was not lost on Lerner. "If I'd have seen myself, in 1984, galloping over the Hampshire Downs with David Rintoul, I'd have said, 'I don't know what I'm on, but I'm obviously dead,'" she says. "'And I've been *good*.'"

PART II

REREADING,
REWRITING

CHAPTER 4

WRITING MR. DARCY

BACK HOME AFTER MY TRIP to England, I was beginning to worry about the progress of The Dress. In six weeks, the musicians would strike up the first dance at the JASNA ball, and I was still waiting for the fabric samples that Maureen O'Connor, my New York City seamstress, had promised to send. When an envelope with her return address finally arrived, I tore it open with relief.

I studied the swatches taped to her letter. For the gown, Maureen was proposing a shiny satin in a deep blue, to be worn with an overdress of a stiffer matte fabric in a different shade of blue. Or she could make me a gown of forest-green brocade, possibly with a black velvet overdress. Could I dance in velvet, in Texas, without dying of heat stroke? I thought not. The blues were beautiful — I could hardly believe I would soon own garments in such lavish fabrics — but did the two shades complement each other? I wasn't sure.

Should we consider an entirely different color for the overdress? I asked Maureen via e-mail.

"This is getting complicated," she wrote back. "I am getting concerned about the time factor."

My stomach clenched as I read her reply. *Oh, no,* I thought. *I'll have no dress for the ball! And I'm turning into a spoiled, demanding ball-zilla of a client!*

Perhaps, Maureen suggested, we should forget about the overdress entirely.

A year earlier, I had happily attended the JASNA ball in a skirt and sweater bought off the rack at the mall. But now the prospect of attending this year's ball wearing nothing but a satin gown felt like a tragic retreat. I wanted my overdress!

I abandoned my concerns about color. What did I know, anyway? "Just go ahead and do the dress and overdress in the fabrics that you chose," I told Maureen. "If you think they'll work well together, then I'll bow to your superior knowledge."

With relief, I left behind the world of clothes, a place in which I invariably felt insecure and inadequate, and returned to the far more welcoming world of books.

These days, when I wasn't examining fabric swatches, I was immersing myself in a literary subgenre that had barely existed a few years before: Jane Austen spinoff fiction. Sandy Lerner wasn't the only Janeite with a hankering to try her hand. Lately, every time I dropped by my local Barnes & Noble, the new-fiction table seemed to be dotted with Austen-inspired paperbacks, their covers featuring mediocre paintings of Regency scenes, their titles — Pemberley this, Mr. Darcy that — advertising their affiliation. Every time I logged on to Amazon, its algorithm suggested yet more possibilities.

The Austen spinoff isn't entirely a contemporary invention. Austen herself apparently imagined afterlives for her characters, telling her family that the fourth Bennet sister, Kitty, would eventually marry a clergyman; that her older sister Mary would settle for a lawyer's clerk; and that Emma Woodhouse's invalid father would die two years after her marriage. The first authors to attempt an Austen spinoff were two of Jane Austen's nieces: Anna Lefroy, who knew Austen well and consulted her for advice on writing, and Catherine Anne Hubback, who was born the year after Austen's death. As a child, Hubback heard Aunt Cassandra read Aunt Jane's books aloud, and she saw the manuscripts of Austen's unfinished novels, *The Watsons* and *Sanditon*. Lefroy never finished her continuation of *Sanditon*, but Hubback, who turned to writing to support her young sons after her husband's mental breakdown, got further. In 1850, Hubback published *The Younger Sister*, a completion of *The Watsons*, dedicating it to Jane Austen's memory.

Admirers with no Austen family connection soon followed in the nieces' footsteps. In 1913 came the first Austen sequel, *Old Friends and New Fancies*, by Sybil G. Brinton, the thirty-eight-year-old daughter of a wealthy carpet manufacturer from Worcestershire. Brinton's book happily mingles characters from all six of Austen's finished novels, pairing off Mr. Darcy's little sister and Fanny Price's older brother, as if Pemberley and Mansfield Park were neighboring estates in a sprawling, interconnected Austen-world. No less a critic than Virginia Woolf mentioned Brinton kindly in an essay about Austen published in the *Times Literary Supplement*. Brinton's book, Woolf wrote, in words that could easily apply to the many similar books that would come after it, was "a work of great love and great ingenuity which, if taken not as fiction but as talk about Jane Austen's characters, will please that select public which is never tired of discussing them."

Between World War II and the early 1990s, a smattering of Austen-related fiction continued to appear: a gothic-tinged *Pride and Prejudice* sequel, completions of both unfinished novels, a handful of books by professional writers trying to re-create the world of *Emma* or *Sense and Sensibility* or *Pride and Prejudice*

—even a tongue-in-cheek pornographic version of *Persuasion* updated to the Edwardian era. I read very little of it. A couple of years before the Colin Firth miniseries aired, someone gave me a *Pride and Prejudice* sequel called *Presumption;* a decade later, one of the participants in my neighborhood Jane Austen reading group passed on her library copy of *Mr. Darcy's Daughters,* an entertaining Regency romance with so little connection to Austen that it might as well have been titled *Mr. Jones's Daughters.* My favorite was a hilarious collection of parodic vignettes called *Pride and Promiscuity: The Lost Sex Scenes of Jane Austen,* which managed to remain true to Austen's characters while placing them in some rather surprising situations. (If any Austen hero were to have a collection of S&M toys and the wherewithal to explain their use to his heroine, I felt sure it *would* be kind, witty Henry Tilney of *Northanger Abbey.*)

Fundamentally, though, I just didn't see the point of Austen spinoffs. In the immortal words of the JASNA bumper sticker I had treasured for decades, I'd rather be reading Jane Austen. But if research could send me across the Atlantic, I could hardly balk at the Kindle downloads and library visits required to acquaint myself with the genre. And acquaint myself I did. I read stories of Elizabeth and Darcy's married life, versions of Austen's novels retold from the point of view of her heroes, and road-not-taken variations exploring how events would have unfolded if, at crucial moments, the plot had swerved in a different direction. I read books in which Jane Austen herself appeared as a crime-solving sleuth, or a vampire running a bookshop in upstate New York, or the heroine of a star-crossed love affair, or an imaginary friend dispensing advice to the lovelorn. I read a "Little Miss Austen" board book for toddlers ("1 English village . . . 4 marriage proposals . . . 10,000 pounds a year") and graphic-novel versions of Austen stories published by

Marvel Comics. I read books that updated *Pride and Prejudice* to the worlds of Jewish retirees in Florida, marine biologists in Massachusetts, and lawyers in California. I read novels in which Austen's characters barely brushed fingertips while passing each other cups of tea, and others recounting inventive bouts of lovemaking (pre-wedding, post-wedding, heterosexual, homosexual) conducted in every imaginable location, from Darcy's library to Lady Catherine de Bourgh's pantry.

Perhaps I should claim that all this Austenesque wallowing was hard labor — research is a dirty job, but someone has to do it — but, frankly, I loved it. Oh, it wasn't like reading Jane Austen, of course — where Austen's novels were richly complex, exquisitely satisfying confections, most of these books were Twinkies. The writing varied from excellent to execrable, the pacing and plotting were frequently amateurish, the temptation to substitute melodrama (war! murder! international drug smuggling!) for Austen's psychological nuance seemed ever-present, but the exuberant silliness was irresistible. Who doesn't feel like devouring a Twinkie from time to time? Some of these writers were probably hacks with rent to pay, but many seemed to be genuine fans driven by their unwillingness to say goodbye to Austen's characters on the final pages of her all-too-short, all-too-few novels. To me, that crazy fondness had its own disarming charm, probably because I recognized it in myself. I too was a member of that select public who never tired of discussing these enchanting people.

Also, some of the sex scenes were pretty hot.

So who was writing all these books?

That Monday morning in mid-January 1996, the faculty lounge at the Texas high school where Linda Berdoll worked as a substitute teacher was buzzing with appreciative female chatter. The day before, A&E had aired the first episode of Colin Firth's *Pride and Prejudice,* already fluttering hearts on the other side of the Atlantic, and now everyone was eagerly anticipating the next installment. "You know that guy that played Darcy?" one teacher said. "I didn't think he was very good-looking at the beginning, but I sure did by the end." Berdoll had been happily married to her high school sweetheart for more than thirty years and had recently become a grandmother, but she was just as Darcy-smitten as everyone else. When the series ended two nights later, she thought, *Oh! Oh! No! It can't be over!*

For Berdoll, as it turned out, it wasn't. Over the next year, she watched *Pride and Prejudice* again and again, read all Austen's novels and letters, and researched the history of the Regency. Then she ornamented her desk with a photo of Colin Firth on horseback — she *really* liked those leather boots — sat down at her computer, and began to write down the story that was filling her fantasies, the story of Elizabeth and Darcy's exceedingly happy marriage. "I wanted to know what happened to these characters — explicitly," Berdoll, a frank sixty-something with a silver-gray pageboy and a Texas drawl, told me one night over dinner in Austin. "No 'the curtain's closed, the camera fades.'" The five-hundred-page sequel to *Pride and Prejudice* that she produced some three years later — an epic historical romance written in a baroque prose style and liberally studded with energetic sex scenes involving two of classic literature's most beloved characters — would eventually sell more than two hundred thousand copies and help turbocharge the Austen spinoff craze.

Berdoll hadn't aspired to be a writer. An Air Force brat who never spent more than a year in the same school, she had lived in Oklahoma, Kansas, and the Philippines before arriving in Texas near the close of her sophomore year of high school. As classes were changing on her first day, she spotted a tall, brown-eyed boy leaving agriculture class.

"Who is that?" she asked the girl who was showing her around.

"Phil Berdoll," the girl replied. "And you don't have a chance of getting him."

A year later, at seventeen, Linda married him. Phil came from a prominent cattle-ranching family and wanted to be a farmer and rancher himself. Linda left high school, got a GED, and went to work to help him save up. Over the next three decades, they raised cattle, grain sorghum, pecans, and two sons. Linda learned to bale hay and castrate cattle, brought Phil brownies when he rode his tractor to the end of a row, wrote a local-news column for the daily paper, and substitute-taught in junior high and high school. She had a busy and satisfying life; there was no Jane-Austen-shaped hole that needed filling. "I wasn't having a midlife crisis, and I wasn't in menopause," Berdoll says cheerfully. "Just the whole story turned me on."

At first, she planned to write only for herself. Then she considered publishing, but changing the characters' names, since what she was doing to Darcy and Elizabeth, or having them do to each other, seemed an impossibly daring affront to English literature. She had never read a romance novel herself—her taste ran more to biographies and classic fiction—so she picked one up, to see how much sexual frankness the genre would allow. "It was something about somebody named Thor, and he had this magnificent erection," Linda says. "And I thought, 'Well, hell, I can do that.'" After dinner every night, she would pour herself a glass of wine ("to loosen things up") and get to work on her story, which was turning out to be a far cry from Austen's sedate domestic tales. Linda's story unfolded against the backdrop of war, economic upheaval, and simmering class resentments. Her Elizabeth survived tribulations ranging from attempted rape to near-death in childbirth; her Darcy dispatched baddies with a couple of well-aimed shots from a pistol. The happy couple made love at the drop of a bonnet — in a carriage clop-clopping along the road to Pemberley, atop a Chippendale dining table, in a forested glade on the grounds of the estate. And Linda, whose research had uncovered a vast number of Regency euphemisms, entertained herself by using a different one ("love torch," "timbered appendage," "larydoodle") every time she needed to mention the male member. Her book wasn't a joke — she cared about her characters' experiences and relationships — but she had a sense of humor about the whole enterprise.

As her novel took shape, Linda read it aloud to Phil. He was no reader — the books she bought him sat unopened by his bedside — but he loved her work. Sometimes, as she upped the erotic ante, she wondered if she'd gone too far.

"Do you think I ought to put that in?" she would ask him.

"*Yes,*" he would whisper back.

Phil was more than an editor and a cheerleader, though. He was something close to a muse, her own strong, silent Mr. Darcy, so gentlemanly that he never used foul language in the presence of a woman. "I knew the man," Linda says.

Finally, the book was finished, and Linda thought — hoped — other people might like to read it. "I knew there were plenty of women out there who wanted to know what Lizzy and Darcy did in bed," she says. "Those were the people that would be my market, those who saw Colin Firth as Mr. Darcy and got all hot and bothered." But the first literary agent she contacted was discouraging. Jane Austen and sex? Nobody would be interested in that.

Rather than risk further rejection, Linda and Phil decided to put the book out themselves, since the burgeoning Internet was making self-publishing far cheaper and easier than it had been in the old days of vanity presses. For perhaps $5,000 they set up a website, christened themselves Well, There It Is Publishers, and bought an initial print run. A friend created cover art of a man on horseback, using a paisley-patterned skirt of Linda's as the backdrop. Linda had considered calling the novel *Mr. Darcy Takes a Wife*, but finally she chose a more esoteric title, *The Bar Sinister*, a reference to the heraldic symbol indicating illegitimacy. She had rejected the idea of abandoning Austen's character names entirely, but she made a few small changes designed to distance herself from her revered predecessor — spelling Elizabeth's name "Elisabeth," for instance, and calling the odious Mr. Collins Thaddeus, instead of William. She wrestled with what to call herself as well. Choosing a pseudonym seemed like a suitable coda to the whole larky enterprise, not to mention a neat way of sidestepping whatever outrage her unorthodox use of Austen's characters might provoke. In the end, though, she published under her own name.

They printed 500 copies. Linda figured that 495 of those would sit in the garage forever.

Hundreds of miles away, in Atlanta, Georgia, another middle-aged woman was sitting at a computer, imagining Fitzwilliam Darcy. Unlike Linda Berdoll, Pamela Taylor had been a Janeite for decades. She had grown up in a blue-collar family in Pennsylvania, in a town with no library; at home, the only books were her mother's old Nancy Drews and the Louisa May Alcotts and Junior Illustrated Classics that had come with the purchase of a set of encyclopedias. In high school, Pamela decided to educate herself by reading the classics lining the shelves of her school library. Like Edith Lank, holed up during the cold Maine winter years before, Pamela started with the A's. She loved *Pride and Prejudice* so much that she bought a copy and read it over and over again, at least once a year, until the book fell apart. She was drawn to the connection between Darcy and Elizabeth, their sparkling repartee and their relationship of equality. "The back and forth, and the give and take — I'd never seen that at that level before," says Pamela, a frosted blond who punctuates her conversation with frequent chuckles. "That was just very attractive to me."

Almost no one in her family had gone to college, but Pamela enrolled at nearby Millersville State and soon began preparing for a career as a school librarian. One day, she decided to attend a meeting of what was reputedly the most intellectually sophisticated of the college's Christian student groups. The organization's brand of evangelical Protestantism was more biblically based and theologically conservative than the liberal Presbyterianism Pamela had grown up with, and in its meetings she experienced a religious awakening intense enough to qualify as a conversion experience. At eighteen, just a year after enrolling in college, she married a man four years older than her who was active in the same organization, and once she finished school, they moved to the Midwest, then eventually to Georgia. He worked in Christian ministry and later in education; she completed a master's degree in library science and gave birth to three sons, whom she homeschooled for years. She held jobs in school, college, and public libraries, and in Atlanta taught at the Christian school where her husband also worked.

From the beginning, the marriage was difficult. Pamela's husband insisted on complete control of all aspects of their lives, kept a stranglehold on the family finances, and monitored her phone calls. A couple of times a year, his anger would spill over into violence: he hit her, threw chairs, left black-and-blue marks in places that didn't show. Pamela told no one. She worried that revealing his behavior could cost him his job or spark a confrontation with her father that could leave one of the men badly hurt; after all, her husband owned a collection of knives and guns. Then her father died, and she didn't want to burden her struggling mother. Most important, she had taken sacred vows before God to remain married, for better or worse. She tried to avoid rousing her husband's anger, or to appease him when he erupted, and she prayed that he would change. In secret, however, she had written an escape plan, spelling out how, if her situation ever became too much to bear, she would gather enough money to travel the hundreds of miles home to her family. "Every once in a while, I'd pull it out and I'd think, 'OK: has it gotten to that point? Am I really going to do this?'" she says. "And then I'd fold it back up and put it away again."

In January 1996, like Janeites across the country, Pamela tuned in to Colin Firth's *Pride and Prejudice.* Pamela had liked the 1980 adaptation that so enthralled Sandy Lerner, and initially she disliked Firth's portrayal. Compared to the polished David Rintoul, Firth looked scruffy. But gradually she began to see in Firth's performance the contours of an inner life that she had never perceived in the character before. She began to wonder about Darcy's transformation, from the arrogant snob Elizabeth scornfully rejects to the generous man who deserves the love she finally gives him. "There was so much more to this man than I had suspected or thought of, even though I'd read the book so many times," Pamela says. "There was a story to be told. Why was he like this, and why did he change?" Her own husband, she had finally begun to realize, was never going to.

By the late 1990s, Linda Berdoll wasn't the only amateur author inspired by Firth's Darcy. All over the fledgling Internet, Janeites old and new were posting their own Austen-related stories and commenting on each other's offerings, taking advantage of a technology that created instant communities of the like-minded. Pamela began haunting the newly minted fan fiction websites, looking for answers to her question: why does Darcy change? No one was answering it in a way that satisfied her. Yes, Darcy falls in love, but to Pamela that wasn't enough to explain his willingness, at the end of the novel, to tie himself irrevocably, through marriage, to his worst enemy, the amoral seducer George Wickham. Darcy's transformation had a spiritual dimension, she felt sure.

Over the years, Pamela had toyed with writerly ambitions. In junior high school, she and a friend had scripted their own *Star Trek* episodes; as a mother of sons, she had considered writing fiction for tween boys. Now she was forty-five, and the time to realize her ambitions was running out. As an experiment, she decided to write a short scene from Darcy's point of view, describing his feelings after his disastrous first proposal to Elizabeth, as he prepares to give her his long letter of explanation. Pamela called her scene "Be Not Alarmed, Madam" — a quote from the opening line of Darcy's letter — and posted the whole thing, five pages or so, on the Republic of Pemberley's fan fiction board, under the name "Pamela T."

"The reaction was just incredible. They loved it. They just loved it," Pamela says. "So I thought, 'Well, you know, it looks like nobody's going to write this, how Darcy changed. Maybe that's what I'll do.'"

Nineteen ninety-eight was Michael Mogen's year from hell, the months in which his college-age son wrecked the car, his father died of cancer, his wife asked for a divorce, and he was laid off from his job as a technical writer. But by the fall, Michael's life was stabilizing. He had found a new and better job, the divorce had proved to be amicable, and he and his ex-wife were sharing custody of their two teenage daughters. That fall, one of the girls was assigned to read *Pride and Prejudice*. As a college English major, Michael had read *Northanger Abbey* without much enjoyment, but at his daughter's urging, he gave this other Austen book a try.

At first, he didn't think much of the priggish hero and the sarcastic heroine, but he kept reading. Halfway through the book, he came to one of Austen's greatest scenes — Darcy's arrogant, insulting marriage proposal ("Could you expect me to rejoice in the inferiority of your connections?") and Elizabeth's passionately angry refusal ("I had not known you a month before I felt that you were the last man in the world whom I could ever be prevailed on to marry"). Michael read it over and over again, memorizing the words, repeating them to himself as he drove home from work. "It just took my breath away," he says, laughing with joy at the memory. "That was one of the greatest reading experiences I ever had."

Like newly minted Janeites before and since, he quickly watched the adaptations, read the rest of the novels — too few! — and, wondering what came next, ended up on the Internet's fan fiction websites. Some of the pieces were terrible; others managed to be simultaneously faithful to Austen's characters and utterly bizarre, like the story written by a chess player, in which Elizabeth and the others hang around Mr. Bingley's house, playing chess. "And then I came upon this little five-page thing. It was called 'Be Not Alarmed, Madam,'" Michael says. "And that one knocked my socks off. I mean, it was almost as good as reading Austen herself." He hunted around and found that the author, this Pamela T, had written more — she was about a third of the way through a retelling of *Pride and Prejudice* from Darcy's point of view, posting five to seven pages every other week. He decided to e-mail her a fan letter. "I think you have captured Darcy's character extremely well," Michael wrote from Idaho. "His proud exterior and his passionate core. His unwilling attraction to this bewitching girl with the vulgar family and low connections, like a moth to a flame."

Pamela's writing life had settled into a rhythm. Every morning, she would wake at five, make herself a cup of tea, descend to her cold basement office, and write for two hours, an Enya CD playing in the background. She wrote a page a day, leaving her terrible marriage behind as she escaped into Darcy's world, where she was in control. Then she dressed and went to work.

She was getting used to gushing online comments and private e-mails from readers hungry for the next installment, an addictive warm bath of praise and encouragement. She had connected with several other women who posted work on the fan fiction boards, and they chatted online regularly, helping each other resolve story roadblocks and discussing how best to incorporate into their writing the Christian faith they all shared. (Pamela had decided to come at the spiritual side of Darcy's journey obliquely, through the story of the religious awakening of his sister, Georgiana, a shadowy figure in Austen's novel.) Eventually, three of those fellow writers visited Pamela in Atlanta, for a mini–Jane Austen conference of their own.

Still, Michael's e-mail stood out. Its author, unlike most of her readers, was male, and his style was restrained and literate. She replied with thanks, pleased that a man found her male character convincing. Michael wrote again, telling her more about which aspects of her work he was particularly enjoying. "I promise not to keep bothering you so you can finish this wonderful story," he concluded.

In her reply, she briefly adopted the voice of a Regency heroine: "'Bother me! La sir,' she responded blushing furiously, 'your comments are rather a spur to my lagging spirits.'" In fact, she told him, she was feeling a bit stuck, not sure she'd have the staying power to carry Darcy's story through the four months still remaining before his proposal to Elizabeth at Rosings, the pivotal moment that had so entranced Michael during his own reading of *Pride and Prejudice*.

This time, his response took the form of a scene at Pemberley between the dispirited author and her creation.

"I confess, madam, I read your words with some trepidation." Darcy's brow furrowed with lines of concern. "Lagging spirits simply will not do! We cannot have it! . . . This is no time to discover a faint heart, woman!"

Michael's Darcy continued for hundreds of words, praising the author for her perceptive portrayal of his inner struggles, taking issue with a few points — she had underplayed his snobbery, he argued — and urging her to complete his story.

"I must remind you," Darcy moved to check the calendar on his desk, "I have a proposal to make to Miss Bennet in April. At Rosings." His eyes slowly rose from his desktop to fix steadily on hers. "Miss T, that is an appointment I intend to keep. I do not know what happens in the interim. That, I'm afraid, is your task."

When she saw Michael's name in her inbox, Pamela expected another chatty note from a fan. As she began to read, however, her heart skipped a beat at the strangeness of the experience — her character, her invention, was talking back to her. She composed her response in the same vein, explaining to Darcy why her progress on his story had slowed.

"I am feeling my way, anxious that I do not take a false step. But, I assure you, my dear Mr. Darcy, you shall get to Rosings! . . . Never fear, you shall have your Elizabeth," she assured him warmly, "but only after you have come to know yourself in truth."

Her scene concluded with Darcy bringing her hand to his lips, "in a tender but chaste salute."

Yes, chaste. By now, she no longer saw the struggling young man she was bringing to life on the page as the smolderingly attractive Colin Firth. Her Darcy had begun to seem more like a son.

Pamela and Michael continued their e-mail correspondence for more than two years, albeit in their own voices, not as Darcy and The Authoress. As she posted each new installment of her story, he offered praise and constructive criticism; after a while, she began sending him her work even before she posted it. Eventually, she suggested a phone call. "I felt like I needed to talk to him and actually hear his voice and say thank you, because I really, really appreciated everything that he'd done," Pamela says. "He'd taken me seriously as a writer and was helping me develop." Maybe this isn't just a fluke, she had begun to think. Maybe I *can* be a writer.

By the summer of 2002, they had spoken on the phone more than once, and their conversations had begun to move beyond her work, into more personal discussions of their lives and their children. As it happened, she was scheduled to attend a conference of Christian schoolteachers in Idaho, two hours away from the nearest airport, an airport not far from Michael's home. She asked if he would meet her plane and drive her to the conference. He agreed, though part of him wondered. Wasn't she afraid that this man she'd never met might be an ax murderer? As she prepared to board her plane, Pamela had her own attack of doubt: *What if he's weird?* she thought. But her nerves vanished when she finally spotted him leaning against the wall of the airport, a lanky, gray-bearded man wearing a baseball cap. On the long drive to her conference, they discovered how much they had in common — childhoods spent in big families, their taste in books, a love of making music. Pamela knew an attraction was growing between them, but she was married, and for her, divorce was out of the question. "It was not in my vocabulary to just abandon my vows," she says. "I went back home determined: I am going to make this marriage work. I am going to do whatever I can."

Linda Berdoll's novel *The Bar Sinister* was selling slowly but steadily. The first five hundred copies were gone in six months, sold over the web to customers as far away as Russia. Linda boxed up the orders and mailed them off, putting pins in the map to mark their destinations. International postage got to be so expensive that it seemed wiser to outsource overseas shipping, so she and Phil arranged to distribute through the Ingram Book Company, the world's biggest book wholesaler; with Ingram's distribution system backing them up, Amazon would sell the book and deal with the mailing costs. Linda promoted her book at literary festivals, convinced a local Borders store to take some copies on consignment, and read the scores of reader reviews that began multiplying on Amazon. Her book, it was quickly becoming clear, was one of those love-it-or-hate-it things. "If only crimes against literature were prosecutable!" wrote one anonymous reviewer. "I laughed and cried and completely enjoyed Linda Berdoll's work," wrote another. "Now where can I find a 21st century Darcy?" Some mocked her for misspelling Elizabeth's name, not realizing she had done it on purpose. Others hated the fact that Linda's Mr. Darcy had slept with a courtesan before his marriage: Mr. Darcy would never do that! they insisted. *That's your opinion!* Linda thought as she read these comments. *Why is your opinion any more important than my opinion? Write your own book!* After a while, she stopped reading the reviews; the mean ones hurt her feelings. But the controversy wasn't hurting sales. Within three years, Berdoll's self-published erotic romp had sold ten thousand copies on word of mouth alone.

Deb Werksman was shopping on Amazon one day when *The Bar Sinister* popped up among her recommended titles. Werksman had been a Janeite since high school, reading *Pride and Prejudice* annually for twenty years; when she ran across Austen spinoffs, she gave them a try, just for fun. "I had run out of Jane Austen," Werksman says. "I couldn't get enough and there wasn't enough." Some four years earlier, Werksman had sold her small book-publishing company to Illinois-based Sourcebooks, joining the bigger publisher as an editor of nonfiction — gift books, parenting books, relationship books with titles like *1001 Ways to Be Romantic*. She added Linda's novel to her Amazon shopping cart.

The Bar Sinister had been lying by Werksman's bed for three weeks by the time she got around to reading it. She couldn't believe how good it was — and how bad. "It was funny, it was sexy, it was epic, it was daring — and the book was riddled with typos and grammatical errors," Werksman says. "Most of the time when I'm reading for pleasure, I just turn off my editorial brain, because otherwise I'd go crazy, right? But I'm reading this book, and I was itching to get my fingers into that language." She began lobbying for the book on two fronts: urging her colleagues at Sourcebooks to make an offer and trying to persuade Linda to sell Sourcebooks the rights.

Linda took some persuading. She knew her manuscript needed editorial help, but she had never cared about fame and fortune, and she didn't want some publisher insisting that she take out all the sex. In the end, however, she decided to give it a try. Phil had years of land deals under his belt, and on Amazon, Linda found a how-to book on negotiating with publishers. Eventually, Linda signed a contract with Sourcebooks to publish her novel under its original, less esoteric title, *Mr. Darcy Takes a Wife.* For the cover, Sourcebooks chose an obscure nineteenth-century painting of a woman in a high-waisted, cleavage-baring gown leaning backward into a passionate kiss.

When I met Linda seven years later, the book was still in print and still selling — 209,000 copies, according to her most recent royalty statement, reportedly the most of any Austen sequel. The book still ignited fierce controversy: the committed Janeites who posted on the Republic of Pemberley usually hated it, but 163 Amazon reviewers had given it a top rating. Elements of what Linda called "the Jane Austen lunatic fringe" still surfaced from time to time to criticize her. One reader sent Sourcebooks a long, detailed letter explaining why the affair Linda had invented between Darcy's father and the famous Regency belle Georgiana, Duchess of Devonshire, was chronologically impossible, as if Linda had written history rather than historical fiction. At an early book signing, a man complained about Linda's word choice: "Jane Austen didn't use the word 'compartmentalize,'" he said. "I don't think she used 'larydoodle' either," Linda shot back. But mostly women told her that they loved the tender and passionate marital relationship she had imagined for Elizabeth and Darcy — elements of which, they apparently assumed, came straight from her own life. "Does your husband know how high he set the bar for all the other men?" one reader asked her. Linda was amazed at how Phil's pride in her accomplishments had softened his habitual reserve. When the local newspaper wanted a photo for a story about Linda, Phil agreed to plop her onto his knee and reenact the book-cover kiss, with the addition of his white cowboy hat. The Berdolls liked the picture so much, they hung a framed print on the wall of their bedroom.

Riding the wave that Linda had launched, Sourcebooks billed itself as "the leading publisher of Jane Austen fiction." Its spring 2011 catalogue grouped the eleven forthcoming Austen-spinoff novels into their own special section, and its backlist included more than forty other Austen-related titles. According to Werksman, who had become the romance-fiction editor at Sourcebooks, spinoffs about Darcy and Elizabeth sold best, especially those with "Darcy" in the title. Books based on *Emma, Sense and Sensibility,* or secondary characters from *Pride and Prejudice* did about one-tenth as well, and books based on Austen's three other novels hardly sold at all.

But by the spring of 2012, the Sourcebooks catalogue listed only three Austen-related books. The wave had crested, Werksman thought, and she was limiting her acquisitions to the more unusual spinoffs, like *Fitzwilliam Darcy, Rock Star.*

Linda Berdoll had continued her story of the Darcy marriage into a second volume, *Darcy and Elizabeth: Nights and Days at Pemberley,* which sold another 114,000 copies, but, disenchanted with her publishers for reasons she would not discuss publicly, she bought out her contract with Sourcebooks for a third volume and decided to hire a copyeditor and return to her roots in self-publishing. The day I drove up the steep, unpaved country road to her modest ranch house, she was going over the proofs of volume three — *The Darcys: The Ruling Passion* — which would be released within weeks. (Twenty-three chapters down, seventy to go.) Without the marketing muscle of a publishing house behind her, she planned to start relatively small, with five thousand copies, which she would store in an air-conditioned shed on her property—"the book house," she was calling it.

She had stopped substitute-teaching when her first novel appeared, lest her sex scenes undermine her authority in the classroom. But fifteen-year-old girls still came up to her from time to time, to say how much they had loved her book. "And I'm like, 'Should you be reading that?'" Linda says. "'How old are you?'"

Pamela's resolve to remain in her marriage lasted for months after her return from Idaho. But it couldn't survive one final betrayal, whose details she won't consign to print. She would never again be able to trust her husband, she realized, and in March 2003 she told him she wanted a divorce. But she had no money and nowhere to go, so for three months, until the school year ended, she continued living in the same house with her angry husband and his gun collection, with only their college-age son to stand between them.

When her decision was made, she told Michael about it. He had never urged her to leave her husband, but he had listened and tried to help. Now they began to discuss the possibility of a future together. That June, not long before Pamela's divorce became final, Michael came to Atlanta, and they packed up her van and drove back to Idaho. She found a job running a public library in a nearby town, and six months later she and Michael were married.

Years later, Pamela's ex attributed his failings as a husband to improperly diagnosed and medicated neurological conditions that changed his personality and precipitated brief, irrational outbursts. He contested some elements of her account of their marriage: he denied that he had monitored her phone calls, estimated that his angry episodes occurred only once every two years, and acknowledged hitting her only once. Mostly, he blamed her relationship with Michael for the breakup of their marriage. And, in a way, he blamed Jane Austen. "Like so many women who do not know how to cope with an unhappy relationship, she retreated to a fantasy world, which only compounded her existing unhappiness by providing a contrast between this ideal world of Darcy and company, and the less happy world of 'real life,'" he said.

As her first marriage reached its end, Pamela was still writing her Darcy story, posting not only to the fan fiction websites that had originally hosted her work but also to a website of her own, which she had set up with the help of a how-to book she'd found at a yard sale. Each week, her site got thousands of hits from readers in 101 countries. Many begged her to publish her story in book form; they were tired of carrying around huge loose-leaf binders filled with printouts of her pages. By the time Pamela arrived in Idaho, she was about three-quarters of the way through what would ultimately become a trilogy nearly a thousand pages long, three times the length of *Pride and Prejudice* itself.

Like Linda Berdoll a few years earlier — and like Sandy Lerner a few years later — Pamela decided to self-publish online. After all, she knew she had a built-in audience, and self-publishing seemed easier than finding a literary agent, shopping a manuscript, and waiting months for it to appear. With the Internet's new print-on-demand services, she didn't even have to commit to buying hundreds of copies in advance; orders could simply be filled as they came in. A fan in California, a book designer by trade, was so anxious to see the story in print that she volunteered to design Pamela's book covers for free. Pamela and Michael created a publishing company named Wytherngate Press — the name had a nice British ring to it, Pamela thought — and Pamela chose a pseudonym, just in case the whole thing flopped and she didn't want to be associated with it. She called herself Pamela Aidan. "Pamela" means "sweet" and "Aidan" means "fire," and she liked the sound of "sweet fire." And, on an alphabetized bookshelf, the Aidans would sit near the Austens.

An Assembly Such as This, the first volume of Pamela Aidan's Fitzwilliam Darcy, Gentleman trilogy, was published in August 2003, followed the next summer by a second volume, *Duty and Desire.* The books shot up online sales rankings, and with no middlemen to take a cut of the profits, Pamela was earning an astonishing five to ten dollars per copy—more when she sold through her own website, less when she worked through an online retailer. She was still writing the third volume of her trilogy when a big New York publisher called. Apparently, someone at Barnes & Noble had told someone at Simon & Schuster to pay attention to this unknown author whose books were selling so well, and now one of the world's largest publishers wanted to give Pamela a contract. She was thrilled—an unsolicited offer from a huge New York publisher!—but accepting it wasn't actually a no-brainer. On the one hand, Simon & Schuster's imprimatur would give Pamela entrée to bricks-and-mortar bookstores and a shot at reviews in mainstream publications that, as a matter of policy, wouldn't look at self-published books. But on the other hand, she and Michael enjoyed being in control of her work. And with tens of thousands of copies sold, they were making a lot of money.

Simon & Schuster kept calling, kept increasing its bid. Eventually, the company was offering $30,000 for all three books.

"And we'd look at that," Michael says, "and think, 'God, you know, we're making that—'"

"We're making that in a month," Pamela finishes.

Finally, they called a prominent publishing lawyer whose name they discovered in the back pages of a monthly magazine for independent presses. Pamela's sales numbers astonished him, and he was amazed by the quality of her self-published products, with their attractive covers and professional printing. Eventually, he offered to represent her in negotiations with Simon & Schuster, winning an advance five times larger than the previous offer. Pamela and Michael even won the right to self-publish the third volume and sell it online until the day the franchise passed to Simon & Schuster. They wanted to see their own project through to completion.

But with the deadline for the Simon & Schuster takeover approaching, Pamela hit a creative wall. "Writers talk about their characters speaking to them, and that's basically how the whole thing had been," she says. "Suddenly, Darcy just stopped talking." One night, as she and Michael drove together to the gym, she burst into tears. She had run out of inspiration; she was under pressure to finish, and she didn't know how to end her story. Originally, she had planned to take Darcy and Elizabeth through their first Christmas together at Pemberley, but her third volume was already far longer than the other two, and the happy couple weren't even married yet. She gave up on Christmas at Pemberley, wrote a wedding scene that concluded with an allusion to the famous opening sentence of *Pride and Prejudice,* and staggered across the finish line. Her fans had preordered more than eight hundred copies of this last volume, *These Three Remain,* from her website, and one day, Michael came home from work to find the boxes of books stacked far up the side of their house. Friends came over to help stuff each copy into a mailing envelope. By the time Simon & Schuster's editions began appearing in mid-2006, Pamela's three self-published volumes had sold a total of seventy-five thousand copies. Simon & Schuster would sell, at a conservative estimate, another quarter-million.

Among Janeites, Pamela's books were perhaps the best-loved

of the many Austen spinoffs, widely praised for sticking close to Austen's language and characterization. Many of the readers who desperately wished that Austen had lived long enough to write another dozen novels found in Pamela's work what Michael had first seen there: something near enough to the original to feel almost as good. Michael collected the fan mail in a burgundy binder he labeled E-MAILS AND LETTERS IN PRAISE OF PAMELA AIDAN. "You are Jane Austen reincarnate," wrote one fan. "There is no other explanation for the ring of true authority you brought to your words." Pamela still found it hard to believe her story had given so much enjoyment to so many, and nearly five years after the publication of her trilogy, she wasn't quite sure what she would do next. Wytherngate Press had published books by two of the women she had met on the fan fiction sites, but lightning hadn't struck twice — none of those books, based on characters from *Persuasion,* had sold as well as the Darcy trilogy. Pamela had turned down a lucrative three-book contract from Simon & Schuster, fearing she would have nothing to write about once she took off the training wheels that Jane Austen's superbly constructed plot had provided her. But she was beginning to feel creative again.

She and Michael shared a relaxed, loving rapport. They had their differences — she was a conservative Republican and he was a Democrat, for one, and more important, although he attended church with her, he was not a believer. He had sat through entire sermons about why Christians shouldn't marry non-Christians. "I feel what a momentous thing she did," he says. Pamela had never imagined she could be happy with someone who didn't share her faith, but she was. "I just love this man so much," she says, rubbing his knee affectionately.

On my last night in Idaho, Pamela and Michael cooked a Chinese dinner and then, after supper, settled down in the living room of their modest house to make music together. "There's nothing like singing to make you feel like a million bucks," Michael had said earlier in our visit. As they played "The Whisky Hornpipe" and another lively Irish tune, she on the hammered dulcimer, he on the guitar, I marveled at how the support and admiration of a worldwide community of Jane Austen fans had made it possible for Pamela to give her own story a happy ending.

She left her seat behind the dulcimer, moved to the couch beside Michael, and spread out the sheet music for the Beatles' "This Boy" on the coffee table in front of them.

That boy isn't good for you
Though he may want you too . . .
Oh, and this boy would be happy
Just to love you.

In two-part harmony, their voices blended in the quiet of the evening.

CHAPTER 5

THE KNOWLEDGE
BUSINESS

DEVONEY LOOSER, THE ONLY Jane Austen scholar ever to star in a roller-derby vampire movie, is introducing the dark, complicated *Mansfield Park* to a class of undergraduates at the University of Missouri at Columbia. She quotes the eminent critic Lionel Trilling on the unlikableness of Fanny Price, the novel's virtuous heroine. She summarizes the scholarly debate over the novel's attitude toward slavery, imperialism, and Britain's colonization of the West Indies. She encourages her students as they draw out the implications of Austen's vocabulary, the significance of apparently unremarkable words such as "obliged," "captivate," and "attached." And she passes around a recent example of the Jane Austen mashup genre, *Mansfield Park and Mummies,* as yet unread ("It's not at the top of my list"). Looser, trim and athletic, with straight blond hair that falls below her shoulders, is a warm, engaging presence in the classroom as she nudges, praises, offers historical context. She is wearing high-heeled black boots and a blazer with a Jane Austen brooch on the lapel. She is not wearing roller skates.

Alongside the Jane Austen who inspires movies, tote bags, fan fiction, and literary tourism lives another Jane Austen—the giant of English literature, the genius novelist whose quill pen launched a thousand dissertations. Since 1883, when a Harvard undergraduate wrote the first academic thesis on Jane Austen, scholars have glorified her and patronized her, sometimes simultaneously. They have called her writing artless and instinctive or conscious and careful, labeled her a conservative or a subversive, a domesticated lady or an ardent feminist. They have burrowed beneath her seemingly placid surfaces to ferret out the sex and the politics. And periodically they have sought to distinguish themselves from those embarrassing Janeites, with their soppy sequels and cutesy costumes. The modern obsession with Jane Austen has "lowered the level of the conversation around her," the Brooklyn College professor Rachel M. Brownstein wrote in 2011. "Familiarity breeds contempt; simplification trumps complexity; writing has driven out reading; Jane-o-mania has gone on too long."

I first encountered this scholarly antipathy to the more enthusiastic manifestations of fandom in the fall of 1983, long before the birth of Brownstein's "Jane-o-mania." Just back from my first JASNA conference, still glowing with the joy of fellowship, I took my seat at the seminar table in my freshman literature class. When the professor heard how I had spent my weekend, she sighed and rolled her eyes. Those Austen fans, with their silly games of dress-up! Only a month into college, I was still insecure enough about my intellectual credentials to feel the need to defend my Janeite clan against this indictment. (It wasn't like that! Nobody dressed up!) It didn't occur to me to point out that dressing up was perfectly compatible with literary appreciation. At seventeen, only a few years removed from the lit nerd who smuggled Dickens out to the playground during recess, I probably didn't believe it anyway. I already knew that Serious Readers didn't wear bonnets.

Twenty-eight years later, however, I had come to Columbia to meet a husband-and-wife team of academics who seemed comfortable in the place where Jane Austen lives now, at the intersection of scholarly importance and pop-culture prominence. Devoney Looser is a well-regarded feminist literary critic, the editor or author of three books on British women writers, including *Jane Austen and Discourses of Feminism.* Her husband, George Justice, has written about the world of eighteenth-century publishing and, when I visited, had recently finished assembling the fourth incarnation of the Norton Critical Edition of *Emma,* a standard classroom text that packages the novel with a selection of scholarly essays and biographical materials. Looser's and Justice's academic credentials were impeccable.

On the other hand, so was their sense of humor. At JASNA meetings, they had delivered a series of talks staged as entertaining marital arguments, posing for a publicity photo back-to-back, their arms crossed, as if preparing for a duel. When Looser took up roller derby at forty-two, hitting the rink in black spandex, knee and elbow pads, and a helmet, she chose Stone Cold Jane Austen as her nom de skate, creating her own mash-up of English literature and professional wrestling. The irresistible contrast between ladylike costume drama and aggressive contact sport captivated journalists and caught the eye of a local director planning a low-budget campus film. He cast Looser as herself—Jane Austen scholar by day, roller-derby aficionado by night—added vampires, and stirred. *Vampyras* was expected to debut some months after my visit.

In the Ph.D. version of that romantic-comedy staple—meeting cute—Jane Austen, the quintessential novelist of courtship, served as George and Devoney's matchmaker. In 1995, age twenty-seven and two years into her first job as an English professor, Devoney put on a little black dress and went off to a party at the conference of the American Society for Eighteenth-Century Studies, held that year in Tucson, Arizona. En route, she and her roommate ran into a mutual friend, who introduced them to her boyish, bow-tied companion, George Justice, the proud possessor of a newly minted Ivy League Ph.D. in English. Two weeks earlier, George had won the academic sweepstakes by landing a tenure-track job in his field, and, exuberantly pleased with himself, he was happy to be introduced to two attractive women.

"I guess I'm naturally of a flirtatious mode, and so I started grilling you," he said, as he and Devoney told the story over dinner, sixteen years and two children later. "Grilling. This is my mode of flirtation."

He knew she worked on Jane Austen, so he asked which was her favorite novel. "And Devoney goes"—here he raised his voice into a higher register and began to round his o's—"'Oh, my favorite's'—"

"You shouldn't do my voice," Devoney said.

They were sitting on the same side of the table, their bodies angled toward each other, tuned in to each other's words. In the public version of their marriage, he plays the irrepressible extrovert who sometimes says more than he should; she plays the sensible introvert who reins him in when he goes too far.

"In her Minnesotan accent, she says, 'I've done the most work on *Northanger Abbey,*'" George continued, in his own voice. "And I said, 'I didn't ask you what you've done the most work on, I asked you what's your favorite.'"

Pressed, she copped to *Pride and Prejudice.* He told her his favorite was *Mansfield Park.* "And Devoney said, 'Oh'—"

"Can I do my own lines?"

"Go ahead, do your own lines."

"I said, '*Mansfield Park* is my least favorite, and I dislike it because I dislike Fanny Price. She's too much like me. She's boring.'"

This is the person I'm going to marry, George thought.

Fanny Price wasn't boring. Fanny Price epitomized integrity, conviction, brilliance, purity. Marry Fanny Price? What could be better?

He's really cute, Devoney thought.

She considered the bow tie. *I hope he's not gay.*

They arranged to continue their conversation later, in the bar at the conference hotel. The friends they had brought along to the bar tired of watching them flirt, and eventually Devoney and George found themselves alone. He chose this moment to propose marriage.

Let's get in a taxi and drive to Las Vegas right now! he said. He was from the Northeast, land of tiny states, and didn't realize that the trip he was suggesting would have taken seven hours. But he was serious about the marriage thing.

She turned him down, of course. She didn't believe in marriage, she said.

"I thought you were kind of teasing me, but I thought you also kind of meant it," she said. "You were being exuberant and impulsive."

"Totally meant it."

"It was around this time that I asked him if he had a girlfriend, and he said yes."

She kissed him anyway.

George went back to Pennsylvania and told his girlfriend of eight months that they had to break up. He found the business card on which Devoney had written her e-mail address and sent her a message, explaining that he had just split with his girlfriend and needed time to process that painful step.

"He needed some time and space," Devoney said. "And so I wrote back, and I said, 'Of course, I understand. Take as much time as you need to heal and deal with your grief.'"

"But I kept thinking about her," George said. "And a couple hours later, I thought, 'Huh . . .'"

"Four hours."

"'. . . I've got this phone number here. I guess it would not hurt for me to make a phone call.'"

"Four hours. He needed four hours to grieve."

"And I grieved for four hours, and then we were on the phone, and we stayed up until about three or four in the morning, talking."

A month later, when the semester ended, Devoney drove to Pennsylvania for a visit. They were engaged before she went home again. For a month or two, they kept their engagement secret, like Jane Fairfax and Frank Churchill in *Emma,* so their parents wouldn't worry about the whirlwind nature of their romance. Their parents worried anyway.

"At the time, I didn't understand that that would be scary," George said. "I just thought it's a good story."

"And it's true," Devoney said. "Which is the best kind of good story."

Devoney Looser's unusual name — pronounce it DEV-oh-nee — came from a book her mother once read. Which book? Devoney never knew. For years, she assumed that when she turned eighteen, her mother would finally pull out a copy, perhaps explaining that its adult content had put it off-limits before, but in fact her mother had forgotten the title. The Loosers were lower middle class; Devoney's father was an insurance underwriter, and her mother kept house for much of Devoney's childhood, eventually going to work in a hospital kitchen. No one in Devoney's family had attended four-year college, but her mother prized education. She took her children to museums and plays, decorated the walls of their house with reproductions of classic artworks checked out of the public library, and organized the family's small book collection, stored on a shelf over the toilet, according to the Dewey decimal system. One book in particular, a volume containing both *Pride and Prejudice* and *Sense and Sensibility,* she repeatedly pressed upon her daughter, but at first Devoney could not master the nineteenth-century language. Only on her third attempt, at thirteen, did she finally fall under the spell of Darcy and Elizabeth's story. Years later, she learned that her mother had never read Jane Austen herself. "It was just a book that she knew that educated people should read," Devoney says, "so she was persistent."

Devoney went to a Catholic high school with a strict policy on teen sex: pregnant girls were expelled, and impregnating boyfriends were allowed to stay in school. The unfairness of this double standard turned Devoney into a feminist. Her excellent grades won her a full scholarship to a small local college, where she studied with single-minded focus to maintain the grade point average she needed to keep her scholarship. Eventually, she chose academia — studying the women writers of the nineteenth century — as the field on which to enact her feminism.

By the time I met her, Devoney was a beloved presence in the classroom, the recipient of teaching awards at four of the five universities where she had worked. Everywhere we went on the Missouri campus, she greeted people with effusive warmth. Introducing me to fellow professors, she offered brief accounts of how wonderful they were as colleagues and scholars. In the university library, she thanked the staff for their help with a recent class activity. Leading the *Mansfield Park* discussion, she praised her students for their comments ("I think that's very perceptive") or thanked them for speaking at all. At home, she told her son's piano teacher how much he was enjoying his lessons. Such unceasing goodwill risked becoming cloying, but Devoney radiated a sunny sincerity. It was hard to imagine her aiming a sharp elbow at an enemy skater on the roller-derby track.

Although Devoney had speed-skated as a child — Minnesotans deliberately flooded their postage-stamp-sized backyards in winter, to create a space for home ice skating — she had taken to the roller rink on a lark, invited by a couple of younger friends from the university. One night, a member of the local roller-derby team spotted their strong skating skills and invited them all to beginners' training. Devoney went home and cried. Once, she would have loved roller derby, but by now, she figured, she was too old. But her friends insisted that she come along to practice, and eventually all three made the team. In her first competitive bout, in May 2010, Devoney — or, rather, Stone Cold Jane Austen — was named Most Valuable Player. Suddenly, everyone she met wanted to know what Jane Austen would have thought of roller derby. (Her standard answer: thumbs up on the camaraderie of strong women, thumbs down on the tattoos.)

Five months later, when university colleagues decided to cast her as herself in a shoestring-budget campus movie shot by a crew mostly made up of students, it just seemed like icing on the whole roller-derby cake. The film — something about a roller-derby team facing competition from a squad packed with vampires — was shot over fifteen days, mostly in grueling dusk-to-dawn shifts. Devoney and her teammates skated through campus in the dark, in pursuit of the villainous vampires. Oscar nominations seemed unlikely to follow.

In her university office — the usual professorial den, with a scratched wooden desk and crowded floor-to-ceiling bookshelves

— Devoney turned to her computer and called up a scene from the work in progress: the fictional Devoney meeting with her white-haired, tweed-jacketed department chair. He points out that she's simultaneously serving as president of the Jane Austen Society and skating with the roller-derby team, and he worries that she's over-committed.

"You know me," Movie Devoney says, a bit stiffly. "British literature, especially Jane Austen, is my passion."

Too bad, Movie Department Chair tells her; she has to choose. Jane Austen must go.

"Roller derby has a much higher profile," he explains. "Both for you and for the university."

The three greatest reading experiences of George Justice's life:

1. Fifth grade — Tolkien's *Lord of the Rings*
2. Senior year of college — Boswell's *Life of Samuel Johnson*
3. First year of graduate school — Jane Austen's *Mansfield Park*

He had read *Emma* in college and had found it rather dull. Perhaps it was because the world he knew was so male: he was the middle of three brothers, had gone to a Quaker boys' school in Philadelphia, and had lost his mother to pancreatic cancer when he was nine. That trauma, eighteen months of chaos before his father's remarriage restored some sense of normality, disrupted an otherwise comfortable life. Though his parents had not grown up with privilege — his father was the son of a West Virginia coal miner, his mother the daughter of Lebanese immigrants — both had finished college, and his father worked as a bankruptcy lawyer. They lived the upper-middle-class life of eastern liberals. By age twelve, George was a member of the American Civil Liberties Union. He majored in English at Wesleyan University, spent two years editing young-adult books at a New York publisher, and then enrolled in graduate school at the University of Pennsylvania.

By then, George had matured enough to appreciate Fanny Price. "I stayed up until three in the morning finishing the book," he says. "It was like a whole world had opened to me. I could not believe how great that book was." That semester, he poured his passionate opinions about *Mansfield Park* into an essay and got a B-minus, which, in the grade-inflated universe of graduate school, was not much better than failing. He might have matured as a reader, but he was still learning how to be a graduate student.

For his doctoral dissertation, he turned to the eighteenth-century publishing industry, devoting two chapters to Austen's older contemporary, Fanny Burney, an important influence on Austen's work — not to mention the author whose first edition my JASNA tour-mate Skip McNeil had bought for his Janeite wife, Debbie, because Austen's name appeared on the list of advance purchasers. At night, George sometimes dreamed he was a talk-show host sitting across a table from Burney, discussing her books. He was half in love with her, even though she had died 150 years earlier.

After that chastening B-minus, he left Jane Austen alone. So many great critics had written about her, he thought. What could he possibly add?

"Unfortunately, so much literary criticism is a kind of mutilated intellectual autobiography," the distinguished literary critic was saying.

We were drinking coffee in a bustling café in central New Jersey, where I had arranged to meet William H. Galperin, a professor of English at Rutgers University, for a tutorial on the history of Austen criticism. Galperin, who goes by Billy, has deep-set eyes, a high forehead, a prominent nose, and dark, bushy eyebrows, and he speaks with a touch of aristocratic drawl, drawing out his words a fraction longer than you'd expect. In his 2003 study, *The Historical Austen,* Galperin had aimed to put Austen in the context of her times, examining how her contemporaries would have read her, what they would have seen — or not seen — in her books. Too often, he said, modern critics read the attitudes of later generations back onto Austen. For decades, a string of critics, mostly male, had assumed she shared the strait-laced values of the Victorian era, even though she was a product of the earthier eighteenth century. In reaction, later critics, often female, had turned her into something like a contemporary feminist. Galperin found fault with both approaches. "They may be able to open up the works to interesting perspectives, but these interpretations are really mostly anachronistic superimposition," Galperin said. "I think if you're going to try to grapple with Austen, you have to grapple with her in terms that she wants to be grappled with."

Grappling with Austen, on her own terms or any other, is so popular a sport that by now, critical works about her could fill every shelf in a good-sized library. It wasn't always so, however; for a long time, almost no one wrote about her. When they were first published, Austen's novels were reviewed only a dozen times, according to the Austen scholar Brian Southam, and in the fifty-nine years after the appearance of *Sense and Sensibility,* only fifty critical articles gave much space to a discussion of Austen, with just six taking her as their main subject. Her admirers included some luminaries, however: two of those six longer articles were written by the best-selling poet and historical novelist Sir Walter Scott and the influential Victorian critic G. H. Lewes, the common-law husband of George Eliot.

The 1870 memoir by Austen's nephew, J. E. Austen-Leigh, which inaugurated the vogue for Austen's works among general readers, also brought her new attention from critics, who argued over how much credit she deserved for conscious artistry. Was she a sweet homebody who produced her charming novels almost instinctively (Henry James compared her to "the brown thrush who tells his story from the garden bough")? Or was she a careful, technically accomplished craftswoman? Both admirers and detractors described her as a novelist of limited scope who confined herself to the domestic sphere, although they were divided over whether this was an advantage (she wrote what she knew) or a disadvantage (she didn't know much). Already, some of her critics were repelled by the preciousness of her fans — not the swooning females of modern caricature, but the clubby, upper-class English men who called Austen "the divine Jane."

Academic scholarship about Austen was born in the early years of the twentieth century, as the study of English literature made its way for the first time into the British university curriculum. The Austen embraced by the academy was no boat-rocker. During World War I, she was seen as so safe and calm that her books were prescribed as a restorative to shell-shocked survivors of the trenches. For the war veteran Robert Chapman, a lexicographer and editor who had studied classics at Oxford, Austen exemplified the solid English values that the war had been fought to protect. In 1923, Chapman produced a still-influential scholarly edition of Austen's novels for Oxford University Press's Clarendon Press imprint. The Clarendon Press Austens were the first-ever scholarly editions of any English novelist; a genre that for much of its history had been disparaged and ignored was just beginning to be thought worthy of serious academic study.

But even in the years surrounding World War I, Chapman's view of Austen — safe, solid, reassuringly English — had dissenters. Some of those disillusioned by the carnage of the war perceived a kindred spirit in a novelist they saw as tough-minded and realistic. "She is the contemporary of a generation whose ideals have blown up," the Princeton University scholar Claudia L. Johnson wrote, "a generation that respects the humor of little things, home things, not because they are darling, diminutive, or manageable, but more tragically because big bombastic things have been shown to be shams."

The split between the reassuring Austen and the disillusioned Austen was an early example of the conflict that would come to define Austen criticism, what the academic Laurence W. Mazzeno calls "the Great Austen Controversy: Was she a conservative or a radical? Did she really believe in the moral values and social structure of Regency England, or was she using her considerable wit and talent for storytelling for subversive purposes?" One of the first and most famous proponents of the Austen-as-subversive school was the psychologist D. W. Harding, whose 1940 essay "Regulated Hatred: An Aspect of the Work of Jane Austen" argued that her satire was far less gentle and affectionate, and its targets far closer to home, than her fans seemed to realize. "Her books are, as she meant them to be, read and enjoyed by precisely the sort of people whom she disliked," Harding wrote. "She is a literary classic of the society which attitudes like hers, held widely enough, would undermine."

As critics focused more and more on Austen's craft and irony, and, later, on the historical context of her work, her novels became firmly entrenched in the literary canon. By the 1970s, she had become such a well-established topic of academic study that, according to Mazzeno, between 1976 and 1990, three hundred doctoral dissertations dealt, in whole or in large part, with her works. Feminist critics were beginning to claim Austen as their own, seeing in her marriage plots a subtle critique of male-dominated Regency society and the limited choices it offered to women. But other voices cautioned against casting Austen in the mold of a twentieth-century liberal, or even a nineteenth-century one. In her 1975 study *Jane Austen and the War of Ideas,* the Oxford scholar Marilyn Butler insisted that Austen's novels took the conservative side in the political and social arguments of their time. In 1993, the Palestinian-American literary critic Edward Said pointed out that the business matters requiring Sir Thomas Bertram, the patriarch of *Mansfield Park,* to travel to Antigua—a crucial turn in the plot—must have involved management of slave plantations. Austen elided this fact, Said argued, and thereby made herself complicit in the unsavory, exploitative economic underpinnings of the leisured world in which she set her stories. Said's argument was controversial— true to form, other critics argued that the text of *Mansfield Park* in fact hinted at a critique of slavery and imperialism—but it was also hugely influential, so much so that eighteen years later, Devoney Looser could not teach the novel to her students without making Said's thesis a centerpiece of the discussion.

Only occasionally did elements of academic discourse make their way into public awareness—and then, not usually with great nuance. A 1995 headline in the *London Review of Books*—"Was Jane Austen Gay?"—provoked raging controversy, although the article it accompanied, a review of a new edition of Austen's letters, never suggested that she was. Among political conservatives, a paper titled "Jane Austen and the Masturbating Girl," which the Duke University English professor Eve Kosofsky Sedgwick delivered at the 1990 conference of the Modern Language Association, became a touchstone, its title alone supposedly proof of the corruption and idiocy of liberal academics. The paper itself, which analyzed *Sense and Sensibility* in relation to issues of sexuality, was actually highly theoretical and far from titillating.

Fundamental disagreements over interpretation are not uncommon in literary studies, but when Austen is the subject, the arguments sometimes seem especially impassioned. Austen matters in a way that many other writers, even some famous ones, don't. "There's just more at stake. People get more invested," Devoney Looser says. "It's like she's a Rorschach test. They want to see themselves in her."

As his career advanced, from tenure-track junior faculty member to tenured professor and then to dean of Missouri's graduate school, George Justice gained the confidence to write about Jane Austen once again. In part, he was inspired by Devoney. In graduate school, he had absorbed an older critical tradition that insisted on confining interpretation to the work at hand, without much reference to historical or ideological contexts. Applying a political notion like feminism to Jane Austen felt a bit earnest and contrived. But Devoney's work had persuaded him that using feminist thinking to interpret literature wasn't illegitimate. "The days of the unacknowledged presence of politics in literature are behind us; the political/social ramifications of literary study are now widely examined," Devoney had written in the introduction to the essay collection *Jane Austen and Discourses of Feminism,* published the year they met. "It is in this respect that scholarship dealing with Austen —feminist and otherwise—must come to terms with contemporary literary theoretical innovations concerning authorship, class, complicity, gender, genre, history, nationality, race, resistance, and sexuality in order to give us a more sophisticated picture of the possibilities for understanding Austen's texts in a critical frame."

Janeites also helped George find his way back to Austen studies. Devoney had spoken at her first JASNA conference a few months before meeting George, and in the late 1990s, the two of them returned to the podium as a double act, applying a template that Devoney sums up as "married couple fights about literature, and you learn something in the process." They staged a he said/she said debate over courtship in *Northanger Abbey,* gave the Myers-Briggs personality test to characters in *Emma,* and argued over whether Cassandra Austen was right to burn most of her sister's personal correspondence, despite the anguish she had caused generations of Janeites mourning the insights those missing letters might have made possible. As the years passed, George and Devoney made good friends in JASNA, acquired a tote bag or two, bought their kids I'D RATHER BE READING JANE AUSTEN T-shirts, and saw most of the movies.

George loved the Emma Thompson film version of *Sense and Sensibility* ("almost as good as the book"), but unlike many Janeites, he was no fan of Andrew Davies, who had written the screenplay for the wet-shirt *Pride and Prejudice.*

"I don't think he's all that great," George said over dinner.

"Oh, George." Devoney sounded exasperated. "You're just wrong about that. You're just wrong. You're wrong. I mean, I don't know how else to respond."

Davies, who had also adapted *Emma,* was on record for disparaging its often misguided heroine and suggesting that the book's secondary romance, between the smooth Frank Churchill and the reserved Jane Fairfax, was disturbing and exploitative. Fresh from editing his Norton Critical Edition of *Emma,* for which he had written an introduction laying out some of the complex questions the novel raised for attentive readers, George disagreed vigorously.

"That is a hack of B-plus quality," he said. "That's just a hack point of view, and a very ungenerous point of view. And the weird thing about *Emma* is it becomes a very strangely generous novel, even though that isn't its impulse from the beginning."

"George usually has to speak in sound bites when he's speaking on behalf of the university, and he gets to shoot from the hip like that," Devoney said.

"I didn't shoot from the hip on that. What, are you criticizing my perspective on *Emma*? Do you disagree?"

"No, but I don't ever get to meet Andrew Davies, thanks to you. You just called him a hack."

Janeite playfulness and exuberance were a far cry from the critical detachment and objectivity intrinsic to the academic code, and in their JASNA lives, George and Devoney enjoyed the contrast. "What I think both of us loved about JASNA from a very early point was that, at most academic conferences, you are not allowed to be enthusiastic. It's not really on the menu," Devoney says. "And so it was a breath of fresh air to go to these conferences and to be able to be excited about something." (Their embrace of enthusiasm did have its limits, though. Although Devoney would have been game for dress-up, George had never agreed to attend a JASNA conference in costume. He worried what his colleagues would think if the photographs ever got out.)

Scholarly discomfort with Austen's ardent fans, a perennial virtually since the beginning of Austen scholarship, flourished anew in the post–Colin Firth world, and not everyone saw George and Devoney's involvement with JASNA in an entirely positive light. "George gets paid to amuse wacko Janeites," one colleague told a newcomer to the English department. To plenty of academics, apparently, the things that went on at Jane Austen conferences were a bit unseemly, a bit *uncritical* — a trivialization of the serious study of literature.

Even Devoney had her doubts about the Janeite predilection for discussing fictional characters as if they were real people. Although her husband had fallen in love with her when she compared herself to Fanny Price, she admitted to feeling some discomfort over the Janeite parsing of such pressing questions as which character you would most like to marry.

"That's an uncritical I'm not willing to go to," she said. "I think there are a lot more interesting questions we can ask than that one. And I think there are more important questions we can ask than that."

"That's very Maoist of you," George said.

He began to talk about Mrs. Elton, the officious social climber who is perhaps the closest thing to a villain in *Emma*. "I've gone through many readings of the novel, and it has taken to number fifteen or sixteen for me just to laugh, and not feel emotionally tugged at by how vile and despicable Mrs. Elton is," he said. "And that takes a lot of readings, because the book is so perfectly constructed to make you despise her."

"Maybe it's a pedagogical problem for me, because this is often the place where students start from," Devoney said. "And I think it's a fine place to start from in reading a novel, but it's a start; it's not where you're looking to conclude. Emotional responses are fantastic, but if what you're trying to do is rethink in a more nuanced way, more deeply, more critically, then that's not going to get you there."

"I completely disagree pedagogically," George said. "In my view, the way you get there is: 'You hate Mrs. Elton. Who hates Mrs. Elton? Why do you hate Mrs. Elton?'"

"But that's pushing it beyond. Now you're asking them to be critical."

"I'm not asking them not to hate Mrs. Elton, though."

JASNA conferences, George said, are conducted in the same spirit. "Let's start with why we hate her, let's figure it all out and have fun while figuring it out, because it doesn't have to be a chore.

And then we end up with a dance and talking about how much we hate Mrs. Elton," he said. "Without the responses, without trying to explain the response, the works die. If you don't love reading them, the works are dead. And you can still love reading them, while you're doing the analysis. And you still hate Mrs. Elton."

"I agree with that part," Devoney said. "And you can still hate Mrs. Elton."

Pleasure had been an integral part of my reading experience since childhood, but, I was learning, it wasn't a response that every scholar saw as, well, scholarly. "Most academics I know take a rather dim view of these galas, where enjoyment rather than hermeneutic mastery is assumed to be the reward of reading," Claudia L. Johnson, the Princeton English professor, had written. Could it be *wrong* to enjoy reading Jane Austen? Or, if not wrong exactly, then intellectually soft, insufficiently rigorous? Did we fans have too much heart and not enough brain?

Devoney took me to the university library, where librarians in the rare-books department showed us first editions of works by Austen and her near contemporaries — *Northanger Abbey* and *Persuasion,* published together posthumously; a tiny volume containing a story by a young Charlotte Brontë; a novel by Jane Porter, one of the subjects of Devoney's next book. Porter and her sister Anna Maria, popular in their day but now largely forgotten, were hardly Austen's equals in literary accomplishment, Devoney acknowledged, but their lives and work were interesting and important nonetheless. Perhaps that was the difference between fans and academics, I thought. Maybe fans read the books they thought were good, while academics read the books they thought were important.

"There are some very, very fine critics, who are telling us new things about literature and literary history, who profess a total lack of interest in whether something is good," George said a few hours later, as we all ate lunch at the University Club. "And I used to be morally offended by that."

Back in his graduate school days, he had argued this point with a fellow doctoral student who was a classically trained pianist and a gourmand, the kind of person who listened to Mozart and ate in Philadelphia's finest restaurants. You judge the quality of the food you eat and the music you listen to, George would say; why do you insist on withholding those judgments about literature, the very sphere in which you have the most specialized training? Over the years, George had become less doctrinaire; he saw now that knowledge could be advanced even by those with no particular love for the books they were studying. But it didn't work for him. "For me, part of being an academic humanist is conveying a very deep appreciation for these glorious works of the human mind, especially at the undergraduate level," he said. He didn't see why you should teach books that you thought were bad.

Devoney didn't entirely agree. In her Jane Austen course that semester, she was teaching a preachy novel by Austen's older contemporary, the religious writer Hannah More. Neither Devoney nor her students much liked it, but it provided interesting context for *Mansfield Park*.

"I think that's OK, if there is enough of the stuff that is really good," George said. "It's going to help you learn Jane Austen more."

Even if they were seeking the interesting as well as the good, academics were hardly immune to Austen's appeal. The Rutgers professor Billy Galperin began writing about Austen after adding her to the syllabus of his course on Romanticism, when he went looking for a novel to vary the course's steady diet of poetry. "For my own sanity, I threw in something I would like to prepare for class and think about," he says. "Austen is a lot more fun to include in your syllabi, because she's just a terrific writer. Jane Austen is the practitioner par excellence of lovable literature."

I had heard Galperin give a dense, highly academic talk on Austen's novella *Lady Susan* at the Philadelphia JASNA meeting, and he said he found JASNA audiences receptive and engaged. Still, he had no trouble understanding the academic discomfort with Austen fandom. "The production of knowledge is linked to change, not repetition," he says. "The JASNA culture is all about repeating and repeating and repeating. People go back to reading the books in a kind of compulsively repetitive way. They already know what they're going to find upon rereading. Whereas the people who are in the knowledge business are trying to get away from repetition, if they can. They're trying to do something new."

The ogling of Regency real estate promoted by the Austen movies, most of them set in houses far grander than those that Austen describes, contributed to the feeling that Janeites were wedded to an idealized, snobbish image of Austen's world. I'd glimpsed that myself, as I trooped through stately-homes-cum-movie-sets with my JASNA tour-mates. "There is a sense, particularly with the ball and all that stuff, that part of what makes Austen so appealing to JASNA people is that she's a kind of one-woman heritage industry," Galperin says. "Austen represents a kind of cultural capital that can somehow be acquired and assimilated simply by reading her."

Galperin's Austen was far more complex and ambiguous, the practitioner of what literary critics call "unstable irony." Her meanings shifted, leaving her readers unsure of where the authority in her narratives lay. As we drank our coffee, Galperin began riffing on the shadows in *Sense and Sensibility* — the ambiguous sexuality of the hero's foppish brother, the hints Galperin detected that

Colonel Brandon, who will eventually marry the passionate Marianne, is working behind the scenes to expose the wrongdoing of his rival for Marianne's affections. Or what about the manipulation practiced by Anne Elliot's ailing friend Mrs. Smith, in *Persuasion,* as she tries desperately to recover family property in the West Indies (another slave plantation, Austen's readers would surely have assumed)? And then there was *Persuasion*'s climactic scene, with Anne Elliot and her new friend, Captain Harville, arguing over whether men or women are more faithful in love, while Anne's lost love, Captain Wentworth, eavesdrops and begins penning "what has to be the tritest letter ever written in the history of—"

I felt a stab of almost physical pain. Trite? Captain Wentworth's love letter? The most romantic passage in all of Jane Austen? Every word of which I knew by heart? "I love the letter!" I squeaked.

"I know you do. I know you do," Galperin said indulgently. "You've got to steel yourself against that."

After work, back in George and Devoney's rambling 1970s house in a leafy faculty neighborhood, George threw together a dinner of bagels and omelets and raced their five-year-old son off to soccer practice. Devoney stayed home to supervise their eight-year-old's strategic deployment of cardboard, tape, and glue in the construction of a *Star Wars* diorama. Later, as he checked up on his Fantasy Football league before bedtime, the eight-year-old asked George for the password to the home computer. "Austen," George said. Most of his computers answered to either "Austen" or "Burney."

The evening felt cozy and familiar. I grew up in a leafy faculty neighborhood near a college campus, studied hard in school, married a graduate student who grew up to be a college professor, and drove my son to soccer practice. My computer password was "Chawton." It felt completely natural to spend hours immersed in conversations about books, and after months of reading Austen spinoffs under the placid gaze of my Jane Austen Action Figure, it was energizing to return to the books themselves — fantastically good, inexhaustibly interesting. George had summed it up the night before: "What could be more wonderful about one's life than to be able to read these books and teach them to young people who also love them?"

In the classroom, Devoney's students are talking about Mary Crawford, the witty, amoral anti-heroine of *Mansfield Park*.

"She's the one I would want to be friends with," says a delicately pretty young woman in a pale-green shirt and denim vest.

Does Austen want us to like Mary, or to dislike her? Devoney asks.

The story is told from Fanny's point of view, and Fanny dislikes her, the young woman says. Fanny sees Mary as a temptress, luring her beloved cousin Edmund away from his duty.

Devoney smiles. "Fantastic," she says. "You took us right away from 'like' and 'dislike' to why it matters. Which I love."

CHAPTER 6

THE JANE AUSTEN CODE

ARNIE PERLSTEIN IS LOST. He's driving me to my hotel, and although he's only a few miles from home, here in south Florida the palm trees and highway turnoffs all seem to look alike. I have a terrible sense of direction too, so I feel nothing but sympathy as Arnie pulls onto a street that turns out to be a driveway, reverses at the entrance to a strip mall, and narrowly avoids going in precisely the wrong direction at the next traffic circle. "Shit," he mutters. "This is all very familiar. I can't believe I screwed it up."

We were talking about Jane Austen when we got lost. We'd been talking about Jane Austen for almost two days — or, rather, Arnie had been talking, and I'd been listening. Arnie talks constantly, almost compulsively, rivers of words overflowing their banks and dividing into hundreds of tiny tributaries, as one topic suggests another and then another. He talks while driving, left hand on the wheel of his 2007 Dodge Charger, right hand slicing the air. He talks while monitoring the championship tennis match on TV, interrupting a digression on biblical interpretation to note a service break. He talks like a man obsessed.

Which he is. If Austenmania were a religion, Arnie Perlstein might be its high priest — or, given the way things have been going, its leading heretic, burned at the stake with a dog-eared copy of his beloved *Emma* clutched in one charred hand.

Since his Austen obsession blossomed in 2002, he calculates, he has spent more than fifteen thousand completely uncompensated hours devising a theory about Austen's novels that most Janeites find bizarre enough to border on the delusional. To the readers of his countless online posts, his wrong turns and false starts behind the wheel of his Dodge could serve as a metaphor for his interpretative method. Still, when I visited him in Florida in mid-September 2010, Arnie Perlstein was convinced he stood on the cusp of something he longed for: acceptance — or at least credibility — in the world of Jane Austen studies. In just over six weeks, he would finally be a featured speaker at JASNA's annual convention, in Portland, Oregon. "If I get, say, one hundred people in the room there, it's going to be crazy, because I'm going to tell them stuff about *Northanger Abbey* that's going to blow their minds fifty times around the room," Arnie said. "I'm going to be telling them things they can't even dream of."

Arnie Perlstein, a rangy, middle-aged man with a head of curly dark hair and a small graying mustache, has been telling Janeites mind-blowing things about Jane Austen for a while, and, as he freely admits, he hasn't exactly persuaded most of his audience. His theory holds that Austen's novels are anamorphic — literary versions of a familiar optical illusion, the picture that can look like either a vase or two faces in profile. Arnie believes that each Austen novel can be read as telling two different stories: the familiar one, with its beloved heroine, witty social satire, and happy ending, and an unfamiliar, far darker version, in which even sympathetic characters lie and scheme, indulge in illicit sex, conceal out-of-wedlock pregnancies, and even commit murder, en route to an ending that may not be so happy after all.

Arnie thinks these parallel fictional universes, which he calls "shadow stories," amount to a radical critique of nineteenth-century patriarchy, adding a compelling feminist dimension to Austen's already rich narrative design. Most other Janeites think he's crazily wrong—and after years of encounters with his online persona, they find him deeply annoying as well. His Internet posts have much the same flavor as his face-to-face conversation. Rambling. Digressive. Long. Really long. He thanks others for the way their completely misguided comments on Austen have helped sharpen his own thinking. He hints teasingly at the textual evidence he can't share because he's saving it for the book he's been promising to write for years. "Treat him like a terrorist," the proprietor of one Austen website privately advised the proprietor of another. Do not negotiate. Just get rid of him before he drives away your other readers. One participant in an online Austen discussion group swamped with Perlstein posts finally begged, "Please, please, please, go away and write your book." Perhaps it was no coincidence that an Austen-themed detective story published in 2012 cast a professor with some strikingly Arnie-esque theories in the role of murder victim.

Closer to home, Perlstein's audience, though fond, remains skeptical, or perhaps just exhausted. His adult children and stepchildren roll their eyes at his obsessiveness. Jackie, his wife of more than fifteen years, has told him to keep Jane Austen out of daily conversation. And when I asked Arnie's ninety-one-year-old father if he had been convinced by a particularly impassioned speech that his son had just delivered, Walter Perlstein said wryly, "I'm convinced of his zeal."

All that afternoon, we had been sitting in the small den of Walter's apartment, with CNBC rolling mutely across the screen of the big TV. Arnie's lanky frame was draped over the brown leather couch; Walter sat on a chair nearby, bushy brows contracted, listening quizzically to our conversation, scanning the scrolling headlines, occasionally dozing. Walter was no Jane Austen fan. Back when he could see well enough to read, his tastes tended toward pulpy thrillers. But his heart had been acting up lately, and Arnie had decided that listening in on an Austen conversation would give Walter a welcome distraction from worrying about a medical procedure scheduled for later in the week.

Walter had few opinions about Austen, but he had plenty of opinions about Arnie's life. The unsuitable first wife, for example.

"He almost disinherited me when I met her," Arnie said. "And probably rightly so."

They argued their way companionably through the details of the story. "And after they were married five years," Walter said, "he came to me and said, 'How could you let me marry her?'"

"I didn't say that to you! You're confabulating that!"

"This is my recollection of history," Walter said, as Arnie chuckled.

Their closeness was a relatively recent development. Arnie's parents had divided their labor in the fashion typical of 1950s American families: Walter worked long hours, and Belle raised their sons. But in 1999, a massive stroke left Belle almost completely disabled, forcing Walter to take on the role of caretaker. For months, Arnie came by daily to offer support and companionship and, after Belle's death in 2001, to help his bereft father adjust to life alone.

Now, as Arnie bustled through the apartment hunting for a list of Walter's medications, his father remembered those years, when their bond was forged in the crucible of Belle's illness. "We both were the only people who could reach her and communicate with her and spend time with her, make her life easier," Walter said. "She couldn't talk, she couldn't write, she couldn't communicate. The way I did it was twenty questions: I would see she wanted to say something, and I would ask her a bunch of questions and narrow it down, and I always found out." Belle grew tired of having a nurse bathe and feed her, so Walter took over those tasks. "She never expected that from me," he said, half sadly, half proudly. "And at night the only connection she would have is I would reach over and hold her hand, and she'd smile and be comfortable."

He paused. "But other times, she let me know she didn't want to live. And I told her it wouldn't be fair to leave me alone."

Arnie was back in the room now, listening.

"The first year after she died, I was a fucking mess."

"We got you through that year of transition," Arnie said.

Now Arnie was the caretaker, visiting Walter once or twice a week and checking in regularly by phone.

"Would you consider staying here tonight?" Walter asked. Arnie was on his way out of the apartment, and the next morning Walter was due at the doctor's for the procedure he was dreading.

"I don't want to!" Arnie said. "You'll be all right."

"Well, I hope I'm able to sleep tonight," Walter said.

"I'm sure you will. You've gotten to sleep under tenser situations than this," Arnie reassured him. "I'll have an extended conversation with you around ten or ten-thirty. I'll talk Jane Austen to you. I guarantee you'll be snoring by the time you put down the telephone."

It's no wonder, I thought, that Arnie loves *Emma,* whose heroine devotedly cares for her anxious, long-widowed father. He *is* Emma.

• • •

Arnie and Jackie live in a spacious, airy, Spanish-style home, with a glassed-in swimming pool, a striking color scheme, and unusual ethnic art objects decorating walls and tables. The home office where Arnie works is something else entirely: a windowless box crammed with books, file folders, DVDs, photocopies, binders, printouts, vacation souvenirs, tennis shoes, family photos, and completed crossword puzzles. Every surface is jammed; every bookcase groans under double rows of volumes. On a table by the door, two Jane Austen Action Figures stand guard over the clutter, the kitschy equivalent of the stone lions flanking the entrance to the New York Public Library. The room is a monument to fifteen years of Arnie's intellectual history — his now-dormant career as a real estate lawyer, his dedication to the *New York Times* crossword puzzle, his enthusiasms for Shakespeare, Agatha Christie, and biblical exegesis, and of course, his Austen research. It's like a physical representation of the space inside Arnie's head, an eclectic amalgamation of the weighty and the trivial, connected in ways that make sense to Arnie but aren't always obvious to an outsider.

The heart of the Austen operation is the computer, with its bookmarks for the websites Arnie trolls daily, its countless digital folders containing the e-mails he's exchanged with everyone from distinguished Austen scholars to fellow amateurs, and its voluminous research files with titles like "Knightley as Jesus," "Lucy Steele Pregnant," and "Love Town." That last file compiles the pervasive sexual references he sees in Jane Austen's work (sample subfiles: "Lesbian Aspects," "Fannies, Rears, and Bottoms," "Music as Metaphor for Sex"). Periodically, he backs up his data and deposits the extra copy in a safe-deposit box, since losing it all to a hurricane or a hard-drive meltdown would leave him suicidal.

Only a fraction of his material makes it into his blog posts and online conversations, Arnie says, which is pretty amazing when you

consider how much he's written online. Over three days one summer, for example, he blogged more than five thousand words about
a brief moment toward the end of *Pride and Prejudice,* when Elizabeth Bennet is serving after-dinner coffee to guests and hoping
that Mr. Darcy will come talk to her. As Darcy approaches, Austen writes, "one of the girls moved closer to her than ever, and said,
in a whisper: 'The men shan't come and part us, I am determined.
We want none of them; do we?'" Generations of readers had seen
this unnamed girl, if they had noticed her at all, as little more than
a farcical roadblock in the way of the inevitable Darcy-Elizabeth romance, but Arnie — who believes that in the shadow story of *Pride
and Prejudice,* Mr. Darcy is more menacing than heroic — was convinced something more was going on. Who was this mysterious
whisperer?

Six hundred words into his argument, Arnie concluded that the
whisperer must be Elizabeth's pedantic younger sister, Mary, who
is trying to keep Elizabeth and Darcy apart because she fears that
Darcy means to seduce and abandon Elizabeth. Some of his evidence seemed less than conclusive — that Mary whispers to Elizabeth in an earlier scene in *Pride and Prejudice,* for instance, or
that the only other person in the novel who uses the contraction
"shan't" is Mrs. Bennet, Mary and Elizabeth's mother, and "after
all, children learn to speak from their parents!" Characteristically,
however, Arnie seemed exuberantly certain of his conclusion —
certain enough to connect a few more speculative dots:

I just realized as I was writing this message that this scene is
JA's masterfully sly rewrite of the most famous scene in Par-
adise Lost, when Satan whispers in Eve's ear while Eve is
asleep, tempting Eve (successfully) to take a bite of the ap-
ple. JA has turned Milton topsy turvy. Mary here is a GOOD

FEMALE Satan in Milton's Garden, whispering a message of female solidarity in Lizzy's (Eve's) ear, as Lizzy is "asleep" to the danger posed by Darcy, as Mary tries to divert her vulnerable sister from falling prey to a seductive man. Ironically, Mary tries to convey "knowledge" to Lizzy, but Lizzy does NOT take a bite. Mary Bennet as a well-intentioned Satan — how cool is that! Isn't it so that Milton's Satan has the power to assume a pleasing shape, and to alter his appearance and voice in order to tempt his victims? Here we have JA's corrective of Milton's sexism, showing how women can stand together and help each other resist dangerous temptations!

The insistence on the significance of an apparently trivial Austen moment, the less-than-obvious link to a major literary forebear, the unearthing of a subliminal feminist message, the reliance on sheer enthusiasm to glue the whole structure together — it was all vintage Arnie.

Yet for most of his life, Arnie hadn't seemed like the kind of guy who would end up blogging about the feminist politics of classic English literature. Growing up, he followed a predictable upwardly mobile trajectory. His parents, both the children of Polish immigrants, were secular Democratic New York City Jews who learned frugality from the Depression and pushed their children toward elite educations and professions. Walter had a long and lucrative career as a Wall Street lawyer, but Arnie, born in 1952, shared a bedroom with his older brother, and the family almost never ate dinner in a restaurant. At twelve, Arnie represented New York City in the National Spelling Bee (he placed twenty-seventh, misspelling "begum"), and he devoured books, working his way through the likes of Agatha Christie and Isaac Asimov. He decided that when he grew up, he wanted to be a writer too.

His parents talked him out of it. You couldn't make a living as a writer, they told him. Do something else and write on the side, his mother advised. Arnie shelved that dream and moved on — so completely that in college, he read little fiction and avoided most of the English department's offerings. Instead, he majored in psychology and went on to law school, although legal practice remained more like a job than a vocation. "I felt really good about myself for a long time doing it, but it never felt like this was what I was meant to be," Arnie says. "It was just a good way to make some good money."

His personal life was complicated and difficult. In the space of eight years, he married, divorced, and remarried, producing three sons along the way. Uninspired by his work, starved for intellectual companionship in the cultural wasteland of south Florida, and increasingly lonely inside his second marriage, he threw his energies into founding a club he called the Intellectual Snobs, a cross between a TV talk show and an eighteenth-century salon. At its height, stoked by newspaper publicity and word of mouth, dozens of Snobs met three times a month for lively group discussions, moderated by Arnie, on everything from psychoanalysis to the films of Ingmar Bergman. He craved community, and for five years, until the collapse of his second marriage sapped his energy and drove him into therapy, he had one.

As it turned out, his life was entering a new phase — a phase that would be dominated by two women, one of whom had been dead for nearly two hundred years.

In 1995, Arnie Perlstein turned forty-three. His second divorce was behind him, his solo legal practice was flourishing, and he was in love with Jackie, a clinical psychologist with two young children from a previous marriage. Jackie had minored in literature in college, and one of her favorite books was *Pride and Prejudice,* by some author whose name Arnie barely knew. When a new film of

Sense and Sensibility arrived in theaters just before Christmas that year, Jackie insisted they go see it.

"You were the one who got him started on Jane Austen," I said, as Jackie, a slender blond, sat curled up on the couch at home, fifteen years after that momentous date.

"Yeah, I know," she said. "It's really unfortunate."

She was joking. At least, I was pretty sure she was joking. Jane Austen was not the other woman in her marriage, Jackie assured me. She liked seeing Arnie so engrossed in his work, animated by a passion he had never felt for the law, and she was impressed and fascinated by everything he had learned about history, philosophy, and literature. Still, even a doting wife has her breaking point. A few years earlier, Jackie had started to notice that conversations with Arnie were morphing into Six Degrees of Jane Austen. When the minor celebrity Anna Nicole Smith died of a drug overdose and one Frederick von Anhalt stepped forward to claim paternity of her newly wealthy baby daughter, Arnie noted that Anhalt is the name of a character in the play the protagonists of *Mansfield Park* decided to stage. Could this modern-day Anhalt be a closet Janeite who had adopted his unusual name as a subtle homage? Eventually, Jackie had had enough. No more Jane Austen, she told him. Fill me in on your latest research topic, but don't mention That Name. She found herself remembering a Gilbert and Sullivan operetta in which one character cuts short his crazy wife's rantings ("Not that you're crazy, honey," she added parenthetically) by saying the magic word — "Basingstoke."

"So I feel like I need to say, 'Basingstoke! Stop that!'" Jackie said.

"She doesn't even know that Basingstoke is about five miles from where Jane Austen lived," Arnie interjected.

Jackie turned to me. "Welcome to my world," she said.

By the time I met her, on my second day in Florida, Arnie had already described Jackie to me as smart, beautiful, strong, sane, independent, supportive, a wonderful mother, a devoted daughter, a talented amateur interior decorator, and an expert therapist. The man was as besotted with his wife as any Jane Austen hero on the last page of his story. And in fact, Arnie said, what really drew him to Austen's work was not so much that film of *Sense and Sensibility* as the electric repartee between Darcy and Elizabeth in the BBC production of *Pride and Prejudice* that he and Jackie had watched together not long afterward. In the witty verbal fencing of two twenty-somethings in bonnet and knee breeches, he had seen a reflection of his own happy midlife romance, an idealized version of his best self, right there on the screen. He decided to read the books.

The fever built slowly. By 2000, he had read most of the novels. From time to time, he discussed them with Jackie, but although she read voraciously, she lacked his appetite for minute, exhaustive analysis. Arnie decided to look online for a place to have those conversations. It didn't take him long to find it—the Janeites discussion group, aimed at anyone, academic or amateur, who wanted to talk about Jane Austen. Almost immediately, he was hooked. "I can't even describe it. It's like I took LSD or something. It was like going to another planet, it was so exciting," Arnie recalls. "And I didn't even need that much input from the other people. I just needed reactions, and then I'd be thinking fifty things based on what other people were saying." Within a month, he had posted dozens of comments, as many as seven in one day.

His far-out theories took longer to develop. For more than a year, he posted typical Janeite speculation, commentary, and insight about what he would later come to call the "overt" stories of the novels, the ones that generations of readers knew and loved. But in June 2002, as he reread *Sense and Sensibility,* a thought popped into his head: perhaps the accidental meeting between dashing, corrupt John Willoughby and passionate, naive Marianne Dashwood — she twists her ankle during a rain-soaked walk, and he arrives on the scene in time to help her home — hadn't been so accidental after all. Perhaps Willoughby had heard about this beautiful young newcomer and had deliberately arranged to run into her. Perhaps Willoughby wasn't just a mercenary rake — perhaps he was a stalker too. Arnie combed the early chapters of the novel for evidence supporting his theory, probing for clues to chronology and motivation; under the heading "Playing Sherlock Holmes," he posted his findings. He found the responses encouraging, even enthusiastic. So he kept going, seeking textual evidence of behind-the-scenes manipulation by another of *Sense and Sensibility*'s unsympathetic characters, the gold digger Lucy Steele. Next, he took a look at Wickham, the callous seducer in *Pride and Prejudice*. Was it *really* a coincidence that Wickham and his childhood friend Mr. Darcy had arrived in the same small town within weeks of each other? His theory began to take shape: perhaps, he hypothesized, Jane Austen meant for careful readers to see that, offstage, the nasty people in her books were pulling hidden strings. But then, as he combed the now-familiar pages, he began to find evidence of behind-the-scenes manipulations by a rather sympathetic character — Charlotte Lucas, the best friend of *Pride and Prejudice*'s beloved heroine, Elizabeth Bennet. And what about kindly Mr. Weston, a secondary figure in *Emma*? Wasn't there something fishy about how readily he had surrendered his motherless young son to the care of his dead wife's relatives? "I started to reread *Emma*. It lit up like a Christmas tree," Arnie says. "And all of a sudden I realized: it's much more than Mr. Weston. It's everybody in the novel, it's every page of the novel. And then I said, 'Oh, my God — it's all the novels. It's everything.' It's not just the bad guys, it's everybody in the novels. There is an alternative way of reading these stories, different than the one that everybody knows."

January 2005: the birth of Arnie Perlstein's Grand Unified Theory of Everything in Jane Austen.

Was it possible, he wondered, that in more than a century of Austen studies, no one else had seen these hints and clues? He started reading. He read biographies, literary criticism, history, philosophy — skimming perhaps a thousand scholarly articles and borrowing 677 books via interlibrary loan, plus countless others already in the collection of his local library. He combed online databases for half-forgotten literary speculations. He scoured the archives of Internet communities, looking for intriguing discussions of problematic oddities in Austen's stories. He took a months-long detour into Shakespeare studies, after realizing that Austen often alluded to the Bard. He was convinced that he was on his way to cracking what he came to call the Jane Austen Code — the "intricate web of clues, hints, allusions and circumstances" in each book that pointed to a buried treasure, the hidden shadow story of the novel. An unusual word or phrase would set him off on a digital hunt through Google Books, to see whether Jane Austen might be alluding to a previous work containing that same phrase, in a complex game of literary association. A throwaway detail or a concealed pun — Jane Austen was full of puns! — might become a wormhole from the overt story to the shadows beyond. Here and there, he found versions of some of his discoveries in the works of published scholars, but no one, it seemed, had taken it as far as he had. He became convinced that he was the first person in two hundred years to see Jane Austen's work as she had meant it to be seen.

As a boy, Arnie had done crossword puzzles, emulating his father, a lifelong solver. But as an adult, he had abandoned them.

"I thought it was a waste of time," he said one afternoon, still draped across Walter's couch. "I thought it's just an intellectual . . ." He searched for a polite way to put this: " . . . self-play . . ."

"Masturbation," supplied Walter.

"Exactly. Because what's the point? All I'm doing is proving to myself how smart I am."

But around the time his love for Jane Austen was growing into obsession, Arnie rediscovered his interest in crossword puzzles. Years later, he was inclined to credit his subconscious. Perhaps something inside him just knew that he couldn't fully understand Austen unless he honed his ability to complete fragmentary patterns. By 2007, he was good enough to place 314th out of 698 competitors in the American Crossword Puzzle Tournament. And filling in the little squares in the super-hard Saturday edition of the *New York Times* crossword puzzle became a kind of mental yoga, giving him the flexibility and endurance to break the Jane Austen Code. "I'm 100 percent certain I turned myself into the world's only real literary puzzle-solver because I trained myself like a maniac," Arnie says. "It's like training for the Olympics. That's why I can do it so much faster and better now. In real time I could get answers to stuff that would have taken me weeks or months back in 2005."

At the time of my visit, Arnie had been working on Jane Austen full time for about two years. By 2008, his legal practice had come to center on a single client, a commercial real estate developer who used Arnie as dealmaker and sounding board. But the crash of the real estate market pushed his client into bankruptcy, and Arnie found himself with a lot of extra time on his hands and, thanks to family money, no financial imperative to return immediately to paid work. Jane Austen expanded to fill the space. For a while, Arnie had been envisioning a book—maybe a series of books—explaining Austen's shadow stories and his method of unearthing them. At last, he seemed to be within striking distance of his child-hood dream of becoming a writer. Once his book was published, he figured, the money would come. He had called it "the Jane Austen Code" in a deliberate echo of Dan Brown's mega-bestseller *The Da Vinci Code*. How much money did he expect to make? I asked. He was thinking $100,000.

I could hardly believe my ears. Six figures? He wasn't writing a beach-read thriller; he was writing a highly technical work of literary criticism aimed at readers with a minute knowledge of the characters and plots of a bunch of nineteenth-century novels. How many copies did he think he was going to sell? But Arnie was optimistic. In recent years, he had lectured on his ideas at two academic conferences in England, and his discussion of *Emma*'s shadow story had drawn a sizable — and, he felt, receptive — audience at a meeting of JASNA's New York City chapter. In his happiest fantasy, his Portland talk would cause a stir, and the Janeites in attendance would invite him to speak to their local JASNA chapters across the country. His book would be published by a mainstream commercial press and respectfully received by scholars. Rank-and-file Janeites would snap it up to read about the shadow stories, and Arnie Perlstein would become a regular on the JASNA circuit. Maybe someday Hollywood would come calling. "The life that I envision is a really cool one, where I'm a public figure in the Janeite world, interacting with other interesting Janeites, maybe even being involved in the making of a movie," Arnie says. "How cool would that be? Even if there were no money to me from it, it would be an amazingly cool and stimulating and exciting experience. But I want the money too. I'm a normal American. I'm not Mother Teresa."

Over the course of his project, Arnie had vacillated about how much of his evidence to share publicly. For years after his epiphany, he had been cautious in his online posts, lest a fellow devotee claim credit for his insights. His paranoia deepened when a brief e-mail-driven mind-meld with a Janeite from Australia deteriorated into mutual recrimination. On the blog that he had set up in 2007, he began appending occasional copyright symbols to his posts, to ensure that his intellectual claims were respected. But in the year or so before we met, his blog posts and online comments had become increasingly detailed, though the significance of his findings was often obscure. (What did it matter that Austen and the chemist Lavoisier had used similar wording? Was *Mansfield Park* really alluding to a little-known essay on friendship, simply because a digital search disclosed that both works contained the phrase "my friend such a one"?) But as we sat in his office one morning, I encountered the limits of his new openness.

Tell me the shadow stories of Jane Austen's novels, I asked.

No, he said. He was saving those for his book.

I pressed. He said no.

Then his native hospitality seemed to kick in, and he relented. Oh, all right—just one. He would tell me the shadow story of *Emma*.

He settled into his desk chair. He spoke, almost uninterrupted, for nine minutes.

Beautiful, orphaned Jane Fairfax was pregnant, and Emma's brother-in-law, John Knightley, was the father. The apparently dim-witted Harriet Smith was a scheming gold digger. Jane's secret lover, Frank Churchill, had wooed the odious Mrs. Elton before her marriage. The governess job that Mrs. Elton claimed to be arranging for Jane was really a one-way ticket into prostitution. Emma's friend Mrs. Weston wasn't pregnant—she was just pretending, so that she could save Jane from disgrace by adopting the baby. The death of Frank's rich aunt was too convenient to be anything but murder. Emma's seemingly doddering father had probably sired a nursery's worth of illegitimate progeny in his time—he was named Henry because his sexual behavior mirrored that of Henry VIII. George Knightley, who might well be one of those love children himself, was scheming to take control of the whole town of Highbury. His marriage to Emma constituted anything but a happy ending.

After a while, the parade of inconceivables began to overwhelm me. Arnie's version of *Emma* was surreal in its distortions, more like the melodramatic Austen sequels that fan fiction writers churned out by the carload than the subtle, understated novels of ordinary life that Austen's readers had grown to love. If this was the story Jane Austen had wanted to tell—or, rather, one of them; Arnie gave the overt stories and the shadow stories equal billing— surely she was history's least successful novelist, leaving all but one of her readers completely in the dark.

"I think she overestimated her audience," Arnie said, when I suggested this to him. Or perhaps, he theorized, she had overdone the secrecy. She had chosen to hide her darkest messages about the corruption of patriarchy inside her shadow stories because the conservative power structure of Regency England would have crushed anyone who spoke such revolutionary feminist sentiments aloud. "She was going to be crucified if she let any of this stuff be open," Arnie said. "So in her caution to hide, she hid too much, maybe."

Or perhaps, he added, her radical message had been buried by her family's posthumous spin-doctoring, which misled generations of readers about the kind of author she was. By now, many scholars felt that the biographical sketch Austen's brother Henry had written for the posthumous edition of her last novels, in which he insisted that none of Austen's characters were based on real-life models, might well have been misleading; even more readers agreed that her nephew's Victorian memoir, which portrayed Austen as a sweet maiden aunt, missed the darker elements embedded in her comic tales of domestic life. But characteristically, Arnie took these insights much further. Maybe, he speculated, Jane Austen wasn't the virginal spinster we'd always assumed. Maybe Jane *Fairfax*'s concealed pregnancy reflected Jane *Austen*'s concealed pregnancy. Maybe Jane Fairfax's baby, who will grow up known as Anna Weston, represented her creator's niece, who grew up known as Anna Austen. Maybe the shadow story of *Emma* was Jane Austen's way of saying that she had given her own baby away to be raised as her niece. And the father of that baby? Well, maybe the self-centered, even tyrannical fathers and brothers in her novels tell us something about Jane Austen's own relatives. No wonder her family wanted to hush it all up.

In his book, Arnie wasn't planning to say much about these explosive biographical speculations, elements of which he credited to his Australian e-mail correspondent, lest they hijack his larger agenda. "That's going to become all that people are going to respond to if I talk about it," he said. "But I happen to think she was abused. I happen to think that very bad things happened in that family."

It all sounded impossibly circular to me, with questionable interpretations of Austen's fiction being used to bolster speculation about her life, and questionable interpretations of her biography being used to bolster speculation about her fiction. Arnie believed that Jane Austen had concealed gothic tales of patriarchal abuses inside serene dramas of daily life, but how much was she really concealing? Thoughtful readers had always found darkness in her novels — razor-sharp satire of the powerful and the foolish, and, amid the happily-ever-after plots, implicit criticism of a culture that made marriage the only respectable way for a middle-class woman to support herself. Arnie had convinced himself that these complexities, the layering that made Austen a great writer rather than a purveyor of nineteenth-century Harlequin romances, amounted to an entire parallel story. Was he ever going to convince anyone else?

Emma Woodhouse, the clever, foolish heroine of Arnie's favorite Austen novel, believes she is an unusually perceptive judge of the people around her. She fashions their lives into romantic narratives that suit her preferences and tries to shape events accordingly, but because her imaginings bear little relation to reality, she leaves a trail of hurt feelings and near-disasters in her wake. Arnie Perlstein had more than a little Emma in him. He said impossibly arrogant things — "I can't imagine someone knowing more than I know about Jane Austen in the entire world," he once told me — with little apparent sense of how they sounded to other people. He fell in love with his own imaginative speculations about Austen's life and works and found it hard to understand why others remained unconvinced. Not everything he said seemed far-fetched. His musings could yield interesting insights into Austen's characters, and even some of those puns looked plausible. And his preoccupations weren't so far from the mainstream of academic Austen studies; for years, Ph.D.'s like Devoney Looser had been combing Austen's novels for traces of sex and violence, colonialism and patriarchy, and Billy Galperin had his own theories about Colonel Brandon's behind-the-scenes manipulations in *Sense and Sensibility*. But Arnie's Jane Austen seemed strangely contemporary, a bonneted version of the Prius-driving Obama voter next door. Arnie's Jane Austen was widely read, politically progressive, and fascinated by puzzles; she sounded suspiciously like Arnie.

Still, maybe we fans all had a Jane Austen like that, an Austen who reflected back to us a mirror image of the selves we'd like to be. Just as Arnie urged us to read Austen's novels anamorphically, Arnie himself looked different when viewed from different perspectives. From one angle, his frequently bizarre speculations were nothing but a fun-house-mirror version of opaque academic theorizing, the projections of an imagination with too much time on its hands. But from another angle, there was something touching about his passionate intensity. He thought of himself, he said, as "some kind of knight," soldiering on, despite the wounding hostility of the people he called "orthodox Janeites," to make the world acknowledge the full dimensions of Austen's genius and grapple with her still-relevant feminist message. He might never muster the discipline to boil down his countless computer files to a few hundred pages of consecutive prose, but nevertheless his obsession seemed a mark of something pure — true devotion, a sincere homage to the power of art. "What matters in life? For some people, it's religion and God, or something like that," Arnie says. "This is my religion and my god. What great artists have done — this is important. They're the spiritual leaders of my world."

On my last morning in Florida, Arnie drove me to the airport early, so he would have time to escort Walter to his doctor's appointment. As we prepared to say goodbye, he was still talking about Jane Austen. "Baron von Anhalt," he mused as he pulled up at the entrance. "I still wonder about that guy."

Six weeks later, as I edged my way through the crowds thronging the Portland Public Library for the JASNA conference's opening reception and rare-book exhibit, I ran into Arnie next to a display case full of first editions. His talk would not take place for another day and a half, but he had already learned from the conference organizers that his projected audience was the smallest among the seven presentations scheduled for his time slot. "Which pissed me off," he said. Especially since the competing sessions included two that, frankly, he didn't think exemplified truly serious scholarship:

a costumed dramatic performance and a discussion of Regency fashion, complete with fabric samples. He had been upstaged by muslin.

But on Saturday morning, the hotel meeting room reserved for his talk was respectably full. The sixty people in the audience listened politely, laughed in the right places, and asked relevant questions. The talk was more vintage Arnie, a semi-convincing, semi-outlandish tapestry woven from the puns he detected in Austen's use of words like "constitutional" and "confinement," the allusions he perceived to works by other writers, the evidence of feminist anger he found in her letters, and the biographical information he had unearthed about long-forgotten contemporaries who, he was convinced, had provided models for her characters. Curiously, Arnie's central thesis — that Austen meant her readers to understand that the mother of *Northanger Abbey*'s hero, Henry Tilney, had died in childbirth, not from the "bilious fever" Henry describes, and that this detail revealed Austen's outrage at the dangerous serial pregnancies that married women of her time often endured — seemed to have little bearing on his controversial theory of shadow stories. "You're absolutely right," Arnie said later, when I pointed this out. "My problem is, I couldn't tell the shadow story of *Northanger Abbey* in less than four hours. This is a piece of the shadow story." Even so, Arnie found himself pressed for time; as the clock ticked down on his session, he spoke faster and faster, squeezing in the last sentence just as time ran out.

In the months after the Portland meeting, it looked as if some of Arnie's fantasies might be coming true. JASNA chapters in Florida, California, and Oregon invited him to speak. A joint presentation with a local college professor drew two hundred Janeites to a kickoff event for a new south Florida chapter of JASNA, which Arnie planned to organize. The *Miami Herald* previewed the meeting and mentioned Arnie's book, which now had the working title *The Shadow Stories of Jane Austen, the Secret Radical Feminist*.

The book itself, however, still existed mostly in Arnie's imagination. "I'm doing the final stage of my book proposal," he told me the week after the conference ended. "I woke up two days ago thinking I'm ready to do this." Nearly three months later, the book proposal remained unfinished. In the meantime, Arnie had written more than one hundred new blog posts — close to ninety-two thousand words about Jane Austen.

CHAPTER 7

———

AUSTEN THERAPY

THE MIDDLE-AGED GUARD at the entrance to Christine Shih's gated community leaned out of his kiosk to get a look at the journalist in the passenger seat of the minivan. Security thing, I figured.

"So, do you like *Mansfield Park* as much as Christine does?" he asked.

A few hours later, half a dozen women of various ages — people Christine knows from church or from the Austen talks she's given at a local historic site — begin gathering in her Nashville living room, chatting companionably over tea and shortbread. Geraldine, a thirty-two-year-old with dark hair piled high on her head, gets the conversation rolling.

"My mom is very similar to Mrs. Bennet," she says. "Her concern for me and my sister seems to stem from the place of self-preservation, how it will affect her. It's not about 'I got three daughters married.' It's about 'I got three daughters married, and they're no longer a burden to me.'"

The topic of discussion is *Pride and Prejudice,* but this is not a typical neighborhood book club. It's the first session of what Christine calls "bibliotherapy," a cross between a do-it-yourself support group and an English class. The women are here to discover whether novels written two centuries earlier can help them cope with relatives in the grip of a psychological condition defined in the standard psychiatric reference manual only in 1980 — borderline personality disorder. These women lead busy lives juggling jobs, volunteerism, spouses, and children, but as they talk about how Austen's characters resemble people in their own lives, years of painful memories bubble to the surface: unstable childhoods scarred by parents who favored siblings, unreasonable and mercurial bosses, manipulative sisters, false friends.

Christine, an empathetic forty-year-old with dark eyes, a wide mouth, and a lilting Louisiana accent, listens intently as a fifty-seven-year-old postal worker named Catherine details a traumatic series of personal upheavals — the deaths of family members, a devastating flood, debilitating conflicts with a work supervisor.

"Were you reading Jane Austen at the time?" Christine asks, as if discussing an experimental medication.

"No," says Catherine, who has already described herself as more of an Austen movie fan than an Austen novel reader. "I was just maintaining and trying to stay sane."

Christine is a warm, appealing woman who smiles often and speaks with intensity and conviction. She is neither a therapist nor an English professor; she's a nurse practitioner who once worked with cancer patients and now stays home with her young daughter. But years of reading in both psychological literature and Austen studies have convinced her that Jane Austen's own mother had borderline personality disorder and that many of Austen's characters are portraits of people with the same condition. "Her novels radiate with her personal story of oppression," Christine has written. Borderline personality disorder, which researchers say affects from 1 to

4 percent of the population, is a psychological state characterized by emotional volatility, unstable relationships, and a pathological fear of abandonment, which paradoxically often leads sufferers to neglect, abuse, or abandon their own children. Christine believes that exposure to Austen's masterful portraits of family dynamics can give the children of borderlines not only insight into their own situations but also the therapeutic tools to heal their pain. The bibliotherapy group is the first road test of this hypothesis.

Although Christine lacks the traditional credentials of an English literature specialist — no Ph.D., no tenure-track university job — she has presented her work at academic conferences and is contributing a chapter to a book of scholarly essays on Austen and aesthetic theory. She considers herself an Austen scholar, not a fan. During my two days in Nashville, she listened patiently to my obsessive musings about Regency underwear and even volunteered to lace me into my corset at the next JASNA conference — sparing me the dreaded self-lacing, monkey-with-a-deck-chair ordeal — but she doesn't dress in ball gowns or buy I ♥ MR. DARCY tote bags herself. At the JASNA ball, she sits out the dancing. "It's not how I connect to her. I connect to her on a psychological level," she says. "You can't really buy coffee mugs that connect on that psychological level. It's the text itself that I connect with, so that's what I stay with."

I knew that Christine wasn't the only Janeite who believed that Austen had anticipated contemporary insights into the dysfunctions of the human mind; I would soon be visiting a speech pathologist who had detected signs of autism in some twenty characters from *Emma, Northanger Abbey,* and *Pride and Prejudice.* I thought Austen was a brilliant psychologist too — few other writers so incisively portrayed self-deception, unconscious motivation, and emotional violence — but I had my doubts about the wisdom of applying categories from the *Diagnostic and Statistical Manual of*

Mental Disorders, the Bible of psychiatry, to fictional people imagined by someone born a few months before the signing of the Declaration of Independence. Austen's world, and her worldview, was so different from ours; how many of our intellectual presuppositions were really transferable? I hoped to find out.

In the beginning, Christine Shih was neither an Austen fan nor an Austen scholar. She was just a child from a troubled family who found salvation in books. At three, she taught herself to read from a copy of *Little Women* borrowed from a bookmobile, and for years she devoured everything from *Anne of Green Gables* to the fairy tales of Hans Christian Andersen. At six or seven, she dreamed of writing something — she wasn't quite sure what — and carried around a notebook, modeling herself on the writer-heroine of *Harriet the Spy.* She excelled in music, first playing the piano and later the marimba, and her books, her music, and the precious hours she spent at school provided a lifesaving escape from home, where two volatile parents battled, sometimes physically, while Christine hid in the closet, waiting for the violence to end. At times, she and her two older brothers were the targets of the anger, and the blows that went with it. When she was ten, her parents split up, and Christine moved with her mother from a comfortable suburban home to a far less pleasant rental in Baton Rouge. On Christmas Day that year, Christine's father arrived on his lost family's doorstep with an ax, threatening to kill them all, until the police came and took him away. As the years passed, her mother drifted from job to job, barely coping with household duties, leaving the children to cook meals and do laundry. They lived on food stamps, government-supplied butter and cheese, and way too many canned goods; by the end of high school, Christine was stick-thin. "It was a real complicated emotional childhood," she says.

She read *Pride and Prejudice* for the first time late in high school and immediately recognized the heroine Elizabeth Bennet's self-dramatizing mother — "a woman of mean understanding, little information, and uncertain temper," in Jane Austen's brutal summation. "I was completely drawn to Mrs. Bennet," Christine says. "I didn't know what was wrong with her, but I just knew she was exactly like my mother, like a clone." Christine found the confidence and humor that Elizabeth brought to the relationship empowering, a reassurance "that it was OK to act that way, it was OK to be that way." As high school gave way to college, she read her way through Austen's books, finding another kindred spirit in *Mansfield Park*'s heroine, Fanny Price, a child plucked from a chaotic home and adopted into an emotionally neglectful second family. But more than she identified with a specific character, she identified with the wise, ironic narrative voice that winds through all Austen's books. "Austen's novels got me through," Christine says. "Her voice got me through not having a voice to guide me. It was a voice of a person with a real self, who understood themselves, who stood up for themselves, who protected themselves. And I took it on as my own."

Christine won a marimba scholarship to Louisiana State University, and although the campus was right there in Baton Rouge, she packed up her car and moved into the dorm, thrilled to escape the financial and emotional burdens of her mother's life. Eating three meals a day in the college cafeteria, she quickly brought her weight to a healthy level. But within two years she was home again. Her mother had threatened suicide if Christine didn't move back. Still, Christine persevered in her studies, double-majoring in music and psychology. "I wanted to know how people ticked, why people do what they do," Christine says. "I wanted to figure out what was wrong with my family." At LSU, she met Kent Shih, a fellow student from a peaceful and loving Chinese-American family. They married in 1994, and, newly secure and free, Christine stopped playing the piano. She didn't need it anymore.

Kent was attending medical school at Vanderbilt University in Nashville, and Christine enrolled in Vanderbilt's nursing program. There, her disparate interests in psychology, nursing, and literature began to come together; for one class, she wrote a paper on how Louisa May Alcott's experiences as a Civil War nurse influenced her writing. Although the professor encouraged Christine to publish her paper, the timing was wrong. She and Kent were about to move to Baltimore, where he was beginning a fellowship in oncology. She took board exams as a nurse practitioner, eventually qualifying to work with both adults and children. And she began a demanding new job, working twelve-hour days with leukemia and lymphoma patients. "When you come from a hard background, working with hard situations just sort of feels normal, I guess," Christine says. "There is a lot of sadness. I could connect to that sadness." As her patients moved on or passed on, she wrote each one a poem and tucked it away.

The Shihs eventually left Baltimore, first moving back to Baton Rouge and then to Nashville. They wanted children, but for years they struggled with miscarriages, an unsuccessful round of in vitro fertilization, and a failed private adoption. Finally, in 2005, Christine became pregnant; during intermittent weeks of bed rest, she read her way through a library's worth of classic fiction, as Hurricane Katrina bore down on the Gulf Coast.

Her profound love for her baby daughter gave Christine a painful new insight. "It really dawned on me how bad my family situation was," she says. "It was not just an issue of not being taken care of. What I learned was that I was unloved. I loved my daughter so much, and the things I would do for her, and the things I would never do to her—it was the opposite of the experience that I had growing up." In the wake of one last emotionally bruising encounter with her mother, she began seeing a grief counselor, who came to believe that both Christine's parents were borderlines. In the books her counselor gave her, Christine recognized her family. "It was an unbelievable relief," she says. "It was just this amazing sense of relief that I had, of knowing that I was not what my parents wanted me to be and that I was OK."

Christine had read the Bible since childhood, finding in its pages another source of the emotional sustenance her family life could not provide, and that February, she attended a women's retreat sponsored by her Presbyterian church. Every year, the retreat included a movie night, and this year's movie was *Becoming Jane,* a highly fictionalized biopic about Jane Austen's abortive, youthful romance with a neighbor's Irish nephew, the lawyer Tom Lefroy. Although she loved Austen's novels, Christine knew nothing about Austen's life, and she was enthralled by the film's depiction of the relationship between the young Jane Austen and her parents, especially her difficult, critical mother. By the end of the movie, the audience was sobbing.

In the middle of the night, Christine woke up. "Jane Austen's mother was a borderline," she said out loud.

Phyllis Ferguson Bottomer spends her days helping children for whom speech itself is fraught and painful—children who lisp, who stutter, who strain to grasp the concept of rhyme or the idea of opposites, who do not even understand what language is for. But over the two days I spent with her in Vancouver, British Columbia, I found myself thinking of Phyllis as a near-virtuoso of conversation. She effortlessly engaged others in dialogue, listened with close but unobtrusive attention, and returned every verbal tennis serve fluidly, in her unhurried, Canadian-accented tones. Her mere presence was calming.

I had come to Vancouver, a continent away from Christine Shih's living room, to meet another Janeite who read Austen with one eye on contemporary psychology. Unlike Christine, however, Phyllis had found Austenesque echoes not in her own family life but in the schools where she worked as a speech-language pathologist. Phyllis had come to believe that more than a century before doctors identified autism, Jane Austen created at least twenty characters whose behavior placed them somewhere along the autistic spectrum. Mr. Darcy, it seemed, had Asperger syndrome.

In the upstairs office in Phyllis's home, a book of Austen criticism titled *A Fine Brush on Ivory* sits on a shelf next to *All About Child Language*. Literary interpretation is something Phyllis squeezes into the spaces in a busy professional life. The school day I spent with her was a whirl of activity from the moment she left home, her sleek gray hair still damp from the shower. In her office, she chatted with workmates while hunting for paper clips on her desk, under a shelf of binders with labels like "Plosives" and "Fricatives." En route to her car, covering the ground with long, fast strides, she stopped a colleague to arrange a meeting about a student. "Speech pathologists have a lot of children in their heads," she said. The trunk of her car was stuffed with the books, card games, folders, and notebooks that she carried between the office and the three schools where she saw students each week. At today's school, she rearranged her therapeutic props as children came and went from the room where she worked with them in ones and twos. She pulled out picture cards, puzzle pieces, and plastic peanut-butter jars full of rings; she offered dinosaur stickers as a reward for hard work. At lunchtime, she inhaled a bowl of microwaved soup in the staff room before dashing off to confer with a graduate student in speech-language pathology whose field training she was supervising. After a session with a jumpy, easily distracted seven-year-old boy, Phyllis and the trainee debriefed: What worked well? What didn't work? The trainee had sometimes spoken imprecisely —saying "house" when she meant "building," or "messy" when she meant "dirty"—which wouldn't help the boy develop the hunger for accuracy he would need in order to do well in school, Phyllis pointed out. "The beauty of language is it's spot-on," she said.

Decades after she first learned the 4-H Club's pledge, Phyllis could still recite the familiar words—"I pledge my head to clearer thinking, my heart to greater loyalty, my hands to larger service, and my health to better living for my club, my community, and my country"—and believed that its call to hard work and service had influenced her life. Although she was born in 1953, her childhood mirrored the experience of an earlier generation. She grew up on the flat central Canadian prairies of Manitoba, first on a farm and then, when her father took a job as a grain buyer, in a series of microscopic hamlets dominated by tall grain elevators. During one stint, she attended a one-room schoolhouse presided over by a nineteen-year-old teacher. During another—a difficult three-year stretch that started when Phyllis was ten—her family of seven (parents, grandparent, and four children) made up almost half the population of a sixteen-person community and owned the only dog in town. Library books were ordered from a government catalogue and arrived three weeks later in a brown paper bag. Sometimes you got what you'd ordered; more often, you got—and eagerly devoured—whatever was going, even if it was book seven in a British children's adventure series whose earlier episodes you hadn't yet read. In each town, Phyllis adapted to her new neighbors and their ways—ice skating here, 4-H Club there. "How I grew up was probably not that different from the sort of rural isolation that Jane Austen experienced two hundred years earlier," Phyllis said over a lunch of dim sum in cosmopolitan Vancouver. "I lived in eight of these little villages, and what there was to pay attention to was who the people were, because even though these places all looked the same if you go zipping past on the highway, they actually all have their own ethos, their own way of being."

Phyllis's father, who had left ninth grade to take over the family farm, set no particular store by education, but he valued it more for daughters than for sons: a boy could support himself with physical labor, as a carpenter or a miner, but the weaker sex needed book learning. At first, he opposed a university education for Phyllis, the oldest girl, but her mother convinced him that everyone was entitled to twelve years of schooling and that, because Phyllis had skipped first grade, she had at least one more year coming. By the time she enrolled at the University of Manitoba, majoring in psychology, Phyllis had set her sights on a career in speech pathology. Her sister, six years younger, had a serious speech problem, and once or twice a month, their mother would take her on a three-hour bus trip to see the speech-language pathologist in the nearest big city—a day of travel for a half-hour of therapy.

For graduate school, Phyllis chose McGill University, fifteen hundred miles and a whole world away. Brandon, Manitoba's second-largest city, where Phyllis had attended university, had offered its own kind of culture shock: Phyllis had had trouble remembering to lock her door, and she had ignored the telephone bell because it didn't sound the two long rings that had been her family's signal to pick up the party line. But Montreal was a far bigger leap. Her mother sewed a ten-dollar bill into her underwear to keep her safe. As the taxi from the airport took Phyllis up University Avenue, she could see ahead of her the stately façade of the Royal Victoria Hospital. *Oh, I've been waiting for this place my whole life,* she thought. The new ideas and new people thrilled her.

A week after her arrival, she was playing doubles Ping-Pong in a dormitory when an Australian graduate student with a black mustache and a big smile burst in, looking for a game. Phyllis noticed how alive he looked. (Later, she would suspect that he had also been rather tipsy.) Lindsay Bottomer, who was studying for a master's degree in mineral exploration, was a geologist who had already spent several years working for the mining industry back home. They married two years after graduation, scheduling their wedding for October, after the busy harvest season in Manitoba. Two months later, they honeymooned in England, and Phyllis bought a few Jane Austen novels to get her through Britain's long winter nights. She had read *Pride and Prejudice* as a teenager and remembered being impressed by the realism with which Austen depicted family life, in marked contrast to so many classic children's books, with their orphaned protagonists or wise, saintly parents. "It was the first thing I read in which teenagers felt uncomfortable with what their siblings were doing, or their parents," Phyllis says. "And I remember thinking that that seemed real, that families existed and weren't perfect." By the time the honeymooners reached Lyme, whose rock formations and fossil deposits fascinate geologists, Phyllis had read *Persuasion* and, just as I did on my JASNA tour decades later, she knew what to look for when she got to the Cobb. "She was pointing out these steps, and I was saying, 'What's the big deal?'" Lindsay remembers.

Their life together took them first to Toronto and then to western Australia, where they lived in three different places, from a sheep town of three thousand souls to the big city of Perth. Lindsay's job as a mineral geologist who helped mining companies find deposits of gold and copper often took him away from home, some-times for weeks at a time. After the fall of the iron curtain and the rise of Latin American economies, he traveled to Russia, to South America, to the Gobi Desert in Mongolia. While he was away, Phyllis raised their two children and worked as a speech-language pathologist in hospitals, rehabilitation centers, and, once they had settled permanently in Vancouver, in the public schools.

Over the years, she reread Jane Austen from time to time, and in 2000, a Vancouver acquaintance invited her to a meeting of the local JASNA branch, where Phyllis found a stimulating new com-munity. Eventually, she and Lindsay began attending JASNA's na-tional conferences. Inspired by their experiences at the JASNA ball, they started going regularly to local country-dance groups back home in Vancouver; at the JASNA conferences, they wore re-strained versions of Regency costume.

At the same time that Jane Austen was becoming an important part of her off-duty life, autism was becoming an increasingly im-portant part of Phyllis's professional life. At one of the local elemen-tary schools where she worked, treating students with everything from simple lisps to severe communication disorders, she had seen a sudden influx of children at the mild end of the autistic spectrum. These children didn't fit the layperson's image of autism, the ste-reotype of a severely impaired person who spun mutely in circles, unable to tolerate even the slightest human contact. These children behaved fairly typically some of the time, especially in predictable, highly structured situations, but they had trouble interpreting non-verbal cues or using language to build relationships. Phyllis found these children fascinating. She began reading more about autism.

One night in fall 2002, Phyllis and Lindsay sat down to watch the Colin Firth adaptation of *Pride and Prejudice,* and a line she hadn't particularly noticed before suddenly stood out in high relief.

Seated at the piano, Elizabeth is needling Darcy about his aloof behavior at the ball where they met, and he tells her that he has trouble with small talk. "I have not that talent which some possess of conversing easily with strangers," he says. In Darcy's words, Phyllis heard an echo of something she had just read in the autobiography of Temple Grandin, an autistic woman who became a famous animal scientist. Describing the ebb and flow of friendly conversation, Grandin had written, "I have always had a hard time fitting in with this rhythm." Jane Austen's Mr. Darcy and Temple Grandin were describing the same phenomenon, Phyllis realized. As she watched the rest of the miniseries, the idea kept percolating. *If she's describing some people that are at the mild end of the autistic spectrum, that affects what this whole book is about,* Phyllis thought. But the school year was in full swing. She had students to evaluate, reports to write. It would be months before she could pursue her idea any further.

Christine Shih knew she couldn't diagnose Jane Austen's mother as a borderline based on a biopic, so she began reading. The more she learned about Austen's life, the more she became convinced that her middle-of-the-night insight had been correct. Austen's mother had fostered seven of her eight babies out to village wet nurses in the early months of their lives, welcoming them home only as toddlers. When the adult Jane fell sick with the illness that would eventually take her life, her hypochondriac mother monopolized the couch while the ailing daughter stretched out on a makeshift settee cobbled together from chairs. During the two months that Jane lay dying in Winchester, her mother never made the seventeen-mile trip to visit her. All of this was abandonment behavior, Christine was certain, the hallmark of the borderline mother's pathological treatment of her children.

Deficient or destructive mother figures were everywhere in Austen's work, Christine thought, and Austen's portraits of borderline behavior tracked the psychological literature so closely that they must have grown out of lived experience, not just artistic imagination. One of the psychological studies Christine had read identified four types of borderline mothers and named each type after a figure from folklore — the waif, the hermit, the queen, and the witch. In *Mansfield Park,* Christine found these types embodied in four important female characters who influence the life of the book's heroine, Fanny Price: the waif in her mother, hapless Mrs. Price; the hermit in an aunt, lazy Lady Bertram; the queen in Fanny's love rival, vibrant Mary Crawford; and the witch in a second aunt, abusive Mrs. Norris. In one of Austen's minor, often overlooked works — a poem she dictated on her deathbed, which had traditionally been interpreted as a piece of light verse about the patron saint of Winchester — Christine detected a metaphorical account of Austen's anger at her mother's abandonment. On the deepest psychological level, Christine believed, Austen wrote what she knew. "I knew she knew it, because she's replicating the same kind of situations that I lived in," Christine says. "I could pinpoint, in my own life, those relationships. And then after I started doing my research on Austen, I could pinpoint those same relationships that she wrote about in her stories, I could pinpoint those same relationships within her own life."

In late 2008, Christine heard of a scholarly conference that would be held at Chawton the following summer, to commemorate the two-hundredth anniversary of Austen's arrival at the cottage. "I needed something to write for, and they were taking essay proposals for the conference," Christine says. "So I'm like, 'I'm a total nobody. I'm a nurse practitioner. I'm going to do it anyway.'" She sent off a proposal connecting borderline psychology to the immoral, manipulative protagonist of Austen's novella *Lady Susan*. The day the conference organizers invited her to speak was one of the greatest of her life.

Her Chawton paper was well received, and over the next two years, she spoke before several more academic or Janeite audiences. She began working with an Australian scholar on an anthology of *Lady Susan* criticism. She considered writing a children's book based on an episode in Austen's unfinished novel *The Watsons*. She linked psychological descriptions of borderline psychology to aesthetic theory, connecting the philosophical distinction between the sublime (that which inspires fear) and the beautiful (that which inspires love) to the tendency of borderlines to conceive of other people, including their own children, in black-and-white terms, as all good or all bad. Every time she spoke about borderline personality disorder in relation to Austen and other writers — she had begun thinking about borderlines in the lives and works of the Brontës and of the gothic novelist Ann Radcliffe — audience members approached her afterward to tell her about borderlines in their own lives. "I feel like I've just been washed in a fountain of truth," a Janeite told Christine, after hearing her speak at JASNA's conference in Portland, Oregon, in 2010.

Not everyone was equally receptive, however. Christine was one of a number of Austen critics who were beginning to sketch a dark version of Austen's family life — a picture radically at odds with the traditional image of a big, close-knit clan of talented people — and the move was controversial. Deirdre Le Faye, an independent scholar known for her painstaking work collecting Austen family records and letters, was hostile to the new approach, and plenty of other scholars and Janeites saw more benign interpretations of the biographical anecdotes whose sinister meaning seemed so clear to

Christine. The resistance, Christine thought, said as much about attachment to an idealized image of Austen as it did about the admittedly fragmentary nature of the evidence about her life. "We know far less about Radcliffe than we know about Austen," Christine points out. "Nobody's complaining with me whatsoever about my interpretation of Radcliffe, but lots of people are questioning me about my interpretation of Austen and her biography." Everyone, it seemed, felt close to Jane Austen.

Phyllis Ferguson Bottomer had not yet written a word about autism in Austen when she encountered the first stirrings of resistance to her ideas. More than a year had passed since she had picked up echoes of Temple Grandin in Darcy's conversation with Elizabeth at the piano; over the summer, Phyllis had reread *Pride and Prejudice* and found subtle signs of autism in the behavior and speech patterns of seven other characters, including both Bennet parents, the sycophantic Mr. Collins, and the overbearing Lady Catherine de Bourgh. "To me, it was relatively obvious from my professional background, and I thought, 'Well, someone else will have done this,'" Phyllis says. A collection of scholarly conference papers called *The Talk in Jane Austen* sounded promising, but when she read the essays, Phyllis was disappointed. Nearly all the contributors were English professors, people who lived in a world where everyone found language easy. They described the same patterns Phyllis had noticed but attributed them to different causes. *They forgot to invite a speech-language pathologist,* she thought.

She was having so much fun linking these hitherto separate aspects of her life, Jane Austen and speech-language pathology, that she thought nothing of sharing her ideas over lunch with a visiting JASNA official. To her surprise, the visiting Janeite was discouraging. More than discouraging, really: at the next day's meeting of the local JASNA branch, she told Phyllis bluntly that she "could not say those things."

Phyllis was stunned. She was no stranger to strong emotion; after all, she had spent her life giving parents sometimes painful news about their children. But unlike those precious flesh-and-blood beings, Austen's characters were, well, fictional. Phyllis's own theory conferred a strange kind of reality on those fictional people, giving them neurological and psychological histories that Austen had never described. But the intense antipathy to her ideas about literary creations, who, after all, had no feelings to hurt—you *cannot* say those things?—amazed her.

And annoyed her. "When you have someone who was raised between two brothers, you should never tell them they couldn't," Phyllis says wryly. Then and there, she marched over to the coordinator of her local JASNA chapter and scheduled a talk on autism in Austen for the following winter. Then she marched straight back to the JASNA official and told her what she'd arranged. Only later did she wonder if the audience would hurl tomatoes. Her college-age son, Tim, a tall, square-jawed rugby player, volunteered to come along just in case she needed protection from scandalized Janeites. (In the event, no tomatoes were thrown, though two different women did ask Tim if he'd like to fill out a JASNA membership form.)

As Phyllis continued to speak about her ideas before JASNA branches and community groups, she, like Christine Shih, found that her talks often prompted audience members to think in new ways about people in their own lives, to reinterpret behavior that had once seemed rude, cold, or overbearing as a symptom of neurological impairment. "Your talk makes me feel I should be kinder to everyone," one woman told her. Another said that Phyllis's presentation had finally enabled her to understand her ex-husband. "Now I can forgive him," the woman said. "Now I'm not angry anymore."

Phyllis had been mulling over the possibility of a book — a London-based publisher with an autism specialty had expressed interest in the project — and one spring weekend when Lindsay was in Peru, she finally found the time to start writing. She had lived with the material for so long that it took her only ten days to produce two hundred pages exploring the evidence for autism in some of Austen's most beloved characters. "It is not pride but subtle autism that is the major reason for Darcy's frequent silences, awkward behaviour at social events and the monologue that he . . . delivers the first time he proposes to Elizabeth," Phyllis argued. "Our recent and growing knowledge of the autistic spectrum is the crucial piece that has been needed to help solve the puzzle of his personality."

When the book, *So Odd a Mixture: Along the Autistic Spectrum in* Pride and Prejudice, was published in 2007, Phyllis's ideas intrigued some Janeites and bemused others. Some accused her of reading her own preoccupations into Austen. "Bottomer is a speech therapist," wrote one participant in the online Austen-L discussion group, "and if your main instrument is a hammer, many things begin to look like nails." Some thought her analysis overlooked moments in the novel in which characters she had placed along the autistic spectrum behaved in notably non-autistic ways. Others just found the whole enterprise bizarre. "The people depicted in all of Jane Austen's novels are fictional characters, nothing more, nothing less," wrote one online commentator. "They cannot have any psychological syndrome or problem, they are *not* real. Jane made them up; they are figments of her imagination." Still others wondered what room Phyllis's theories left for moral judgment about Austen's characters. Phyllis had suggested that it was unfair to blame Darcy for his stiffness in social situations, since it stemmed from a neurological deficit: "People with obvious physical and mental disabilities are not held to be responsible for their shortcomings; however, the milder the difficulties the less visible their causes are to outsiders—hence they are seen as something occurring by choice or lack of effort," she had written. "This is akin to telling someone with a hearing loss to 'listen' or someone with limited vision to 'look.'" But some readers were unconvinced. "You know, sometimes people aren't autistic," wrote a blogger called This is Fit Crit. "They're just dicks."

I found myself agreeing. Something felt off-kilter about Phyllis's interpretation of Austen, and perhaps about Christine's as well. I didn't know enough about the autistic spectrum or borderline personality disorder to assess how accurately they were applying the concepts, but regardless of the scientific basis for their theories, I found it unlikely that Austen would have had much sympathy with their approach. Because the mental space of twenty-first-century North Americans is shaped by therapeutic categories, ascribing people's bad behavior to their neurological deficits or personality disorders, rather than to their moral failings, seems perfectly natural to us. But Jane Austen inhabited a very different mental space. Unlike that woman in Phyllis's audience, she didn't necessarily want to be kinder to everyone. With a few swift sentences, she pinned Mrs. Bennet down as mercilessly as an entomologist labeling a butterfly specimen. Her nasty characters behaved badly because they were bad people, not because they had bad genes. Her flawed heroes and heroines might be survivors of poor parenting, but they still had to redeem themselves by taking responsibility for their own choices and trying to do better. Austen cut characters no slack because they were young and unformed, poorly educated or badly treated. She demanded rational, ethical behavior from everyone and pitilessly exposed those who fell short. That ferocious moral clarity was one of the things I loved about Austen, even if I sometimes wondered how I'd measure up against her terrifyingly high standards.

Phyllis was far more forgiving than Jane Austen. "I do believe that certain things are truly harder for some people than others," she says. "We still have to hold people responsible for their actions, but we can understand more where they come from." Whereas Austen apparently assumed that many of her secondary characters would never change — even Elizabeth Bennet's younger sister Lydia, it seems, will forever be as vulgar and thoughtless as she is at sixteen — Phyllis envisioned brighter futures for many of them, especially those who were barely adults when Austen finished with them. "I have to believe that people can change," Phyllis says. "Any therapist or any clinician has to believe that people can change."

Back in Phyllis's room at school, a ten-year-old boy named Andrew sat in a plastic chair, facing her. "One thing you did really well today was you were reading Tony's body language," she told him. Andrew, she explained to me later, falls somewhere on the autistic spectrum; during his session, he had fidgeted and rocked his chair, and while working with another student, he had sometimes had trouble interacting over a simple card game designed to teach the "th" sound. But Phyllis was focused on the positive. "The other thing I noticed today that I was very pleased with was there were three times today you laughed, and the third time your volume was perfect," she said. "That's really a big improvement."

As Andrew prepared to return to class, she sent him off with one last word of encouragement. "You did really well today," Phyllis told the struggling little boy.

By the time I visited her, Christine Shih had not seen her father for over a year or her mother for more than five, and she found the separation liberating. Her reading, her writing, and the therapy she had undergone had given her a sense of peace and freedom. Her bibliotherapy group, she hoped, would help others find a similar release. Children of borderlines grew up without the support of nurturing families; she wanted her group to fill that void. "My desire is for people to connect with each other and find relationships," she says. Saved by reading, she hoped to encourage others to read; in the months ahead, she planned to assign her bibliotherapy group not only *Pride and Prejudice, Mansfield Park,* and *Lady Susan,* but also works by Charlotte Brontë, Louisa May Alcott, and the contemporary memoirist Jeannette Walls. As they read the stories others had created in order to come to terms with their lives, group members would learn to narrate their own stories, she hoped. Psychotherapy was expensive, but reading was free.

I was beginning to see that for all of us Austen fans, the enterprise of Austen interpretation involved us in the narration of our own lives. We all seemed to be engaged in a version of the "mutilated intellectual autobiography" that Billy Galperin, the Rutgers professor, had seen in so much literary criticism. Phyllis's Austen was a meticulous observer of speech patterns and communication problems. Christine's Austen was an abused daughter who worked out her private pain through storytelling. Arnie Perlstein wasn't the only Janeite who seemed to have fashioned an Austen in his own image. I had to admit that I did the same thing: my Jane Austen was a coolly objective observer with high standards and a sharp edge, a plausible version of my own imagined ideal self. We all wanted a Jane Austen who would reflect back to us the best in ourselves.

In Christine Shih's living room, the bibliotherapy group is winding on. Andrea, a slender thirty-nine-year-old woman with short, curly hair, is describing her favorite scene in *Pride and Prejudice* — the moment when Elizabeth Bennet stands up to the insults of the arrogant, highborn Lady Catherine de Bourgh and asserts her right to privacy, dignity, and respect. "These people can think they're so hot and so high above you and just degrade you," says Andrea, who has already told the group about her demoralizing conflicts with her mother-in-law. "I just love how she just levels her."

"I think Jane Austen would have been that way," says Carina, a lively thirty-eight-year-old with long, highlighted dark hair. "She may have had to lay someone out at some point."

"Or wished she had," Christine says. "And did—by creating it in a story."

PART III

THE
COMPANY OF
CLEVER,
WELL-INFORMED
PEOPLE

CHAPTER 8

TALKING JANE

LIKE ELIZABETH AND DARCY, they met at a ball. Jack wore a blue coat and white breeches. Joan had rented a black dress once featured in a film about a mistress of Lord Byron. The year was 1975, the place a country house in Hampshire, the occasion a costume ball commemorating the bicentennial of Jane Austen's birth in nearby Steventon. Jack and Joan spoke only briefly on their way out, but years later she remembered the conversation vividly. "He was the first person I had ever encountered who loved Jane Austen as I did, and the first person who knew as much, in fact a great deal more, than I," she wrote. "It seemed to me like a miracle."

Her trip to England to celebrate Austen's two-hundredth birthday had already made an impression on Joan Mason Hurley. A few days earlier, an official of the British Jane Austen Society had refused to let Joan's husband, Denis, use the bathroom at Chawton House before the JAS's annual meeting under a tent on the grounds. That night, as the Canadians Joan and Denis drank sherry with Lorraine Hanaway, an American they had met at the meeting, Denis urged them to found their own Jane Austen society on the other side of the Atlantic—a friendly, democratic society that wouldn't refuse anyone the use of a bathroom.

Although they laughed off the idea, it wasn't entirely far-fetched. Before her marriage, Joan Mason Hurley had been Joan Austen-Leigh, a four-generations-removed niece of Jane Austen. She was a direct descendant of the oldest Austen brother, James, and his son, James Edward Austen-Leigh, whose memoir of his aunt had sparked the Victorian-era rebirth of interest in her work. In a bank vault back home in British Columbia, Joan kept Jane Austen's portable writing desk—the one my JASNA tour group would see years later at the British Library—which she had inherited from two English aunts, who displayed it on top of their grand piano. And Joan too was a writer: after marrying young, raising four children, and running a lakeside hotel with her husband, she had started college in her forties, earned bachelor's and master's degrees, and begun a second career as a playwright and novelist. She had been raised to revere Austen and to wear her family connection with the author as a badge of honor. Still, Joan had no intention of founding a Jane Austen society.

In the mid-1970s, the world of Jane Austen fans was a smaller, quieter place than it would become decades later. Britain's Jane Austen Society, launched in 1940 with the mission of preserving Chawton cottage, was a well-established, if rather stuffy, institution. Each July, its members met under a tent at Chawton, elected a management committee consisting largely of prominent Hampshire citizens, listened to a lecture on some aspect of Jane Austen's life and works, drank a cup of tea, and went home. Overseas members who could not make the long trip to Chawton each year made do with the JAS's report, which was mailed to them annually. Every few years, the BBC produced a respectful new adaptation of *Pride and*

Prejudice or *Emma* or *Sense and Sensibility.* For the festival celebrating the two-hundredth anniversary of Austen's birth, teams
representing Chawton and Steventon faced off in a tug-of-war and a
cricket match. Colin Firth was fourteen years old.

Despite their instant connection at the bicentenary ball, Joan
Mason Hurley hadn't expected to see Jack Grey again, since she
lived in Victoria, British Columbia, and he lived a continent away,
in New York City, where he worked as the assistant principal of a
junior high school in East Harlem. But Jane Austen kept bringing
them together. Four months after the ball, the Pierpont Morgan Library in New York invited Joan to bring her Austen writing desk to
their bicentenary exhibit, and Jack took her to dinner at an expensive restaurant where — unimagined luxury! — she ate fresh rasp-
berries in November. The friendship flourished, and the next summer Jack traveled to Victoria to visit Joan and Denis. Start a Jane
Austen society, Denis urged again. They refused. They were busy
with other projects. "We loved to read Jane Austen, of course," Joan
wrote years later. "She was our greatest joy. But that was enough.
We did not need the stress of organizing any society."

Eventually, of course, Denis wore them down. In late 1978,
Jack wrote to Sir Hugh Smiley, the honorary secretary of the British Jane Austen Society, asking for a list of the JAS's American and
Canadian members, who Jack hoped might form the core of a trans-
atlantic spinoff. In November, Sir Hugh mailed back thirteen pages
of hand-copied names and addresses. "I do hope that you can read
my handwriting," he wrote. "I have never indulged in a typewriter."
Sir Hugh asked only one favor in return for his labors: "Should you
find that any members are dead, it would be a help to let me know
so that I can take their names out of my files."

In deference to Joan's Canadian sensibilities, the new organization was to be named the Jane Austen Society of North Amer-

ica. (The acronym, JASNA, was unfortunate, the founders felt, but surely no one would actually call the group JAZZ-na.) In January 1979, Jack and Joan drafted a third cofounder. They considered asking Lorraine Hanaway, the American whom Joan had met during the Austen bicentennial and who had by now become a friend, but in the end they settled on Henry G. Burke, a prominent Baltimore Janeite whose wide-ranging expertise as both lawyer and accountant would be invaluable for a fledgling volunteer-run nonprofit. Jack would serve as president, Joan and Harry Burke would become vice presidents, and Joan would edit the annual newsletter, to be called *Persuasion*. In March 1979, Jack and Joan sent a "Dear Fellow Janeite" letter to the North Americans on Sir Hugh's membership list, proposing a new society and a kickoff dinner in New York City in October. "We will dine, exchange ideas, and have the pleasure of being able to 'talk Jane' with others similarly afflicted," they wrote. More than three hundred paid the membership fee— three dollars for one year, five dollars for two.

From the beginning, JASNA was intended as a place where Ph.D. professors and Austen fans without scholarly credentials— "deconstructionists and just plain groupies," as one former JASNA board member put it years later— could meet on equal terms. The only membership requirement would be a love of Jane Austen, the same passion that had brought together the organization's three founders.

Joan Austen-Leigh, who turned fifty-nine the year of JASNA's founding, was indomitable, adventurous, and commanding. Although she was Canadian-born and -bred, she spoke with the poshest of British accents, acquired during two years at school in Suffolk before World War II. She was tall, blue-eyed, and statuesque, her hair—first blond, then white—styled in an elegant pageboy. Long before the Internet made self-publishing easy, she founded

A Room of One's Own Press to publish her plays and her novels, which eventually included two sequels to *Emma*. Well into her seventies, she took solo voyages in her twenty-nine-foot sailboat, *Elizabeth Bennet,* which towed a little dinghy named *Mr. Darcy.* "A spitfire," the Austen scholar Devoney Looser called her. Early in her academic career, Devoney had spotted Joan at a JASNA conference, deep in conversation with someone else. As Devoney waited to introduce herself to the famous founder, Joan suddenly looked up, seized her by the arm, and said, "I've been waiting for you! We need to go into the bar and have a drink." As they sat down, Joan confided to the slightly bewildered Devoney, "That was the most boring man of all time, and I couldn't think of a better way to get rid of him. You look like an interesting person." Not everyone liked Joan—those who hadn't acquired the taste found her imperious and overbearing, too invested in her status as the keeper of the Austen family flame. But those who loved her, Devoney among them, found her charming, witty, and vibrant, a big personality with a voice and a laugh to match.

Joan had grown up with Jane Austen, but forty-four-year-old J. David Grey, Jack to his friends, hadn't discovered her until after college, when he stumbled across an Austen site while vacationing in England. He was already an Anglophile, a Catholic kid from Elizabeth, New Jersey, who was given to eclectic, consuming passions: collecting memorabilia of the vintage *Dick Tracy* comic strip, or following the fortunes of the New York Knicks basketball team, or acquiring rhinoceros knickknacks. Jane Austen soon eclipsed his other interests, and he began amassing a vast Austen collection—books, pictures, theater programs—that eventually filled the second bedroom in his Manhattan apartment. "It was famous among Janeites," his JASNA friend Diane Levine recalls. "People would write to ask permission to come see it." And although he had never earned a doctorate, Jack also became an amateur Austen scholar, eventually editing or co-editing two collections of essays on Austen.

Jack Grey did everything with extravagant flair. He chain-smoked a couple of packs of cigarettes a day, dressed elegantly, loved to travel, ate at fine restaurants. An international basketball tournament was underway in Portland, Oregon, while he was in town to visit another JASNA friend, and he bought tickets to eight games over five days. "And then we fit in two trips to the theater, trips to the four best restaurants in Portland, and we still had time to spend an entire day in Powell's bookstore," the friend, Susan Schwartz, remembered years later. "It was so Jack. He was going from the time he woke up in the morning until the time he went to sleep at night."

Some of his friends saw incongruity in the juxtaposition of his cultured elegance with the gritty world of public education in East Harlem, but his passion for people was as intense as his other commitments. He adored his younger sister, Dorothy Thompson, and her five children, squired his stepmother on overseas vacations, and gave his friends quirky gifts. He was also gay, a fact that was no secret to friends who met his live-in companion, Marino Romero, at JASNA events and offered comfort when Marino died of AIDS in 1985. "Despite the fact that I have never felt so alone," Jack wrote Lorraine Hanaway that year, "thanks to a few knowing and understanding friends like you, my grief has been lessened." Later, he planted a tree in Marino's memory — at Steventon, of course.

Harry Burke, who turned seventy-seven the year of JASNA's founding, was the oldest of the triumvirate, a prominent Baltimore estate lawyer who was also a certified public accountant and held a Ph.D. in political science. Burke, who came from a Lithuanian Jewish family, was a sophisticated, dryly witty man who wore bespoke three-piece suits befitting his formal Old World manner. In 1930, he married Alberta Hirshheimer, a Wisconsinite he had met while she was a student at Goucher, the small women's college in Baltimore. Alberta had inherited a fortune from a businessman grandfather, and the Burkes filled their lives with music, theater, travel, and literature. Although they had no children, they owned two apartments in a Baltimore high-rise: one to live in, and one to house their books. They kept a radio on hand solely for emergencies. Each night, as one spouse bathed, the other read a favorite book aloud. They got through all of Austen's novels every year. "He loved the style, and I think he loved the good sense, and he loved the structure of it," says Elsa Solender, a freelance journalist nearly forty years younger than Burke who met him not long before the founding of JASNA. "And he loved the fact that you could return to it every year, and it was always new."

Beginning in the mid-1930s, Alberta Burke became an avid Jane Austen collector. Like Jack Grey, she collected Austen ephemera —programs from theatrical adaptations of the novels, newspaper clippings mentioning Austen, still photographs from the Laurence Olivier film of *Pride and Prejudice*—which she compiled into ten notebooks that eventually held some twenty-eight hundred items. But unlike Grey, she had the money to give wider scope to her passion, Sandy Lerner–style, and soon she became a dedicated collector of first editions, Austen family letters, and other expensive treasures. "The J.A. collection is the perpetual pleasure of my life," she wrote to a book dealer in 1948. "I have bought each thing because I felt I could not live without it, and because Jane Austen is 'St. Jane' in my private hagiology." Among her acquisitions was a lock of Jane Austen's hair, auctioned by Sotheby's in 1948. The following year, the Burkes attended the annual meeting of the Jane Austen Society under the famous tent at Chawton and listened as the man who had recently spearheaded the purchase of Chawton cottage complained that a lock of Austen's hair had lately been bought—by an *American*. "Alberta muttered under her breath, 'I will give them the damn hair,'" her husband wrote years later. She rose and offered it to the society, and "at that point, the tent in which the meeting was being held almost collapsed." For Janeite pilgrims, including the members of my JASNA tour group, viewing the lock of hair became an indispensable part of every visit to Chawton in the decades that followed.

By 1979, when Joan Austen-Leigh and Jack Grey invited Harry Burke to cofound JASNA, Alberta had been dead for four years, her first editions and notebooks of Austen ephemera donated to Goucher, her valuable manuscript letters to New York's Pierpont Morgan Library. No one seemed to know why Jane Austen had so captured her imagination; like Edith Lank, the real estate columnist who quoted Louis Armstrong when asked to explain her Austen obsession, Alberta seemed to think that her reasons went without saying. "Alberta was frequently asked how she came to be interested in Jane Austen," her husband wrote to the Morgan Library's director the year she died. "But the expression on her face in response to that question was very much the kind of expression that you would see on the face of someone sitting over a filet mignon and being asked how he came to like steak."

JASNA's kickoff dinner, attended by one hundred Janeites, took place on Friday, October 5, 1979, in a mirrored, gold-draperied room at New York City's Gramercy Park Hotel. The menu featured boneless stuffed chicken and pecan pie. The after-dinner speeches were given by two prominent academics, members of a distinguished cadre of scholars whom Jack had invited to serve as

JASNA's patrons, "to lend an air of credibility to what seemed to us both at the time an extremely shaky enterprise," Joan wrote years later. There were white chrysanthemums, a printed program decorated with Jane Austen's lace pattern, a quiz, and a vote for favorite novel conducted by a Pulitzer Prize–winning playwright, Tad Mosel (*Pride and Prejudice* won handily). The *New York Times* covered the dinner; *The New Yorker* featured it in a Talk of the Town piece ("Some people who like Jane Austen got together the other evening").

At the before-dinner business meeting, Harry Burke had volunteered to host the next annual meeting, with the dependably controversial *Mansfield Park* as the theme, and when the Janeites reassembled in Baltimore the following year, the problematic novel did indeed provide the occasion for plenty of fireworks. During one lecture, an academic described Mary Crawford, the novel's clever, corrupt anti-heroine, as "the wickedest woman in English literature since Lady Macbeth," recalls Edith Lank, who had traveled from upstate New York for the occasion. "At which point a man got up in the back and started shouting and said, 'Sir, I have been in love with Mary Crawford these twenty years! Kindly go on to your next topic!' That's a moment you don't forget."

As the years passed, JASNA's traditions took shape. Every fall, members gathered in a major American or Canadian city for the Annual General Meeting, which pretty much everyone began calling an AGM — a JAZZ-na AGM, since Joan and Jack had turned out to be entirely wrong about the popularity of that dreaded acronym. Often, the AGM included a Jane Austen quiz and Tad Mosel's after-dinner vote, the TadPoll, on the best-loved character in the novel under discussion. By 1987, when it was Jack Grey's turn to organize a conference in New York City, he insisted on a characteristically extravagant venue, the legendary Waldorf-Astoria Hotel, and an innovative theme—Jane Austen's novella *Lady Susan* and her juvenilia, the boisterous short tales she had written as a teenager. The weekend began on Thursday night and stretched through Monday, with lectures, music, a performance of a *Lady Susan* theatrical adaptation, and a field trip to Princeton, New Jersey, to examine rare books and manuscripts. The kickoff reception, modeled on the fashionable gatherings in the Pump Room in Regency-era Bath, was held in an elegant peach-and-green room and featured, for the first time at a JASNA conference, a critical mass of revelers in Regency costume. In another first, the lavish conference failed to make money for JASNA.

There were other growing pains, of course. A printer's error morphed the title of JASNA's journal, published every year on the anniversary of Austen's birth, from *Persuasion* into *Persuasions,* which, as it turned out, everyone preferred. Board members juggled sometimes straitened finances and debated whether JASNA was becoming "too academic"—and what "too academic" meant, anyway. The national organization worried about regional JASNA chapters that seemed insufficiently committed to the national organization or that groaned under the yoke of dictatorial locals. Volunteers took offense at perceived slights and quit in dramatic flurries of pique. The 1994 annual meeting in New Orleans almost ran off the rails when a bitter dispute between local and national JASNA officials ended with the locals quitting en masse and destroying their files, leaving JASNA's board to pick up the pieces. The conference came off successfully, but in place of the usual glowing conference write-up, the next issue of *Persuasions* carried an anonymous, uncharacteristically snarky report complaining about everything from the audiovisual equipment to the refreshments. ("Alas! the food! Sushi chicken? 8 pink corpses atop mushroom mush carried out from our table!") Hurt feelings and furious behind-the-scenes letter writing ensued, and the following year's *Persuasions* carried a semi-apology ("We certainly regret any pain the article may have caused") and no narrative report on the 1995 conference.

Through it all, JASNA grew. Jack Grey had figured the new organization might attract three hundred members, but within two months of the New York dinner, membership swelled to 500 and, five years later, to 1,300. Joseph Costa, a New York schoolteacher who became JASNA's second president in 1981, wrote hundreds of longhand letters each year, urging new members who lived far away from other fans to celebrate Jane Austen's birthday over dinner with a friend. He heard from a Janeite in the Canary Islands and from a woman who had clutched a copy of *Pride and Prejudice* while bailing out of a disabled seaplane over the South Pacific. "We're not a country with a strong intellectual tradition," a white-haired Costa told me decades later, as we talked at his assisted-living community in Westchester County, New York, and over lunch at a nearby Greek restaurant. "So a lot of people think they're outsiders, or they're loners. What we discovered was that this was an incredibly common enjoyment among readers."

At the next table, a blond, fortyish woman in a yellow rain slicker finished her lunch and got up to leave. She leaned toward us.

"I couldn't help but overhear 'Jane Austen,'" she said. "I just finished reading *Pride and Prejudice* for the fifth time. Just finished on Monday."

"Good for you!" Costa exclaimed, slipping automatically into proselytizing mode. "Take a look at *Persuasion* too, because that's a beautiful, beautiful — short novel, but ever so beautiful."

As she went on her way, he chuckled delightedly. "There you

go. Is that a Jane Austen experience? For the fifth time! Isn't that super? And she looked rational."

By 1985, JASNA had more than 1,800 members, and by 1995, more than 2,500. By then, Colin Firth was all grown up. As wet-shirt-driven Austenmania picked up steam, JASNA added 1,000 new members in just two years, 850 of them in 1997 alone. In 1998, Elsa Solender, Harry Burke's journalist friend, who was now JASNA's president, warned members that not everyone making noise about Austen out there in the public realm was, well, up to JASNA's standards. " 'Jane Mania' and 'Jane Fever' have produced a corps of instant Jane Austen experts," Solender wrote. "They have seen a film or two, and may even have read through the entirety of one of her novels. Beware!"

Disgruntlement with other Jane Austen fans — the stuffy, bathroom-withholding kind — had helped propel JASNA into existence, so perhaps it wasn't surprising that mutual dissatisfactions — the tensions between community and exclusivity that had always been endemic to the fandom — still percolated. In 1986, a regional JASNA organizer wrote, with apparent wistfulness, about the local Sherlock Holmes organization, which, she said, "requires each aspiring member to pass an examination on the works of Conan Doyle. We could never do that, but at times I feel our members have read *P&P* and *Emma,* the truly devoted have also read *Persuasion.*" Joan continued to hold a grudge against the British Jane Austen Society. "I have the idea that the English society likes to ignore us, (JASNA) and that they think of us as a lot of vulgar rednecks (a Jane Austen Club) until they need money, of which they think we have lots," she wrote to JASNA's president in 1989. "Heaven knows, time and again when Jack and I have been at Chawton we have hardly received even a cursory How de do."

But mostly, JASNA members who had spent lifetimes in solitary worship reveled in the fellowship of like-minded devotees, just as I had as a college freshman at my first AGM. Edith Lank had been nervous about attending the 1980 Baltimore conference —after decades of marriage, she wasn't used to traveling alone —but she quickly fell for the Janeite camaraderie. "What got me was that you could talk Jane Austen from morning to night," says Edith, who had been reading all six of the novels every year since 1947 but knew no one else who was interested. "Everybody there wanted to talk Jane Austen. It was such a relief." Over and over, JASNA members recapitulated the joyful experience of instantaneous affinity that had first drawn Joan Austen-Leigh and Jack Grey together. "This is the greatest experience of my life!" the 1980 edition of *Persuasions* reported hearing a sixty-nine-year-old bookkeeper saying at the Baltimore conference. "I could hardly believe it this morning, hearing all those people up there talking and thinking about things I've been thinking about all my life." A New York magazine editor replied, "That's just how I feel—as if it's a feast which someone miraculously invited me to share."

Harry Burke was the first of JASNA's founders to die, two days before Christmas in 1989. Visiting his bedside a day earlier, Elsa Solender had found him angry at the doctors, who, he believed, had botched a routine operation and left him in perilous straits. Although he was eighty-seven, he wasn't ready to die, she thought.

Three weeks earlier, Harry had offered the traditional toast to Jane Austen at the birthday meeting of Baltimore's JASNA chapter, reading the closing stanza of a poem by Rudyard Kipling called "Jane's Marriage":

Jane lies in Winchester, blessed be her shade!
Praise the Lord for making her, and her for all she made.
And while the stones of Winchester — or Milsom Street — remain
Glory, Love, and Honour unto England's Jane!

Harry and Alberta's personal bookplate had quoted the first line of the same poem.

Joan Austen-Leigh was the last of the founders to die, in 2001, on the cusp of her eighty-first birthday. Two years earlier, she had donated Jane Austen's portable writing desk to the British Library, where it instantly became another can't-miss stop for Janeites like those on my JASNA tour. Joan had docked the *Elizabeth Bennet* when she became too old to land it alone, converting the boat into a cottage where she could entertain friends over gin and tonics. In the spring of 2001, Goucher College presented her with an honorary doctorate in recognition of her service to Jane Austen's memory, but Joan was too ill with pancreatic cancer to travel so far from home. Friends in academic regalia gathered at her hospice, listened to the ceremony on speakerphone, and presented her with a faxed copy of Goucher's scroll. Afterward, she refused to let them write "Dr. Austen-Leigh" on the door to her room. Too pretentious, she thought.

By the time Joan died, cancer had already claimed Jack Grey. Despite his diagnosis, he had attended the 1992 AGM in Santa Monica, California—the same conference at which Sandy Lerner had decided to buy Chawton House—and he had spent the ensuing days taking in a Los Angeles Lakers game and visiting Disneyland, Universal Studios, and the rhinos at the San Diego Zoo. In a photo published in that year's *Persuasions,* he looks hollow-cheeked and gaunt. He had already booked a suite with a lake view for the 1993 AGM, to be held at the spectacular Lake Louise in the Canadian Rockies, but months before the conference, he began selling his treasured collections of Dick Tracy and Jane Austen memorabilia. "It was as if he was letting go," says his friend Susan Schwartz. "He was just depleting himself of layers of his life." He couldn't eat the food with which his friends filled his refrigerator, though he managed to drink the bottles of French orange soda that Diane Levine supplied. Too ill to get around Manhattan, he spent long fall days at his beloved younger sister Dorothy's house on the Jersey Shore. They baked cookies and bread, and he played with her children. On New Year's Eve, he and Dorothy went back to his apartment in New York and watched the ball drop in Times Square. "How special it was!" Dorothy wrote later. "We laughed, we yelled out over the terrace, 'Happy New Year to all!' and we cried in each other's arms."

The day Jack died, Dorothy summoned Diane to his bedside, where Dorothy, a faithful Catholic, was praying over her unconscious brother. "Say something in Hebrew, Diane," Dorothy urged. Diane was as lapsed a Jew as Jack was a Catholic, but she dredged up the prayer over the Friday night Sabbath candles. As she held the dying man's hand and intoned the familiar, inappropriate words, Diane thought, *Jack is getting a kick out of this.* It was two days before his fifty-eighth birthday.

Seven months later, JASNA met at Lake Louise to discuss *Persuasion,* the last novel Jane Austen completed before her final illness overtook her. "It was a gorgeous place," Diane Levine said years later. "But we kept looking around for Jack." The conference was dedicated to his memory, and early on Saturday morning, friends gathered to share their reminiscences. They paid tribute to his intellect, his energy, his gift for friendship, his passion for Jane

Austen—all the qualities that had brought JASNA into being and had helped weld a small band of enthusiasts into a community. Joan Austen-Leigh told the story of their momentous meeting at the bicentennial ball. Their long friendship had become strained in the years before his death, but she had visited his bedside days before the end. "Jane Austen and the Society were at the very center of his life," she told the Janeites at Lake Louise. Jack was thin and weak, Joan recalled, but, one last time, he summoned Jane Austen's wit to his aid. When Mr. Darcy walks to the piano to hear Elizabeth Bennet play, she teases him, insisting that she will not be cowed by his presence. Facing death, Jack quoted Elizabeth's words. "My courage always rises with every attempt to intimidate me," he said.

CHAPTER 9

JANE.NET

THE BROOKLYN BOOK FESTIVAL was in full swing as I
threaded my way through the crowds in front of Borough Hall,
looking for the booth hosted by the Metropolitan New York branch
of JASNA. On this sunny afternoon in September, I had arranged
to meet my seamstress, Maureen O'Connor, for an official fitting of
The Dress. I was never going to look as good in a Regency gown as
Baronda Bradley did, but with less than a month to go before JAS-
NA's Texas AGM, it was time to see how Maureen's work was coming along.

Near a table covered with Austen-related books, fliers, and merchandise, I found Maureen in an Empire-line day dress, her dark
hair pulled back and styled into short sausage curls. Or not: Maureen had mentioned to me that she often used a hairpiece to sim-
ulate the proper Regency look, and indeed, it turned out, today's
curls were detachable. As we walked to the bus stop for the short
trip to her home, she told me about her recent stay at a Vermont inn,
where each guest had spent the entire weekend interacting in character, as a person from one of Jane Austen's novels. Maureen had
prepared carefully for her role as *Emma*'s officious Mrs. Elton, go-

ing through the novel and highlighting all Mrs. Elton's speeches, in order to study them for turns of phrase.

When we reached the brownstone where Maureen lived with her two beloved cats, she took off her curls while I checked out the family photos. Pictures of Maureen's husband — at their wedding, dancing with a niece — were displayed prominently. His death four months earlier was still a raw wound, Maureen had made clear in one of her e-mails. "I know sewing these dresses will perk me up," she had written.

In Maureen's bathroom, I took off most of my clothes and stepped into the partially laced corset I had brought along in my Philadelphia AGM tote bag. When I emerged, Maureen finished lacing me up and began holding pieces of fabric against my body — adjusting the bust line, making sure the sleeves would fit, checking for length. We discussed which color braid I preferred for the trim and which kind of fastener Maureen would use on the overdress. Standing in a bedroom wearing almost nothing while a woman I hardly knew assessed my measurements was a strangely soothing, old-fashioned experience, like confiding secrets to a hairdresser. By the time I left, I was feeling calmer. *Maybe this whole dress thing will work out after all.*

Back home in the days that followed, while I waited for Maureen to finish stitching, I started my mornings as I always did: dropping in on the discussion boards at the Republic of Pemberley, checking the headlines on AustenBlog, following up any interesting Jane Austen links unearthed in my daily Google Alert. Only seven years after my first foray into the online Austenworld, it seemed perfectly natural that a passion for books written two hundred years earlier should manifest itself via technologies that their author could scarcely have imagined.

There were Jane Austen fans before there was an Internet, but

Jane Austen fandom—an international community of people bound together by a shared love for Austen's books and their film adaptations—is a creation of the digital age. In 1991, when a McGill University English instructor founded the first Jane Austen Listserv, the World Wide Web did not yet exist, let alone a Tumblr feed called Fuck Yeah, Jane Austen. Just twenty years later, countless bloggers were extolling Austen on sites with names like Bitch in a Bonnet, The Secret Dreamworld of a Jane Austen Fan, and Jane Is My Wonderland. Facebook hosted Austen fan pages in Polish, Italian, Greek, Romanian, Portuguese, and Turkish, as well as groups with names like "I am going to marry one of the men in Jane Austen's novels," whose members seemed likely to end up migrating sadly to the group called "Jane Austen gave me unrealistic expectations of love." Hundreds of pages were registered in the name of Jane Austen herself (variously described as being "in an open relationship," working as a baker for Stella's Muffin Shop, and living in Rome). The plot of *Pride and Prejudice* had been retold in the form of a Facebook news feed, complete with emoticons and tagging; on YouTube, "The Lizzie Bennet Diaries," a year-long serial recasting the novel as a video blog created by a twenty-first-century graduate student, drew tens of thousands of passionate fans. Android offered the free Ask Mr. Darcy app, a Magic Eight Ball that dispensed cryptic advice in the form of quotations from *Pride and Prejudice*. Mr. Darcy, *Persuasion*'s dashing Captain Wentworth, and Elizabeth Bennet's sycophantic cousin Mr. Collins all had their own Twitter accounts, and Austen herself had more than a hundred—not counting Hipster Jane Austen, Jane Austen's Ghost, or JaneAustenNBA, which featured tweets like "Jason Kidd is the Elinor Dashwood of 3 point shooting." In cyberspace, Jane Austen was inescapable.

"It's so unlikely that people who love Jane Austen would also be online," says Myretta Robens, the head of the Republic of Pemberley's fourteen-member management committee. "Her characters are riding around in carriages and writing with quills, and you'd think that her fans would be emulating that. But no. They're developing websites."

The water pistols, lace handkerchiefs, and bottles of soap-bubble solution were distributed first, before the plastic wrap was ceremoniously removed from a brand-new set of videotapes of the 1995 adaptation of *Pride and Prejudice* (Colin Firth version). Then the founding members of the still-fledgling Republic of Pemberley, soon to become the Internet's largest Jane Austen fan community, settled into their hotel room for a marathon interactive viewing of the five-hour adaptation that had brought them all together, first in cyberspace and now in Las Vegas. "It was the first *Rocky Horror Pride and Prejudice*-watching," says Amy Bellinger, the creator of the electronic bulletin board that evolved into Pemberley. The women followed an audience-participation script that one of them had prepared ahead of time, chiming in with the actors on such favorite Austen lines as "I am all astonishment!" and "Are the shades of Pemberley to be thus polluted?" as well as some Austenesque lines invented by the screenwriter. When Elizabeth Bennet's overwrought mother got the vapors, they fluttered their lace handkerchiefs. When Darcy took a bath, they blew bubbles. When he got wet, they deployed their water pistols. By the end of the day, someone had complained to hotel security about the noise. Two days before, most of these eighteen women would not have recognized each other by sight, but over that weekend in August 1997, "we just talked and talked and talked until we were hoarse," Bellinger says. "It was like meeting people you'd known all your life for the first time."

I knew what she meant. That was how I'd felt when I first logged on to Pemberley, soon after my neighborhood Jane Austen book club read *Pride and Prejudice.* I was looking for background information on the property laws barring Elizabeth Bennet and her sisters from inheriting their father's estate, but my desultory research project quickly turned into something more absorbing. Here at Pemberley, I realized, were my people, the ones who could argue for hours — days! weeks! — about whether Anne Elliot and Captain Wentworth plan a long engagement, about the relative merits of the Kate Beckinsale and Gwyneth Paltrow *Emma* adaptations, about the moral worth of Fanny Price's suitor Henry Crawford. I returned more and more often. I couldn't stay away. I loved everything about my new community. I loved the way it fostered civility by requiring participants to sign their comments with some version of their real names. I loved the handy abbreviations (who wants to write *Sense and Sensibility* all the time, when *S&S* is so much quicker?). I loved the ease with which you could access searchable texts of the novels, the better to pursue arguments about whether Elizabeth is really flirting with Darcy in the *Pride and Prejudice* piano scene. Make that the *P&P* piano scene.

One night, immersed in the organized "group read" of *Persuasion,* I stayed up past midnight, waiting for the moment when we could begin posting comments on the next chapters, so I could be first up with my brilliantly perceptive analysis of Wentworth's immortal missive, which we Pemberleans call The Letter. The next day, feverish with anticipation, I logged on to read the reactions to my post. I basked happily in the electronic praise for my perceptive brilliance. I felt so loved!

My husband wasn't jealous, exactly, but he monitored my obsession with wary bemusement. Glancing over my shoulder at the computer screen, catching a glimpse of the familiar font, he would sigh, "Pemberley-ing again?" I started logging off quickly when I heard his step on the stairs, as if I was engaged in a sordid Internet affair with an old boyfriend.

As Jane Austen herself would have predicted, this head-over-heels, can't-stop-thinking-about-you, Marianne-and-Willoughby level of infatuation couldn't last. I knew things had changed when, amid the furor over Keira Knightley's star turn as Elizabeth Bennet in the latest Austen film, I logged on to the *Pride and Prejudice* discussion board and found that eleven hundred new messages had been posted in the day or two since my last visit. Weeks earlier, the avalanche of Janeite opinion would have exhilarated me. Now, I realized, it exhausted me. My passion for Pemberley had subsided into a more manageable, less time-consuming love. I no longer lay awake at night composing clever quips for tomorrow's online exchanges. But I still checked in every day, and when an interesting discussion thread caught my eye, I threw in a comment or two. Or five.

It all began because Jacqueline Reid-Walsh didn't want to stop talking about Jane Austen. A Canadian with a recent Ph.D. in English from McGill University, Reid-Walsh had just finished teaching a yearlong course on the eighteenth-century novel, including works by Austen and some of her female contemporaries. "It ended in 1991, and I was so sad," Reid-Walsh says.

"I want to keep talking about Jane Austen and Fanny Burney and Maria Edgeworth," she told her husband, Michael Walsh, who worked in computer services at McGill.

"Well, you can, you know," he replied.

And then he told her about a relatively new communication method called the Listserv, a discussion group whose conversations were conducted via e-mail messages automatically delivered to every subscriber. Walsh set up the Austen list — Austen-L — on McGill's mainframe computer; then he and Reid-Walsh posted a description on Usenet, the bare-bones computer network that pre-dated the World Wide Web. A handful of people signed up. One lived half a world away, in New Zealand; another was at sea aboard a U.S. Navy ship, like a twentieth-century version of one of Jane Austen's sailor brothers. "It was always global," Reid-Walsh says. "That's what we loved."

Via word of mouth, Austen-L's membership grew rapidly, reaching the hundreds within a year. Reid-Walsh had envisioned the list as a forum for the kind of civil, academic discussions that she had so enjoyed in her classroom, but from time to time, the discourse on Austen-L lost its civil tone. A few members seemed to enjoy provoking others, and with the etiquette of the young Internet still a work in progress, conflicts quickly escalated. "It was something they hadn't encountered before, and they really didn't know what it was and how to react to it," Walsh says. "That's how things got blown a little bit out of proportion." Fanny Price, the controversial heroine of *Mansfield Park,* was a particular flashpoint. "You should be careful about casually throwing around words such as the following in reference to Miss Price: 'insignificant,' 'moralizing prig,' 'feeble,' 'dull,' or 'nebbish,'" one Austen-L participant warned new members. "Not because these are necessarily objectively wrong, but because on Austen-L they are what the U.S. Supreme Court has termed 'fighting words.'" The periodic verbal battles, which raged so furiously that they became known as "the Fanny Price wars," startled Reid-Walsh. In the classroom, she had seen passion, but not the kind of nasty, personal rudeness that the relative anonymity of the Internet seemed to encourage. "I'm just a timid academic," she says. Once or twice, in those early days, she and Walsh had to expel particularly difficult members from the list.

In 1996, Amy Bellinger, a forty-something freelance writer from Chicago, joined Austen-L not long after watching the Colin Firth *Pride and Prejudice* for the first time. Bellinger had always enjoyed seeing films of her favorite books—at ten, she had taken along her father's copy of Shaw's play *Pygmalion* when she went to see the movie *My Fair Lady*—and Austen had been one of her favorite writers since early adulthood. But her passion for the Firth *Pride and Prejudice* was something new. "It's kind of hard to describe," she says. "It just took my breath and my heart away." She wanted to share her reactions with other fans, and she turned to the barely two-year-old World Wide Web to find them. Although she had trained as a journalist and worked in public relations, Bellinger had an affinity for computers, and the community-building aspects of the web had appealed to her from the start. In a neighborhood, or even a city, you might never find more than a few people who shared whatever your esoteric interests might be, Bellinger had realized, but when you reached out to the whole world, you could always find kindred spirits.

With a spate of Austen adaptations arriving in American movie theaters and living rooms that year, Bellinger's kindred spirits were flocking to Austen-L, and list membership swelled to more than eight hundred. Quickly, though, some of the new members began to feel inhibited. "You had this invasion of this scholarly literature list by all of these fans of the movie," Bellinger says. "We were all holding back. We wanted to feel free to gush over Colin Firth's portrayal, but we felt that these academics might be looking down their noses at us." Movie fans began discussing the possibility of spinning off a new list where Firth-gushing would be welcomed. Initially, Bellinger recalls, other Austen-L members urged them to stay. "They said, 'Oh, no, no, no, don't go. If we don't like the post, we'll just delete it,'" she says. "And I remember thinking, 'No, no, you don't understand. We are holding back *a lot*.'"

In July of 1996, Bellinger created the spinoff, a bulletin board —a simple messaging site—that she called P&P2BB. (The BBC's 1980 *Pride and Prejudice,* starring Elizabeth Garvie and David Rintoul, was P&P1.) Immediately, fans began posting two hundred messages a day, a rate of traffic that would have swamped Austen-L. Soon, it swamped P&P2BB as well, and in November, the site finally crashed for good.

From New England, a technology manager named Myretta Robens contacted Bellinger to offer help restarting the site. Robens, who was in her late forties, had been reading Jane Austen so long, she couldn't even remember when she'd started, and she still read the novels on a regular biannual rotation. In later years, during a hiatus between jobs, she would try novel-writing herself and eventually find a publisher for two romances set during the Regency. Austen-L was Robens's base for Janeite socializing, but she too had loved the Firth *Pride and Prejudice* and had joined the discussions at P&P2BB.

Over the next few months, Bellinger and Robens reconceived the bulletin board as a broader Jane Austen site, and in May 1997, they registered the Republic of Pemberley's domain name, www .pemberley.com. As Pemberley grew into the vast online Austen resource that I found on my first visit, its norms—often aimed at keeping community life harmonious—evolved. Discussions of politics, sports, and religion were off-limits (too divisive), as were gossiping about celebrities' private lives (too intrusive) and explicit conversations about sex (too racy for pre-teen Janeites). The real-name requirement was another tool for keeping the peace. "Our initial inclination was that, when people used aliases, they were more capable of being rude, because they were less responsible," Robens says. Fifteen years later, Pemberley's list of nearly eight hundred registered members would include at least twenty-two variants of Elizabeth, but not a single DarcyChick.

On a hot July day in 2004, in a Philadelphia apartment with a dial-up Internet connection and no air conditioning, Margaret Sullivan launched AustenBlog, promising her readers a sober, objective compendium of news about Jane Austen's afterlife in popular culture. "We have other places to rant and vent about eejits who don't get it," Maggie wrote. "Please do not take our dispassionate demeanour as endorsement or condemnation."

The sober, objective thing lasted for exactly twenty-two days. On July 23, Maggie posted the first pictures from the set where Keira Knightley was filming a new version of *Pride and Prejudice*. Knightley-as-Elizabeth-Bennet was wearing a green dress so hideous that it would later be compared to a garbage bag. Maggie could not resist. "That popping sound you hear is the simultaneous explosion of the heads of costume geeks worldwide," she wrote. Calm and dispassionate were out; witty and caustic were in.

That summer, Maggie Sullivan was turning forty-two, a fast-talking, intense woman with short dark hair, big glasses, and a sarcastic sense of humor. She had spent the first half of her childhood in a row house in northeast Philadelphia, the youngest of four children in a working-class Catholic family. Although neither of her parents had attended college, both were readers — Harlequin romances for her, Ian Fleming spy thrillers for him — and Maggie read voraciously even before she turned six and was old enough to get her own library card. At eight, she came home from the library at the top of the street with *My Darling, My Hamburger,* a not-exactly-appropriate-for-tweens young-adult novel about love and

sex among high school students. As she read, she had a few questions ("Mom, what are 'knockers?'"), but her mother never cen-
sored her reading. "She knew it would all go over my head anyway,"
Maggie says. "I've always been a very precocious reader, and I think
that's done me good. I've never been afraid to read anything."

When Maggie was nine, her child's world began to fall apart.
That year, her father died during open-heart surgery, and two
years later, her mother had a fatal heart attack, orphaning Maggie
at eleven. Like the heroine of a children's story, or *Mansfield Park*'s
much-maligned Fanny Price, she was sent to live with an aunt, albeit one who lived in the suburbs. Maggie repressed her feelings
about her parents' deaths and went on with her life, though she
identified intensely with the orphaned heroine of *Jane Eyre*. She
was a competent student and, despite a weakness for wisecrack-
ing, a mostly well-behaved kid who limited her rebellion to wearing
Earth shoes with her Catholic-school uniform, instead of the man-
dated green saddle shoes.

In the years after high school, Maggie started college, left without finishing when her money ran out, took dead-end clerical jobs
to pay the rent, and finally earned her degree at thirty-five, after
three years of night school. A few years earlier, she had been browsing on the cheap-paperback rack at a local pharmacy when she'd
happened across a copy of *Emma,* marked down to two dollars. Although what she'd heard about *Pride and Prejudice* had never appealed to her, at that price, she figured Austen was worth a try. "I
didn't know it was going to be how it was—funny and light," Maggie says. Laughing over the endless chattering of the old maid Miss
Bates, she flipped to the front of the book to check Austen's dates.
"It said she died in 1817. I was shocked," Maggie says. "It seemed
so modern." *Pride and Prejudice* came next, but it wasn't until she
read *Persuasion* that she was completely hooked. Captain Went-

worth's love letter to Anne Elliot—The Letter—did it. "Chills, hair standing on end: it was thrilling," Maggie says. "I loved the language, I loved the passion, the emotion." Instantly, she became a devoted fan. She completed Austen needlework kits, collected bookmarks and T-shirts, and acquired a Jane Austen finger puppet, a Jane Austen rag doll, and the Jane Austen Action Figure. And she joined the discussions at the Republic of Pemberley, even before she had seen the iconic Firth *Pride and Prejudice*. ("What are all these people talking about?" she found herself thinking in those early days. "What wet shirt?")

Since childhood, Maggie had been a writer. In fifth grade, it was a story about a talking dog that went to the moon; in high school, it was spinoffs from the books, movies, and television shows she loved, fan fiction before fan fiction had a name. She had made abortive attempts to write ever since dropping out of college, and when she discovered Jane Austen, she channeled her efforts into short stories based on Austen's characters. At first, they weren't very good, but she had learned enough in college writing classes to diagnose her own shortcomings. She posted her earliest efforts at online fan fiction sites, including Pemberley, and slowly, as she practiced her craft, she improved. "I had to find my own voice, I guess," Maggie says. "I learned how to write from writing fan fiction."

Her facility with computers was growing too. During the tech bubble of the late 1990s, she worked for a dot-com, taught herself the programming language of the web on a lark, and enjoyed the free bagels, the games of Ping-Pong, and the barbecues on summer Fridays. When her company was sold and she was left with little to do, she spent the downtime creating her online presence: a blog called Sick & Wicked—a reference to a line in one of Austen's letters—where she wrote about everything from her opinions of Austen to her crochet projects; and a website called Tilneys and

Trapdoors, after a line in *Northanger Abbey,* whose hero, the witty Henry Tilney, had become her favorite Austen man. Eventually, she posted all her fan fiction on her own site.

The dot-com laid her off in early 2003, and in the months before she was hired as a webmaster for a Philadelphia law firm, Maggie decided to work more seriously on her writing. One afternoon, she sat down and wrote a bittersweet story about love and marriage from the point of view of a secondary character in *Persuasion,* and a new magazine called *Jane Austen's Regency World* accepted it. Not long after, a tiny Canadian press invited her to write something about Janeites for a collection of essays on fandom. Maggie wrote about the divisions among Janeites—academic purists versus Colin Firth fans, pretentious poseurs versus true enthusiasts—and the eccentricity of her own preference for Henry Tilney over Mr. Darcy. "Being a Janeite has become part of my identity," she wrote. "Nearly everything that I do or experience is viewed through a filter that is colored by my understanding of Jane; I call it my inner Henry Tilney." But her deepest bond, it was clear, was not so much with any particular Austen character as with the writer who had created them all, a woman Maggie imagined as something like herself, another "genteel spinster with a yen for scribbling."

By the spring of 2004, Jane Austen news was proliferating. Fans were eagerly anticipating the Keira Knightley *Pride and Prejudice,* the first big-screen version of the novel since the 1940 film starring Laurence Olivier and Greer Garson. A Bollywood update titled *Bride and Prejudice* was also in the pipeline, a biopic called *Becoming Jane* was rumored to be seeking financing, and journalists were name-dropping Austen every week. Maggie Sullivan sensed an unfilled niche: the world needed a news blog that fans could turn to for accurate information about the burgeoning pop-culture appropriations of Austen. AustenBlog—tagline: "She's everywhere"

—was the result. The month after her launch, Maggie scored her first coup when she reached a publicist for the Knightley movie and was able to definitively debunk the persistent but false rumor that the older sister of the heartthrob actor Orlando Bloom was going to play Elizabeth Bennet's friend Charlotte Lucas. That was the kind of tidbit that Janeites and Bloomites alike were hankering for.

Ironically, when the Knightley film that had started it all was finally released, to mixed reactions from Janeites, Maggie was among those who deplored it—"No Taste, Less Filling," her review was headlined. Still, she acknowledged that the film had its merits, first among them Matthew Macfadyen's Darcy. "What a very fine, strapping, juicy hunk of British woof on the hoof," she wrote. "Bring that gaping frilly shirtage over here, sir, and you can leave your boots on."

As the months wore on, the voice of AustenBlog evolved into a mix of good sense and good snark not unlike that of Jane Austen herself, albeit an Austen reinvented as a blogger who called herself "The Editrix," used the royal we, and wasn't afraid to raise readers' hackles. AustenBlog's comments section became a place where the eternal conflict over who was the *right* kind of Janeite could be worked out, or at least worked over. In one memorable exchange that ran to sixty-nine back-and-forth comments, Maggie and some of her readers tangled with Arnie Perlstein, mingling accusations of arrogance and discourtesy with substantive arguments over the historical context of *Northanger Abbey*. Another day, she posted two less-than-glowing guest reviews of a new *Pride and Prejudice* sequel, and her comments section filled up with overwrought defenses from the writer and her friends, relatives, and fans. "Sarcasm is the lowest form of wit, I am sure Miss Austen would agree if she were alive today," wrote one of the affronted, who had apparently not read much of Miss Austen's often sarcastic work. A baseball fan as well as a Jane

Austen fan, Maggie armed herself with an imaginary weapon she called the Cluebat of Janeite Righteousness, which she used to administer virtual whacks to especially clueless commentators — those who referred to "Jane Austin," for example, or who outrageously misrepresented her stories, or who described her as a Victorian novelist, even though she had died two years before the birth of the future Queen Victoria. The Cluebat became such a treasured part of the AustenBlog repertoire that, three years into Maggie's Austen-Blog career, the organizers of a Jane Austen Festival in Louisville presented her with a genuine Louisville Slugger, in pink.

Among Janeites, AustenBlog was soon widely read, and in 2006, a small Philadelphia-based publisher invited Maggie to write a historical primer for Austen readers, *The Jane Austen Handbook: A Sensible Yet Elegant Guide to Her World.* Maggie dedicated it to her mother, "who let me read everything." (The book sold respectably — although not nearly as well as the same publisher's next foray into Austeniana, the surprise bestseller *Pride and Prejudice and Zombies*.) At JASNA conferences, Maggie came in costume, or in a T-shirt reading TEAM TILNEY, and she professed some exasperation with Janeites who looked down their noses at manifestations of fandom they perceived as unserious. Although she liked to caricature the Editrix as an Austen purist — a "tar-hearted dried-up purist spinster Janeite," to be exact — Maggie's usual view of the fandom was tolerant. "Janeite-ville is a big tent," she says. "I'm trying to live and let live."

As the 2000s went on, more and more Austen-inspired bloggers joined Maggie Sullivan on the Internet. One was a Virginia grant writer named Vic Sanborn, who had read *Pride and Prejudice* annually from her teens to her thirties, savoring the close relationship between the acerbic Mr. Bennet and his favorite daughter,

Elizabeth, which reminded her of her bond with her own father. "It was almost as if it was a friend," Sanborn says. "Every year, in summer, I would read *Pride and Prejudice*." For years, she hadn't known Austen wrote any other books; in college, when she finally learned differently, she tried *Mansfield Park* and, uninspired, returned to *Pride and Prejudice*. But Sanborn still found the history, fashion, and social customs of the Regency fascinating, and in 2006, she and a friend decided to start a book club to read Austen and her twentieth-century imitator, Georgette Heyer. Now, reading with the hard-won wisdom of a fiftyish woman who had survived professional setbacks and a painful midlife divorce to build a satisfying life, Sanborn found new riches in the books, even the relatively inaccessible *Mansfield Park*. "All of a sudden, the treasure of Jane Austen just unfolded for me," Sanborn says. "I started reading books about her life, I started reading articles that critiqued her books. I just became totally immersed and have been ever since."

Sanborn had always been the kind of person who committed deeply to absorbing enthusiasms — she had been a lab researcher, a watercolor painter, an unpublished novelist — and blogging became her newest passion. Like Maggie Sullivan two years earlier, she found an unfilled niche: the Internet lacked blogs offering well-sourced information about the English Regency. Sanborn filled the niche with Jane Austen's World, where she posted carefully researched and copiously illustrated pieces on life in Georgian England, covering everything from prostitution to road conditions.

Soon, she was trading tips on search-engine optimization with another Austen blogger, a Barnes & Noble bookseller in Washington State named Laurel Ann Nattress. Nattress fell in love with Austen in college when, like Sandy Lerner, she saw the BBC's 1980 version of *Pride and Prejudice*. Compared to the stressed-out America of the Carter administration — the Iranian hostage crisis! disco!

—Austen's world seemed reassuringly civil and uncomplicated. "I was probably searching for something, searching for different things that I connected to. And it just happened to be Jane Austen," Nattress says. "And I didn't really talk about it with people. I just read her books every year and thought about her a lot." Rereading *Pride and Prejudice* was an annual ritual that Nattress usually performed in the fall. By the early years of the twenty-first century, however, the joys of solitary fandom had given way to a longing for connection: Nattress wanted a place to communicate her passion for Jane Austen to the like-minded. "I thought, 'Well, what the heck? I'll just do this blog, and if nobody reads it, no big deal,'" she says. "Every day, I decided that I was going to write something about Jane Austen, just a little paragraph or two, and it would just be for me, if nobody else wanted to read it."

At first, Nattress's blog, Austenprose, offered a daily meditation on the significance of a particular word in Austen's letters or novels. Eventually, Nattress branched out into reviews of Austen movies, television shows, and spinoff books, and some two years after her blog launch, a literary agent e-mailed to thank her for a friendly interview with one of his clients. For six months, Nattress had been mulling over a book idea of her own, and now she seized the opportunity to make her pitch for an anthology of Austen-related short stories by some of the leading practitioners of the Austen spinoff genre. Within days, the agent got her a contract, and a year and a half later, the book, *Jane Austen Made Me Do It,* was a reality. The seller of books had become a creator of one. "I am like the poster girl of 'Follow your bliss,'" Nattress says. "And it was all Jane. She did it all for me."

Jane Austen's afterlife on the Internet embodied the tension at the heart of passionate fandom, the desire for both community and exclusivity, the yen to keep the big tent open and simultaneously wield the Cluebat. Some of the people immersed in online fandom reveled in the joy of finding other Janeites. "I keep thinking how fortunate we are to have Jane Austen's novels, and how easily she could have died with them unpublished and possibly consigned to flames," wrote one participant in the online Janeites discussion group on Yahoo. "I love the way her novels bring us together as a particular community. Would they not have been published, most of us would probably be devoted to other lists — and some of us on those lists together — but we wouldn't be this exact community." But others seemed more ambivalent about Austen's newly globalized popularity, worrying about whether she was being smothered in the embrace of people who didn't really understand her. "I remember when the doings of both the English Jane Austen Society and JASNA used to be the province of the educated, congenial, delightfully slightly dottily eccentric amateur and enthusiast," wrote another Janeites participant. "Today the JA world is so commercialized and dumbed down, it's hard not to be in despair at a deep and private love reduced to popular media pandering."

It was with mixed feelings, then, that some of the women who had first brought Jane Austen to life on the Internet watched as the wave of her popularity seemed to crest and, perhaps, to recede. For years, new film and TV versions of Austen novels had stoked Janeite fervor, but as the second decade of the twenty-first century began, the passions seemed to be cooling, the size of the audience for each new blog post shrinking. "At first, there was this hunger for anything about Jane Austen," Sanborn said in early 2012. "But last year, Laurel Ann and I e-mailed each other, and Laurel Ann says, 'I think the party is over.' And it's true — that kind of frenzy for the films is over. But now, see, this is what I'm enjoying: the serious Janeites have stayed."

Fifteen years after P&P2BB first came into being, the website of the Republic of Pemberley was getting five to ten million hits each month from 150,000 unique visitors hailing from 165 countries. The community paid for its server space with donations, advertising, and links to retail sites, and Myretta Robens, now retired from her tech career, spent thirty hours a week handling technical issues and checking the traffic on the discussion boards, just to keep her finger on the community's pulse. Janeites were still discovering kindred spirits there, with the same feeling of joyful homecoming I had experienced when I first logged on. In the mid-2000s, Laurie Michael, a homeschooled teenager from an evangelical Christian family, went looking for Austen online because her Maine town was short of fellow Janeites. She found AustenBlog and Pemberley, and if the discussions sometimes felt daunting—so many people knew so much more than she did—it was thrilling to see that she wasn't alone in her passion. "I was really excited when I first found out there are other people who like Jane Austen too," Laurie says. "This community of fans—it amazed me."

The Austen-L list was still generating conversation and controversy, much of it these days revolving around Arnie Perlstein and his periodically heated disputes with his antagonists. Although list membership had dropped from the mid-1990s highs, it had stabilized at 250 or 300. Many of those people also belonged to the second Austen discussion list, Yahoo's nearly thousand-member Janeites group, which two Austen-L members had founded in 1998 partly to escape the sometimes vitriolic free-for-all on the original list.

Jacqueline Reid-Walsh's research interests had moved on, and she no longer joined the conversations at Austen-L. But she still thought of its early days with affection, remembering the list members who had told her they were shut-ins who looked forward to their daily dose of Austen discussion. With its kindly neighbors and its grouchy eccentrics, its talkative protagonists and its silent lurkers, the list — like the world of Janeite fandom that it embodied in miniature — had become a digital analogue of the country villages where Austen set her novels. "I was so pleased to see them as a community, because Jane Austen writes about communities," Reid-Walsh says. "You can look at Austen-L as something out of *Emma*, perhaps."

At AustenBlog, Maggie Sullivan too was slowing down. By the 2010s, her day job was becoming increasingly intense and exhausting, and she often came home at night too tired to blog. The rush of Jane Austen news had slackened, in any case, and cyberspace was far more crowded with Jane Austen outlets than it had been when she began. By late 2012, she had decided to make the transition to a new, more personal blog that would give her room to write about a wider range of her interests; she was, she decided, suffering from a bad case of Austen-blogger burnout. "I really always have joy in JA when push comes to shove," she e-mailed me, when I wrote to ask why AustenBlog had been dormant for months. "I just need to get away from the fandom for a bit and get back to my own, admittedly quirky pleasure in Jane." Still, Austen was too much a part of Maggie's life to be left behind entirely; the latest Austen-related inanities would still call forth the Cluebat, she promised. She was planning to call her new blog This Delightful Habit of Journaling — quoting Henry Tilney, of course.

Late one night, I sat at the computer, wondering if I should e-mail an enquiry to Maureen O'Connor. A week after my fitting, my relative calm was evaporating. The AGM was approaching, and I still had no ball gown. As if Maureen had read my mind, a message from her suddenly appeared in my inbox, quickly followed by three more—photos of the nearly completed outfit. "I am sure you are going to love it," she wrote. Two days later, she e-mailed again: the parcel was in the mail, scheduled to arrive a few days later, barely a week before my departure for Texas. I began imagining nightmare scenarios—frantic calls to the postal service to track down a lost box, dancing at the ball in street clothes . . .

To tamp down my anxiety, I went looking for the long gloves I needed to complete my ensemble. In an online guide to Regency dress-up, Lisa Brown, a Syracuse Janeite who rents out her collection of period costumes, had issued strict instructions about gloves: "Please don't buy shiny satin." It was so important that she said it twice. But during a morning of shopping in the Halloween departments of two local party stores, I found nothing but shiny satin, and I didn't have time to troll vintage shops on the off chance I'd find an unshiny pair discarded by someone's great-grandmother. Online too, satin was everywhere; the only cotton gloves I could find in the matte fabric that Brown demanded would cost me fifty dollars. I grimaced and paid up.

A week before my flight to Texas, I went out to check the mail and found a Federal Express box from Maureen on my doorstep. With studied casualness, I collected the contents of the mailbox and began flipping through envelopes.

Perhaps I'll open the credit card bill and sort out the letters from school before I look at the dress.

Oh, screw that.

I sat down and, with hands that were actually kind of trembly, ripped open one end of the box and pulled out the bundle inside. A flash of blue, a glint of gold braid . . . I unfolded the tissue paper, spread out the dresses, and began to laugh. I had never owned any piece of clothing this beautiful, let alone worn it. The high-waisted underdress was a deep blue iridescent satin with a square neckline trimmed in gold braid and short, bell-shaped sleeves threaded with ribbons in a contrasting blue. A rope of the same gold braid cinched the sleeveless blue overdress under the bust. Maureen had even thrown in a matching drawstring reticule. I e-mailed her a rapturous thank-you. The $314 price tag, which would bring the total cost of my outfit to more than $600, seemed a bargain.

That evening, my daughter tried and failed to lace me into my corset. By the time my husband took over, I had become a stressed-out, unpleasant Mom from Hell, and my daughter retreated to her bedroom close to tears. "I'm sorry I don't know how to lace a corset!" she wailed when I came in later to apologize. "I'm only eleven, and I live in the twenty-first century!" The real source of my stress, however, was the dress, which had looked far better lying flat on my bed than draped over my un-Paltrowesque frame. I could only hope that the magic of the JASNA ball would somehow transform me into the heroine of a Jane Austen movie.

CHAPTER 10

THE TRIBE

Day 1

Nestling in the middle of my Jane Austen goody bag is a black lace thong.

It is the first day of JASNA's Annual General Meeting, and I am sitting on the bed in my Fort Worth hotel room, examining the contents of the free tote bag I collected a few minutes earlier from a registration-desk volunteer wearing a TEAM WILLOUGHBY button. In *Sense and Sensibility,* Willoughby is the handsome, manipulative serial seducer who breaks Marianne Dashwood's heart, precipitating her deep depression and near-fatal illness, and I am, frankly, a bit shocked to see a Janeite on his team. It's not as if she had no choice: other volunteers are wearing TEAM BRANDON buttons, boosting Marianne's eventual husband, the devoted and selfless Colonel Brandon. "For the weekend!" the Willoughbyite explains, laughing. "Who would you rather be with for a weekend?"

The souvenir tote bag has become a fixture of the JASNA AGM, and this year's has a satisfying heft, signifying a large quantity of freebies. We've come a long way since the 1983 AGM I attended as a college freshman, when the swag consisted primarily of a laminated bookmark illustrated with a scene from *Emma*. Today, the pile on my hotel bed includes Post-it notes and hand sanitizer from Southwest Diagnostic Imaging; a pen from American Airlines; a bar of soap; a lime-green stuffed dog emblazoned with the LOVE PINK slogan of Victoria's Secret; a mouse pad with an armadillo on it; a tea bag of English Breakfast, courtesy of a store in Grapevine, Texas; a bottle of Victoria's Secret perfume; a plastic 7-Eleven coffee mug; a CD of songs from a new musical version of *Sense and Sensibility;* and countless publicity materials — postcards, bookmarks, fliers, a coaster, a fridge magnet — advertising Austen-related books, from *Approaches to Teaching Austen's* Emma to *Jane Austen: Blood Persuasion* ("She sips tea in the afternoon, drinks blood at night").

And of course, the thong, considerately provided in a one-size-fits-all version. It comes with a tiny card reading, "Call me! XOXO, Willoughby," accompanied by a real phone number, which is answered by a recording of a silky male voice, flirtatious and British-accented, urging me to attend next year's AGM in New York City.

The whole thing leaves me slightly depressed. All the product placement — the thong is also brought to us by Victoria's Secret, one of twenty-three conference sponsors — smacks of a level of commercialization that would have been unimaginable back when Jack Grey and Joan Austen-Leigh were soliciting members for their Jane Austen society. The discontent that washed over me during my summer visit to Chawton cottage returns: *Too many people want a piece of Jane Austen these days! Give her back to me! I can appreciate her the way she was meant to be appreciated!* Most days, I'm happy to share Jane Austen; I even enjoy her crossover appeal, her status as both highbrow and lowbrow, intellectual and popular. Just now, though, I feel a bit wistful about that laminated bookmark and the small, homespun Janeite world it represented.

Still, as I pack away, or throw away, the contents of my goody bag, my malaise passes quickly. Nothing can long dampen my enthusiasm for the four days of unapologetic Jane Austen wallowing that lie ahead. Nearly seven hundred people are attending this year's conference celebrating the two-hundredth anniversary of the publication of *Sense and Sensibility,* and the program is a testament to Austen's crossover-artist status, a vivid demonstration of JASNA's time-honored melding of highbrow academia and swooning fandom, serious study and unserious fun. We will hear lectures with titles like "The Iconography of Sensibility," and we will take English country-dance lessons. We will listen as university professors closely parse Austen's language, and we will munch popcorn during a marathon showing of *Sense and Sensibility* movies. We will learn about land transportation and political economy in the time of Jane Austen, and we will buy wine charms reading W.W.J.D. — WHAT WOULD JANE DO? I can't wait.

Day 2

" . . . slap Edmund upside the head," someone is saying.

My day is starting with the first of what are sure to be many visits to the conference Emporium, and a snippet of conversation has floated over to the spot where I'm browsing amid booths selling Jane Austen earrings and CARPE DARCY — SEIZE MR. DARCY T-shirts. *Ah,* Mansfield Park *— always gets the juices flowing.* Edmund Bertram, the novel's hero, spends most of the book panting for the temptress Mary Crawford while remaining pathologically oblivious to virtuous Fanny Price's love for him. Janeite frustration with Edmund is so widespread that the Republic of Pemberley created a special acronym, ENASUTH, for the frequently used phrase "Edmund needs a slap upside the head." On AustenBlog, Maggie Sullivan refers to him as "the Lord High Mayor of Wankerville." The JASNA AGM is the perfect place for Janeites to indulge such emotions, secure in the knowledge that no one within earshot is going to ask who Edmund is, or point out that he isn't a real person. As if that mattered.

But I have no time to join the Edmund bashing, since I'm scheduled for a workshop on English country dance, run by Beverly Francis, the dance caller I met during last summer's JASNA tour of England. As I walk in, I spot a number of people wearing bonnets and Regency day dresses. At 8:30 A.M. On the first morning of the conference. "Oh, my goodness," says the woman beside me, who is wearing slacks. "I should have worn my dress." Over the next ninety minutes, as we amateurs follow along in our clumsy, enthusiastic way, Beverly takes us through three relatively easy dances dating from around Jane Austen's lifetime, dances with picturesque names like Sprigs of Laurel and the Duke of Kent's Waltz. Then she teaches us a much older, more difficult dance, Mr. Beveridge's Maggot, from 1695. (*Maggot*, in this context, means a whim, not a disgusting, wormy larva-thing.) We are learning this dance because Elizabeth and Darcy danced it in the BBC's famous 1995 *Pride and Prejudice* miniseries.

Nearly every filmed adaptation of a Jane Austen novel includes a ball scene — lines of women in long dresses joining hands with lines of men in knee breeches, stepping gracefully forward and back, turning away and coming together, in a symbolic enactment of the push-pull of Austen's courtship plots. It's a folk dance form that was popular in England for centuries, though dance aficionados don't see Austen's era, when two-person dances like the waltz were only just beginning to arrive in Britain from the European continent, as a moment of especially great creativity for the art form. In any case, the English country dancing shown in Jane Austen movies owes more to the choreographic needs of the screenplays than to an accurate reading of dance history—Mr. Beveridge's Maggot, Beverly tells us, is not a dance that Elizabeth and Darcy would likely have done. Still, the hundreds of English country-dance groups that convene regularly for casual evening dances or occasional fancy balls are happy to initiate Austen fans, however poorly informed. In a bid for a wider audience, local groups sometimes dub their more formal evenings "Jane Austen balls." "Jane Austen, with dance, is becoming code for something that you might vaguely think of based on the movies, which are historically inaccurate," says Allison Thompson, a Pittsburgh Janeite who is also a dance scholar. "But you have this image, and it's a pretty image, and so I think it's—I don't know if 'gateway drug' is too strong a word."

Until the 2010 AGM in Portland, Oregon, I felt about Regency dancing the same way I felt about Regency costuming—I was Not That Kind of Jane Austen fan. But that year, research compelled me to join in, and to my surprise, English country dancing turned out to be curiously absorbing. The flutter of anxiety over finding a partner for each new dance, the concentration required to follow unfamiliar steps (is it the left foot this time? the right hand? the counterclockwise turn?), the uncomfortable intimacy of locking eyes with a stranger across the set—it all made for an oddly intense way to spend an evening. After a lifetime of Jane Austen fandom, I finally understood why Austen so often threw her heroes and heroines together at a ball. I probably won't seek out my local country-dance group between AGMs, but I am looking forward to dancing at this year's JASNA ball.

After the workshop, I drift back to the Emporium, where I am alternately charmed and repelled by the merchandise on display. For every apron or tea towel or mirrored compact bearing a genuine Jane Austen quote, there seems to be a key chain or plaque or note card adorned with a line found only in an Austen movie. The real Jane Austen, I'm sure, would have died rather than write anything as maudlin as "Sometimes the last person on earth you want to be with is the one person you can't be without" or "Perhaps it is our imperfections that make us so perfect for one another." *Hasn't anyone around here READ THE BOOKS?* I find myself wondering. The movies have made Jane Austen more accessible than ever, broadening the base of her fandom and diversifying her appeal, and even as I register my silent squawk of protest, I feel a bit churlish, like some mean Alpha Girl patrolling the boundaries of the high school clique. (But really — "Sometimes the last person on earth — ?" That one wasn't even in an Austen movie! It was on the *poster* for an Austen movie!) Once again, I'm face to face with the contradictions of fandom: I've come to a Jane Austen conference to enjoy the company of other Janeites, but I can't help turning up my nose, just a little, at the gross ignorance — the sheer bad taste! — of people whose idea of *Pride and Prejudice* owes more to Keira Knightley than to Jane Austen.

But of course there are genuine Janeites, my kind of Janeites, among the small-business owners who are hawking their wares here. At the Bingley's Teas booth, Julia Matson is selling loose-leaf tea packaged in boxes designed to look like hardcover books. Matson was a massage therapist and young mother who discovered both a passion for tea and a love of Jane Austen in the mid-1990s, around the time she first saw the Colin Firth *Pride and Prejudice*. In 2009, she had been selling tea online for a year — she had named her business after Mr. Bingley, Darcy's sociable, openhearted best friend — when her husband began urging her to put an Austen twist on her marketing. At first, she resisted. "I snapped at him," she says. "I said, 'I'm not just going to slap some tea with her name. I take Jane Austen seriously, I take tea seriously, and I would like to be taken seriously.'" But one night a sudden inspiration woke her from her sleep: like each of Austen's characters, she realized, each flavor of tea has its own distinctive personality. Two years after that middle-of-the-night epiphany, Matson is selling more than a dozen teas named for Austen's people, from Wicked Wickham ("dashing tart flavor with a candy like after taste") to Mr. Knightley's Reserve ("true and balanced"), and her Jane Austen Tea Series accounts for most of her sales.

Not far away is the booth for Jane Austen Books, where three women from Ohio, Jennifer Weinbrecht and her adult daughters, Amy Patterson and Beth Dean, sell Austen-related titles, from the scholarly to the popular. Weinbrecht read Austen aloud to her girls when they were barely old enough to read themselves, and in sixth grade Patterson dressed in a reasonable facsimile of Regency costume to present a book report on a Jane Austen biography. Their first Christmas together, Patterson's future husband gave her an 1837 edition of *Sense and Sensibility*, bought online for just a hundred dollars, and her mother was so impressed by his taste that she warned Patterson, "Don't screw this up!" The women of Jane Austen Books are the kind of people who characterize friends and relatives with pitiless Austen shorthand — this one is Aunt Norris (abusive and overbearing), that one is Marianne Dashwood (impulsive and emotional). "I am always thinking about Jane Austen," Patterson says. "She's always on the couch next to me."

In front of the book display, I run into Christine Shih, who updates me on the progress of her work on Austen and borderline personality disorder. A paper she wrote on Jane Austen's deathbed poem has been accepted to a conference in Oxford, and she is talking to Vanderbilt's nursing school about team-teaching a course on borderline personality disorder in literature. Her bibliotherapy group has gained so many new members that it threatens to overflow her living room, and after discussing *Mansfield Park* and *Lady Susan,* participants have moved on from Austen to spend two sessions on *Jane Eyre.* I remind Christine of her promise to lace me into my corset on Saturday night, and we make arrangements and exchange phone numbers. Phew! I have secured my lady's maid.

The rest of the day passes in a busy blur. A cosmetics executive lectures on the sometimes lethal ingredients in Regency-era beauty products. A romance writer describes weddings in Jane Austen's day. A British crime writer previews her about-to-be-published historical mystery novel, which attributes Jane Austen's last illness to arsenic poisoning at the hands of a homicidal relative bent on covering up an adulterous liaison. Baronda Bradley — dressed in sky blue, with a giant white feather in her hat — offers tips for assembling a JASNA-ready wardrobe, her many gowns arrayed around her on portable racks. Afterward, audience members finger the fabrics and snap pictures.

At one of the sessions, I meet sixteen-year-old Heather Gehrman and her mother, Hollie, who have driven three hours from Oklahoma to attend their first JASNA AGM. (Bill Gehrman, husband and father, is watching TV in the hotel room. "He said it's a girly thing," Hollie explains.) Fandom seems to run in the family: Bill once attended a *Star Trek* convention, Heather has been to a *Twilight* convention, and back in January, Hollie stumbled across JASNA when she went looking for something to feed her Jane Austen enthusiasm. Heather has brought along a wardrobe's worth of Austenesque dresses that she sewed with her mother's help, and today she is wearing pale-purple satin trimmed in antique gold braid.

Moriah Webster, seventeen, comes over to introduce herself to Heather, a rare fellow teenager in a sea of middle-aged women. Moriah too is a first-time AGM attendee accompanied by her mother. "We didn't know that there was a big dress-up thing," Moriah says. "I bought a dress here — it's red — for the ball."

"If you want to change, you could always borrow one of mine," Heather offers. "I have five."

Later, I catch up with Moriah's mother, Mindi, a tiny woman with a head of curly brown hair, who teaches middle-school English in Virginia. Mindi, who describes herself as a conservative, likes Austen's psychological insight, subtle characterization, and moral rigor. Today's parents, Mindi says, too often sidestep moral judgment because they want to seem hip to their children, but Jane Austen has no such hang-ups. "She's not afraid to say something is improper," Mindi says. "I think that's one of the things that our kids yearn for — I see it in my classroom. They want something to tell them when they've crossed the line."

"Jane Austen is like a guide where there's nothing else that's guiding," Moriah says.

Mother and daughter are both wearing TEAM BRANDON buttons. "Willoughby was a jerk," Moriah says.

I am in a hotel elevator filled with Janeites wearing conference name tags, bonnets, and Empire-waist dresses. Gradually, the elevator empties out, until no one is left but me and a youngish man in a baseball cap. He eyes my JASNA name tag. Clearly, I'm with the bonnet people.

"What's going on here?" he asks.

"It's a Jane Austen convention," I reply.

He looks blank.

"Jane Austen? The writer?"

Still blank.

"The author of *Pride and Prejudice*?"

He shakes his head. "No, I'm not familiar with that," he says.

I'm embarrassed. For him. "Umm . . . she's actually . . . a pretty famous writer . . . ," I mutter.

A thought seems to strike him, and he brightens. "Is she here?" he asks.

Day 3

A roomful of women armed with needles and embroidery floss sit companionably, counting stitches, and the BBC is filming it all.

We are making cross-stitch bookmarks featuring Jane Austen's silhouette and signature. They are making a documentary on Jane Austen's popularity through the ages, which will air two months later in Britain as *The Many Lovers of Miss Jane Austen*. A brunette in a black pantsuit — Amanda Vickery, a well-regarded British historian with a sideline in popularized history TV — is traveling from table to table, asking earnest questions about why we love Austen. Later in the day, I will spot Vickery in the book display at the Emporium, holding up titles and commenting for the camera: "*In the Arms of Mr. Darcy* — Jane Austen as Mills & Boon. *The Importance of Being Emma* — Jane Austen as chick lit. *Mr. Darcy, Vampyre* — Jane Austen and vampires."

On Sunday, JASNA is holding a giant book-signing for authors of Austen-related fiction and nonfiction, and in preparation for that event, the book exhibit here is crammed with titles. So many of the Janeites I've met were writers manqués who found in Austen the inspiration they needed to finally realize their dreams, whether on-line or in print. Surely, this isn't an inevitable result of fandom. (Do admirers of Picasso rush to pick up paintbrushes?) Apparently, however, something about Austen makes her acolytes think that they too can write. Perhaps she seems at first glance an unintimi-dating figure—the country clergyman's daughter, without much money or formal education, who traveled little, socialized mostly with relatives and neighbors, and wrote about the stuff of ordinary life, the family conflicts and love stories that we've all lived through ourselves. If she could write like that, surely we can too! To me, though, it's the very ordinariness of Austen's life that is the most in-timidating thing about her: nothing explains her achievement ex-cept the ineffable quality of her mind, and who among us can lay claim to that?

The chairwoman of the Scottish branch of Britain's Jane Aus-ten Society, resplendent in dark blue taffeta and pearls, is singing lovely, melodic songs with titles like "The Highland Laddie," while slides of Scottish landscapes fade in and out on the video screen. The connection to *Sense and Sensibility* is a bit tenuous—although Marianne Dashwood is musical, Jane Austen never tells us whether she sang Scots songs—but never mind; it's a delightful way to spend a morning.

Next up is Elisabeth Lenckos, an instructor in the University of Chicago's continuing education program. In German-accented English, Lenckos describes the Chawton House Library's col-lection of Austen-era novels that, like *Sense and Sensibility,* cen-ter on pairs of sisters. She summarizes the plots of gothic thrillers and moral tracts, all of which sound far less engaging than Austen's complicated, sardonic tale of self-contained Elinor and expressive Marianne. In conclusion, Lenckos passes out a quiz that will allow each of us to determine if we are an Elinor or a Marianne ("Must your boyfriend be handsome, charming and reckless, and then you wonder why your heart is broken?").

In the question-and-answer session, the ambivalence that *Sense and Sensibility* often provokes in Janeites bubbles to the surface. Some people dislike the passionate, self-absorbed Marianne; others can't reconcile themselves to her marriage to the much older Colonel Brandon, a marriage that Austen tells us is initially founded, on Marianne's side, on "no sentiment superior to strong esteem and lively friendship."

"It seems to me, being a Marianne, that people are awfully hard on Marianne," one audience member argues. "She's a teenage girl, after all."

"Her extremes seem to be excessive because she is so young," Lenckos agrees. Other novels of Austen's time deal far more harshly with straying young females, she adds. "Given the context of the other novels, she is not punished," Lenckos notes. "She'd be dead in the other books."

"I've never been convinced that Marianne and Colonel Brandon were happy," another woman in the audience says. "I think at night, when she and her husband were making love, she thought of Willoughby."

"But that's not forbidden!" Lenckos exclaims.

A few rows ahead of me, I spot a ponytailed man wearing earrings, whose collared shirt proclaims, I READ JANE AUSTEN AND I GOT THE GIRL. His name is Jameson Stalanthas Yu, and seven months earlier, he tells me, he proposed to his girlfriend, Alice Villaseñor, a Ph.D. in English who wrote her dissertation on Austen. He staged the big moment in the most romantic setting imaginable: the grounds of Chatsworth, the palatial Derbyshire home of the Duke and Duchess of Devonshire, which some believe was Austen's inspiration for Mr. Darcy's estate, Pemberley. Jameson sounds like a devoted Janeite spouse-to-be: he has read and enjoyed the novels, and he has bought Alice Chinese and Thai translations, as well as all the Marvel Comics versions. Dress-up, however, remains out of reach. "I can't afford that yet," he says. "It's harder for the guys to get costumes. They don't make men's brocade as casual wear."

I have been in Fort Worth for two days, but everything so far has been prequel; JASNA's AGM opens officially only this afternoon, with a plenary talk by Joan Ray, a university professor from Colorado who is a past JASNA president. She is an accomplished and entertaining speaker, unafraid to court controversy with her slashing criticisms of Edward Ferrars, Elinor Dashwood's future husband, whom many readers find pallid and dull. He's far from dull, Ray insists. "There is a lot more to say about Edward," she says grimly, "and it is not good." Mercilessly, she fleshes out her critique, indicting Edward for aimlessness, for dishonesty, for allowing the woman he loves to suffer needlessly while he dithers over an unfortunate secret engagement. I am taken aback — Edward isn't my favorite Austen hero, but surely he isn't this bad? — but next to me, a Japanese scholar who will be speaking later on Austen and *Frankenstein* chimes in softly, "Yes! Yes!"

The rest of the afternoon is taken up with shorter breakout sessions, our choice of three out of twenty. A college instructor describes how *Sense and Sensibility* subtly engages with nineteenth-century debates between Whigs and Tories over societal responsibility for the poor. An antiques dealer explains how to buy nineteenth-century furniture, china, and glass on a budget. A self-published Regency romance novelist champions Colonel Brandon's "sheer, unadulterated romance and derring-do." I skip the session on snuff, guns, and cravats, led by an amateur historian whose conference biography cheerfully reports that he has attended four previous AGMs as "an accessory to his wife" and that he "has very nearly read almost half of *Emma*."

On the way back to my room, I notice a Jane Austen jigsaw puzzle lying partially completed on a side table in the lobby. Arnie Perlstein is standing in line for the elevator, chatting animatedly to one of the breakout speakers, a community-college teacher who discussed attitudes toward primogeniture in *Sense and Sensibility* and the biblical book of Genesis. "What gets me is when people say 'Would she do it on purpose?'" Arnie is saying. "It's like Will Shortz. You don't say, 'Did he put that clue in on purpose?'" I can't tell if his interlocutor knows that Will Shortz is the crossword-puzzle editor of the *New York Times*.

Since 1950, *Sense and Sensibility* has been adapted for the screen at least eight times, and for tonight's movie marathon, we will be treated to three of those adaptations: the 2008 TV miniseries, with a script by the revered Andrew Davies, author of the wet-shirt *Pride and Prejudice;* the 2011 movie *From Prada to Nada,* which transplants Austen's story to the world of Latinos in contemporary Los Angeles; and a never-before-seen modern update called *Scents and Sensibility.*

As I settle down with my popcorn next to a Denver Janeite named Jennifer Petkus, I am already worrying about *Scents and Sensibility.* At this afternoon's plenary session, a producer of the film promised that we would find it "wholesome" and "adorable," adjectives that seldom come to mind when I think about Jane Austen. And, as I feared, the movie never rises above the level of an after-school special, as its barely differentiated heroines—call them Perky and Plucky, since neither seems much endowed with either sense or sensibility—navigate their romantic dilemmas while launching a home hand-lotion business to pay for their little sister Margaret's leukemia treatment. By the closing wrap-up, which gravely informs us that Margaret recovered from her leukemia and "moved with her mother to a ranch in Colorado, where she raises therapy horses," Jennifer and I are speechless with mirth.

Day 4

"Elinor here was up at five-thirty," the young mother is saying to her breakfast companions, as a bright-eyed toddler sits stolidly in the stroller beside her. Yes, I confirm a moment later: Amanda Himes's baby was indeed named after one of the heroines of *Sense and Sensibility*. We Janeites do that kind of thing. Among the sponsors of a past AGM was an anonymous donor making a contribution "in Memory of Fitzwilliam Darcy, Feline, Esq."

In the hotel lobby after breakfast, I run into Baronda Bradley, who is wearing an aqua-green, classical-Greece-inspired gown, one of five new ones she is debuting at this AGM. She has found a part-time gig at a local university, but the promising job lead she was counting on months earlier has fizzled, and she's still looking for full-time work. Here at the AGM, however, she's not just another casualty of economic collapse; she's a star. "Love that dress!" a passerby calls out. Someone else stops to take her picture.

Saturday—a full day of speakers, culminating with the banquet and ball—is the heart of the JASNA conference, and as I look around the meeting space where we're all gathering, I notice more people than ever in costume or sporting evidence of recent visits to the Emporium: coffee mugs decorated with Austen quotes, T-shirts listing the titles of all the novels, proliferating TEAM BRANDON and TEAM WILLOUGHBY buttons. Heather Gehrman is wearing blue satin and a fashionably mismatched pair of earrings—a nickel-sized disk bearing a picture of Colin Firth's Darcy on one ear, a second disk reading KEEP CALM AND AUSTEN ON on the other.

The morning plenary and breakout sessions fly by. A college professor from Canada lectures on the literal and metaphorical duels in *Sense and Sensibility;* at her waist hangs a small sword she had to get special permission to transport across the border. I hurry from a fascinating, thoroughly academic session on Chinese and Eastern European translations of Austen's novels to a breezy, entertaining talk by a video-game editor on digital and pop-culture responses to Austen. (Note to self: check YouTube for Jane Austen drinking games.) From dueling to tweeting, in a single morning: such is the Janeite world in the early twenty-first century, sixteen years after Mr. Darcy donned a wet shirt just as digital technology was creating the virtual space where we could all talk about it.

For lunch, I join a reunion of our summer JASNA tour, and we pass around photos and share messages from those who couldn't make it. I have already run into many of my fellow tour members in the halls of the conference. In the Emporium, I found Debbie McNeil, who has never before dressed in costume or danced at the ball but who is thinking of buying a feathered headband for Saturday night. As we eat lunch, the conversation turns to *Sense and Sensibility,* and Sue Forgue, the creator of the online Regency Encyclopedia, says she worries more about Elinor's marriage to the diffident Edward than about Marianne's marriage to the reserved Colonel Brandon, which more often raises Janeite hackles. We discuss Joan Ray's harsh assessment of Edward. Was she fair to him? Everyone has an opinion. As the Janeite conversation swirls around her, Judi Roth, a bubbly sixty-year-old from Ohio who took the summer tour with her twin sister, sighs happily. "This is my favorite," she says.

• • •

We are almost late getting back to the ballroom for the most anticipated talk of this AGM. On the video screens next to the podium,
a montage of scenes from *Sense and Sensibility* adaptations is playing, to the accompaniment of "Nessun Dorma," the stirring Puc-
cini aria that served as the theme for Italy's 1990 World Cup tournament. As the aria reaches its climax, with the tenor declaiming,
"Vincerò! Vincerò!" ("I will win! I will win!"), a succession of Eli-
nors and Edwards passionately embrace. Apparently, Jane Austen
happy endings are the female equivalent of soccer victories.

Soon, the video screens fill with a new montage. As Connie Stevens purrs "Sixteen Reasons (Why I Love You)," familiar scenes
unspool before us. Elizabeth and Darcy kissing on their wedding
day, in the BBC's 1995 *Pride and Prejudice*. Colin Firth in a rein-
deer sweater, as the Darcy-inspired hero of *Bridget Jones's Diary*.
Colin Firth as Darcy, gazing at an off-screen Elizabeth with an ad-
oration so naked that the moment is known in Janeite lore simply
as The Look. Then, as Stevens's song fades out, a man in a white
shirt strides toward Pemberley, dripping wet. And onto the stage
steps . . .

. . . a white-haired, seventy-five-year-old screenwriter, and we
leap to our feet in a spontaneous standing ovation for Andrew Davies.

Davies is this AGM's biggest draw, the author of much-praised
adaptations of four of Austen's six novels, as well as TV and film
versions of many other classic and contemporary works of fiction,
including *Bridget Jones*. Not every Janeite likes his work — he is
famous for making explicit on the screen the sexual tension that
remains implicit on the page — but no one can ignore it. He is
almost *too* big a draw: months earlier, an AGM volunteer acci-
dentally discovered that a small group of fans of the Victorian

writer Elizabeth Gaskell, whose novel *Wives and Daughters* Davies had adapted for TV, was planning to attend his JASNA talk without registering, or paying, for the whole conference. Partly in response to this tip, volunteers have been carefully checking AGM name tags at the door of each event all weekend. Secretly, I am hoping that the Gaskellites attempt an entrance — I'm not sure I can die happy without witnessing a smackdown between Regency hostesses in Empire-line dresses and party crashers in hoop skirts — but alas, they seem to have thought better of their scheme, and no one materializes.

It's their loss, for Davies proves to be a diverting raconteur, entertaining us with an hour's worth of funny, self-deprecating tales from the Austen-adaptation trenches. He explains some of the choices that made his *Pride and Prejudice* "a very pro-Darcy adaptation." He riffs hilariously on the sixteen-year age difference between Emma and her future husband George Knightley, recasting the story of their lifelong friendship as a Tennessee Williams–style plantation drama replete with overtones of pedophilia. In a Brit's version of a Southern accent, he impersonates a faithful retainer slyly telling Mr. Knightley, "You sho' do like Miz Emma."

"We cannot allow ourselves to think such thoughts, not if you're going to write a nice adaptation," Davies continues, his audience in stitches. "So I just wiped that as far as I could from my thoughts."

He discusses his controversial decision to spell out something that Jane Austen leaves ambiguous in the pages of *Northanger Abbey:* that the shallow coquette Isabella Thorpe not only flirts with, but also sleeps with, the amoral rake who is courting her. "I do feel sorry for her," Davies says. "To be shagged and abandoned like that was a very bad situation. 'Are we engaged?' she says."

He pauses. "Oh, that's in my version. I keep forgetting Jane Austen didn't write that."

"She meant to, of course," he continues, as we giggle. "It was in the draft, but Cassandra said, 'Leave it out. The people will guess what happened to her.'"

Finally, we reach his *Sense and Sensibility* ("a very anti-Willoughby adaptation"), which opens with a moment kept decidedly offstage in the novel — Willoughby's seduction of Colonel Brandon's teenage ward, imagined by Davies as a fire-lit scene of whispered come-ons and half-naked limbs. "Why did I start off with such a sexy scene?" Davies asks rhetorically. "Well, because that's the sort of man I am."

I could happily listen to Davies's stories for another hour, but the punishing AGM schedule demands that he close after taking almost no questions, disappointing several people waiting for their turns at the mike, including Arnie Perlstein. During the tea break, as Janeites cluster around Davies, snapping pictures and requesting autographs, Arnie tells me what he'd planned to say — that although Davies had sometimes been accused of over-sexing Austen, he had actually *under*-sexed her, because *Emma*'s Jane Fairfax is pregnant with John Knightley's baby.

After one last breakout session — yet another college professor, this one analyzing the bond between Elinor and Marianne — I head for my room. The banquet and ball are less than three hours away. It is finally time to put on The Dress.

Christine is late for our corset-lacing appointment, and I am quietly panicking. I have managed to achieve the requisite shelf look by lacing the corset in front, rotating the lacings to the back, and slipping my arms into the loops of ribbon at the shoulders, but I will definitely need help tying the drawstrings on my dress. *Where is she?* I call her phone and get voicemail.

I am standing in front of the mirror, adjusting the corset, when, with a deceptively tiny, sickening pop, one of the ribbons tied atop my left shoulder rips from its seam. My $260 corset sags abruptly, and I stare at the detached ribbon in stunned disbelief. *This never happened to Elizabeth Bennet!* Was the corset poorly made? Did I damage it while slipping my arms through the loops of ribbon? Have I gotten that much bigger in the three months since its arrival? I have no time for analysis. I rush to the bathroom for a safety pin, but the tight-fitting corset restricts my arm movements, and I can't manage to reattach the ribbon. I decide to wait for Christine and hope she has better luck.

Five minutes later, Christine arrives — delayed by an absorbing discussion of plans to found a literary society honoring Ann Radcliffe, the gothic novelist whose works Austen both loved and mocked. Christine commiserates over my corset catastrophe, quickly discovers that safety pins are hopeless, and instead decides to restitch the errant ribbon. Fortunately, she turns out to be remarkably handy with a needle — that nursing training has obviously paid off — and she sews the ribbon back into place with tiny, neat stitches. She ties the strings of my dress, helps adjust the overdress, and steps back to admire the effect. "You look great!" she coos supportively, in her warm Louisiana accent. I thank her effusively for her lady's-maid skills, and she goes off to change her own clothes. Alone again, I take a deep breath and look in the mirror.

The news is not good. The dress is as lovely as ever, but on my body, its horizontals accentuate every unflattering line, while its straight drop obscures every compensating curve. I resemble nothing so much as a small blue refrigerator. I don't feel like a princess, a Jane Austen heroine, or an authentic Regency lady; I feel like a twenty-first-century woman who's about to appear in public in precisely the wrong dress. *A pox upon these dress-up Janeites and the mess they've gotten me into!* But there's no help for it now. I pull on my expensive gloves, pick up the matching reticule in which I've stashed my room key and my camera, and head for the elevator.

The crowded pre-banquet reception is a riot of costumed Janeites. Everywhere I look, I see silk, satin, and taffeta, cutaway coats and knee breeches, tall headdresses and cameo brooches, as well as plenty of modern cocktail dresses and sober suits, plus one green T-shirt emblazoned MRS. DARCY. The speech-language pathologist Phyllis Ferguson Bottomer, a feathered headdress atop her gray pageboy, is there, accompanied by her husband, Lindsay, who is wearing a vest and a billowy white shirt. My seamstress, Maureen O'Connor, elegant in a light-blue gown with ribboned sleeves, finds me and surveys her handiwork. She's smiling, but I can't help wondering if she's thinking that I should not make a habit of wearing clothes like these. Still, people keep asking to take my picture; the gown is so beautiful that even my failure to do it justice doesn't seem to matter. Bizarrely, after all my years of disdaining dress-up, I have somehow become one of those picturesque Janeites whose photo will end up in a scrapbook in Albuquerque or Louisville.

We adjourn to our banquet tables, where I discover that sitting in a corset is remarkably uncomfortable. I am silently praying that Christine's stitches hold until the end of the evening. Elsa Solender, JASNA's former president, rises to give the traditional toast to Jane Austen, but first she recalls JASNA's founders — Jack Grey ("he looked adorable in knee breeches"), Joan Austen-Leigh, and Solender's dear friend Henry Burke. "Tonight, I shall be toasting our goddess," she says, "but also the trio of titans, American titans, who founded our society." And then she offers again the familiar lines from Kipling: "Jane lies in Winchester, blessed be her shade!

/ Praise the Lord for making her, and her for all she made . . ." As Solender concludes, we all rise and clink champagne glasses. Tears spring to my eyes, because suddenly none of the bad stuff—the faulty corset or the unflattering dress or the cheesy commercialization—matters as much as being part of a community of people bound together by a love of books.

Naturally, Baronda Bradley is leading the costume promenade. We costumed Janeites head out the door of the hotel and into the balmy October night, our procession stretching for a full block through the streets of downtown Fort Worth, as passersby snap pictures with cameras and cell phones. "Do you have a couple extra dresses? We might join you," call out two young women in stilettos and skinny jeans. A street-corner preacher ignores us. "Jesus says you must love Him more than your brother and your sister, your husband or your wife," he announces. Back at the hotel, I run into Sonya Samuels, the red-haired Angeleno from the summer JASNA tour. She isn't in costume, but watching the promenade, she seems to have caught the bug. "I want to get a dress now," she says.

Our ballroom is a low-ceilinged hotel basement carpeted in a hideous green-and-burgundy leaf pattern, a far cry from the salons of Pemberley. But more than a hundred people are dancing, as an all-female band reels off centuries-old tunes and Beverly Francis calls the figures of the Margate Hoy and the Midnight Ramble. I find a partner, join a set, and try to concentrate on learning the new steps while ignoring the ominous creaking noises that I very much fear are coming from my corset. Halfway through a dance, I realize that my worst fears have been realized: a ribbon on the other shoulder has snapped, and now the right-hand side of my corset is sagging under my gown. The BBC camera crew is on hand again, filming the Janeites at play, and Christine's needlework may be the only thing standing between me and an internationally televised wardrobe malfunction.

Still, the music is beautiful, Beverly's calling is expert, and the ball has moments of magic, as I look down the room at rows of people in Regency costume moving semi-gracefully through dances Jane Austen might have known. Out of the corner of my eye, I see Phyllis teaching the basics of English country dance to several young men in black T-shirts who have wandered in from another convention. Midway through the ball, Andrew Davies, in jeans and a black Oxford shirt, joins the dancing. When the last country dance ends, the band strikes up two final waltzes. Baronda circles the room in Eric's arms, and Andrew Davies partners a woman young enough to be his daughter.

By midnight, a group of us are making our way tiredly through the lobby.

"It was a lovely ball," the Janeite beside me sighs wistfully. "It went so quickly."

Andrew Davies is a few steps behind, but as some of us stop at the elevators, he sweeps past, surrounded by women in Regency gowns.

"We're carrying right on to the bar," he calls out cheerfully.

The rest of us gaze after them. "He has groupies," somebody murmurs.

Back in my room, I peel off my damaged corset—Christine's stitches held after all, God bless her—and briefly consider slipping into something less precarious and joining the Davies acolytes in the bar. But I don't have the energy. Instead, I crawl into bed with my Kindle and stay up way too late finishing my latest *Pride and Prejudice* spinoff, a charming young-adult version updated to a snooty Los Angeles private school. Of course I know that Derek and Elise will end up together, since they share the initials, not to mention the major plot points, of their famous prototypes. But it doesn't matter. I just want to see that wonderfully familiar story play itself out one more time.

Day 5

In a cavernous foyer, more than two dozen authors are signing their Austen-related books. Pamela Aidan is on hand with a novella about the thirteen-year-old Fitzwilliam Darcy, her first foray back into fiction since the success of her trilogy. I recognize some titles from my adventures in fan fiction, others from the postcards that filled my goody bag. Laurel Ann Nattress of the Austenprose blog launched her collection of Austen-inspired short stories at a nearby Barnes & Noble two days earlier, and the AGM's attendees have welcomed her with open arms, she will tell me later. "People chasing me down in the elevator for signatures!" she says. "I felt like a Jane Austen celebrity."

I run into Christy Somer, a self-described former flower child whose graying hair cascades luxuriantly to her waist. Christy contributes frequently to the online Austen discussion groups, usually arguing for the traditional view of Jane Austen as a fundamentally contented person securely rooted in a supportive family. In cyberspace, she and Arnie Perlstein are often locked in combat, though their conversations seldom take on the venomous tone of his disagreements with other list members. Christy and I chat about Edward Austen Knight's wife, Elizabeth, and her attitude toward her brilliant sister-in-law, and about Jane Austen's love for her oldest nieces, Anna and Fanny. Arnie joins us, and our conversation turns to Austen-L's ongoing discussion of Austen's letters, with their sometimes affectionate, sometimes caustic observations about relatives, neighbors, and family friends.

"I'll tell you," says Christy, "she loved Mrs. Harry Digweed, because —"

"She was mocking her!" Arnie cries.

And they're off . . .

The AGM will not close officially until noon, but as we gather for
brunch, a morning-after atmosphere already suffuses the room.
Most people have packed away their feathers, reticules, and gowns,
although a few die-hards are still sporting bonnets and Baronda
is wearing her denim Regency dress. As we eat our waffles, actors
portraying the married couples of *Sense and Sensibility* circulate,
answering questions in character, until Colonel Brandon drives
Willoughby from the room at sword point. Before we scatter to our
homes, the organizers of upcoming AGMs urge us to attend their
parties too. In New York next year, with no publication anniversary to commemorate, the theme will be "Sex, Money, and Power
in Jane Austen's Fiction," and Sandy Lerner will be speaking about
— what else? — money. And in 2013 we will reconvene in Minneap-
olis to celebrate the big kahuna, the two-hundredth anniversary of
the publication of *Pride and Prejudice*.

We are a tribe, we Janeites. We name our children and our pets
after people who never existed, treat an elderly screenwriter like
a rock star, and seek twenty-first-century life lessons in two-hun-
dred-year-old books, or the tarot cards based on them. Our love for
Jane Austen unites us, and yet sometimes it seems that we all love
something, or someone, different. In Austen's novels, Linda Berdoll finds inspiration for racy sex scenes, and the evangelical Christian Laurie Michael sees a commitment to biblical values. Sandy
Lerner's Jane Austen is confident and contented; Arnie Perlstein's
is angry and rebellious. We make our Austen into a reflection of our
own preoccupations, a teller of our own stories.

I am ending my travels more convinced than ever that those tempting, pat explanations of Austen's appeal—Anglophilia or escapism, feminist sensibilities or romantic longings—can never account for the diversity of Austen-love. What single theory could encompass Joan Austen-Leigh's revered ancestor and Christine Shih's abused child, Devoney Looser's literary scholarship and Debbie McNeil's Elizabeth Bennet soap? Yet if my journey among the Janeites has taught me anything, surely it is that Austen's work is not just a Rorschach test, a collection of inkblots with no meaning beyond the mind of the viewer. The rich diversity of responses to Austen captures something real about her—the depth and complexity of her writings, which, like diamonds held up to sunlight, reflect something different from every angle. Her stories are not blank canvases onto which we project ourselves; they are complicated, ambiguous pictures of lived reality. We all find ourselves in her because, in a sense, she contains us all.

I know now that I will never be the kind of Janeite who wears satin Empire-waist gowns in public, and I doubt I'll ever pen my own *Pride and Prejudice* sequel, write a scholarly monograph on *Emma,* or travel long distances to shake Colin Firth's hand. Although I no longer have to hide my books from the recess monitors, I'm still the kind of Janeite who is happiest curled up alone with my old copy of *Persuasion* or discussing the finer points with friends, in person or online.

Like the members of any tribe, we Janeites don't always see eye to eye, whether it's about zombie mash-up or Regency dress-up. But maybe the diversity of the fandom suggests something hopeful about the possibility of human connection. Beyond our passion for Austen, what most obviously unites our disparate group is something we have in common with the members of every subculture—of every culture, really: the desire to share with other human beings the things that bring us joy. Until the day he joined an Internet discussion group, "it never dawned on me how amazing it would feel to talk about the books with other people," Arnie Perlstein once told me. And despite the vitriolic responses his ideas sometimes draw, he keeps coming back. "It would be horrible to be all by myself with it," Arnie said. "I want to connect to those who feel the same way about this." As we turn the well-thumbed pages of our *Pride and Prejudice* paperbacks, perhaps, unconsciously, we Janeites are looking for ourselves. But in the community of fandom, we find each other.

Brunch ends, and suddenly the lobby is crowded with Janeites dragging wheeled suitcases, arranging taxis to the airport, saying goodbye. I run into Debbie McNeil, getting ready to go home to Skip. She bought that feathered headband from the Emporium after all, she tells me, and she wore it to the ball. Next year, she thinks she may dance.

THE NOVELS OF
JANE AUSTEN

Sense and Sensibility (1811)

Sisters Elinor and Marianne Dashwood must leave home when their father dies and their older half brother inherits his estate. The restrained, cautious Elinor loves Edward Ferrars, but inexplicably, Edward fails to declare himself before the Dashwoods move to Devonshire and begin life on a greatly reduced income. In Devonshire, emotional and demonstrative Marianne falls deeply in love with the dashing John Willoughby, taking no notice of a reserved older man, Colonel Brandon, who is clearly smitten with her.

Just as Willoughby seems on the brink of proposing to Marianne, he leaves for London, offering unconvincing explanations for his sudden departure. Meanwhile, Elinor gets crushing news: a new acquaintance, the penniless Lucy Steele, confides that she and Edward have been engaged for years but have kept their relationship secret lest they anger his snobbish family. Elinor realizes that as a man of honor, Edward cannot break his engagement. Sworn to secrecy by Lucy, Elinor carries her emotional burden alone while Marianne indulges her grief about Willoughby.

On a trip to London, Marianne encounters Willoughby, who cruelly rejects her; he is about to marry an heiress. Soon, the Dashwoods learn why: by seducing, impregnating, and abandoning Colonel Brandon's teenage ward, Willoughby has alienated a rich relative whose money he hoped to inherit. Marianne sinks into depression, contracts a fever, and narrowly escapes death. Meanwhile, Edward's family learns of his secret engagement to Lucy. Edward's mother disinherits him and settles his fortune on his younger brother.

Back home in Devonshire, the sisters are coming to terms with disappointment when Edward arrives unexpectedly. Lucy has broken their engagement in order to marry his newly wealthy brother. Edward and Elinor marry, and Marianne eventually accepts the faithful Colonel Brandon.

Pride and Prejudice (1813)

"It is a truth universally acknowledged, that a single man in possession of a good fortune must be in want of a wife." That famous opening line launches the story of the five unmarried Bennet sisters, who face an uncertain future because their father's estate will pass on his death to a distant male relative.

When the wealthy Mr. Bingley rents a house in the neighborhood, he and the eldest Bennet daughter, Jane, fall in love. The second Bennet sister, Elizabeth, takes a dislike to Mr. Bingley's even wealthier friend, the proud and aloof Mr. Darcy, but she is drawn to the handsome George Wickham, whose late father worked on the Darcy estate. Wickham tells Elizabeth that Darcy cheated him out of a promised job, confirming her prejudices.

Elizabeth rejects a marriage proposal from her father's heir, the sycophantic Mr. Collins, and to her hysterical mother's dismay, he marries Elizabeth's friend Charlotte Lucas instead. Even worse, Mr. Bingley leaves suddenly for London without asking Jane to marry him.

On a visit to Charlotte's new home, Elizabeth again meets Mr. Darcy, whose aunt, Lady Catherine de Bourgh, is Mr. Collins's employer. When Darcy asks Elizabeth to marry him, insulting her family in the process, she rejects him angrily, accusing him of ruining Wickham and talking Bingley out of marrying Jane. Darcy writes her a letter explaining his side of both stories: he believed Jane to be indifferent to Bingley, and Wickham is a cynical seducer who tried to elope with Darcy's teenage sister, Georgiana, in order to get his hands on her considerable fortune. Elizabeth realizes that her first impressions of both men were mistaken.

On vacation with her aunt and uncle, Elizabeth visits Derbyshire and, assured that the family are away, tours the palatial Darcy estate, Pemberley. Darcy returns home unexpectedly while she is there and treats Elizabeth and her relatives with politeness and generosity. But the rapprochement is cut short when Elizabeth learns that her sixteen-year-old sister, Lydia, has run off with Mr. Wickham but has apparently not yet married him, a family disgrace that will likely ruin the marital prospects of all the Bennet daughters. After days of suspense, however, Lydia and Wickham are found, and they do marry. Only later does Elizabeth learn that it was Darcy who tracked them down and bribed Wickham into the marriage that saved Lydia's reputation.

Elizabeth is now in love with Darcy and hopes he will renew his proposal. Instead, she receives a visit from his overbearing aunt, Lady Catherine, who has heard rumors that Elizabeth is engaged to Darcy and demands that she promise never to marry him. Elizabeth refuses, and when Darcy hears of the conversation, he is emboldened to propose again. This time, Elizabeth accepts, and she and Darcy marry in a double wedding with Jane and Bingley.

Mansfield Park (1814)

Ten-year-old Fanny Price leaves her struggling family in Portsmouth and is sent to Mansfield Park to live with her wealthy aunt and uncle, Sir Thomas and Lady Bertram. She is patronized or ignored by most of the family — and tyrannized by another aunt, the nasty Mrs. Norris — but her sixteen-year-old cousin, Edmund Bertram, treats her with kindness, and she falls in love with him. When Fanny is nearly eighteen, Sir Thomas leaves on an extended business trip to the West Indian island of Antigua. Back at Mansfield, the family circle is enlivened by the arrival of new neighbors, Henry Crawford and his beautiful, witty sister, Mary. Fanny's cousins Maria and Julia compete for Henry's attention, even though Maria is engaged to the rich but stupid Mr. Rushworth. Meanwhile, Edmund falls in love with Mary. She is also drawn to him, although as a younger son and a clergyman, he is a far less eligible match than she had hoped for.

With Sir Thomas away, the young people decide to put on a play, the racy *Lovers' Vows*. Only Fanny firmly insists on the inappropriateness of the theatricals, and her misgivings are justified as Henry's flirtation with Maria and Edmund's attraction to Mary flourish during rehearsals. Sir Thomas's sudden return scotches the performance, and when Henry fails to declare himself, Maria marries Mr. Rushworth and takes Julia with her on her honeymoon. With nothing else to amuse him, Henry decides to engage Fanny's affections. She resists, but before long he discovers that he has fallen genuinely in love with her, and he asks her to marry him. She refuses, even when Sir Thomas pressures her to change her mind. Most painfully, her beloved Edmund urges the match, although he is still dithering over whether to ask the worldly Mary to be his wife.

Sir Thomas decides to send Fanny home to Portsmouth, for the first visit since her departure eight years earlier, hoping that the squalor of her family's life there will persuade her to think better of marriage to the wealthy Henry Crawford. But while Fanny is in Portsmouth, catastrophe strikes the Bertram clan. The dissipated oldest son, Tom, falls desperately ill; Julia elopes with Tom's callow friend Mr. Yates; and news comes that Maria has deserted her husband to run off with Henry. When Edmund goes to Mary to discuss the situation, her cynical assessment of Henry and Maria's adultery — behavior that Edmund views as a grave sin — opens his eyes to her true character. Sir Thomas and Lady Bertram, who have learned to appreciate Fanny, welcome her home to Mansfield, and eventually Edmund recovers from his attachment to Mary, falls in love with Fanny, and marries her.

Emma (1816)

Rich, self-satisfied Emma Woodhouse lives alone with her anxious, invalid father and presides as queen bee in the small village of Highbury. Bored and lonely after her best friend and former governess marries a neighbor, Mr. Weston, she takes an interest in pretty but dimwitted Harriet Smith. Although Harriet's parentage is uncertain—she is probably illegitimate, which rules out marriage to anyone of high social standing—Emma decides Harriet must marry well and fixes upon the local minister, Mr. Elton, as the perfect man for the job. To further her plans, she talks Harriet out of accepting a proposal from a respectable local farmer, Robert Martin, earning a stern condemnation from George Knightley, a longtime family friend whose brother, John Knightley, is married to Emma's older sister.

To Emma's shock, Mr. Elton proposes to her instead of to Harriet, and when she refuses him, he quickly decamps to Bath, where he meets and marries the vain and officious Augusta Hawkins. Meanwhile, a stranger has come to Highbury: handsome Frank Churchill, Mr. Weston's son by an earlier marriage, who was raised by an aunt in faraway Yorkshire after his mother's death. Frank and Emma flirt and gossip, indulging in spiteful speculations about Jane Fairfax, the beautiful but reserved niece of an impoverished, talkative neighbor, Miss Bates.

At a ball, Mr. Elton ostentatiously refuses to dance with Harriet—his revenge on Emma for trying to marry him off to a woman so far beneath him—but George Knightley saves her from humiliation by dancing with her instead. Walking home not long after, Harriet is accosted by gypsy children, but Frank Churchill arrives in time to drive them away. Emma is certain this romantic episode will inevitably end in the marriage of Frank and Harriet, but she refrains from telling Harriet about her speculations; she's trying to learn from the disastrous Elton episode. Meanwhile, the pushy Mrs. Elton adopts Jane Fairfax as her protégée and offers to find her work as a governess, though Jane resists the interference.

Everyone assembles for a picnic at Box Hill, but the day goes badly.

As she flirts with Frank, Emma publicly insults silly Miss Bates, and Mr. Knightley sternly reprimands Emma for abusing her social power. She is overcome with remorse and tries to make amends.

Frank Churchill's overbearing aunt dies suddenly, and shocking developments ensue: Frank, it turns out, has been secretly engaged to Jane Fairfax, has concealed the relationship lest his aunt disinherit him, and has flirted with Emma only to divert suspicion. Emma fears that Harriet will be crushed, but Harriet announces that she has fallen in love with George Knightley and believes that he returns her feelings. Only then does Emma realize that she is in love with Mr. Knightley herself.

Mr. Knightley, of course, believes that Emma loves Frank, and as he tries to console her for her disappointment, she steels herself for what she is sure will be his declaration of love for Harriet. Eventually, the misunderstandings unravel, and to Emma's surprise and delight, Mr. Knightley confesses his love for her. They marry, and Harriet accepts a renewed proposal from Robert Martin, the farmer Emma had once thought so far below her.

Northanger Abbey (1818)

Naive Catherine Morland, the daughter of a country clergyman, accompanies her neighbors on a vacation trip to Bath. There she meets Isabella Thorpe, a vain coquette on the lookout for a good marriage, and Isabella's boorish brother John, a college friend of Catherine's older brother James. Catherine and Isabella bond over a shared love for sensational gothic novels, and their bond seems to deepen when James and Isabella become engaged.

Meanwhile, Catherine has also met another set of siblings, the Tilneys. Gentle, well-bred Eleanor becomes her friend, and Catherine falls in love with Eleanor's brother, the witty, charming Henry—though she is less taken with the oldest Tilney brother, Frederick, who is pursuing Isabella despite her engagement. The Tilneys' father, General Tilney, takes an immediate shine to Catherine and invites her to stay at the family home, Northanger Abbey. There, Catherine learns that the engagement between Isabella and James has ended because Isabella has taken up with Frederick Tilney. When Isabella realizes that Frederick has no intention of marrying her, she tries to patch things up with Catherine and, through her, with James, but by then Catherine sees Isabella for what she is and will have none of it.

Under the influence of her gothic reading matter, Catherine begins to wonder whether the dictatorial General Tilney might have murdered his wife, who died when Henry and Eleanor were teenagers. When Henry discovers Catherine's speculations, he is horrified and quickly explains away the circumstances that she had found so suspicious. They are back on good terms when Henry leaves Northanger to return to the parish where he works as a clergyman.

Soon after Henry's departure, however, Eleanor comes to Catherine late at night with the unaccountable demand that she leave the house at once, on General Tilney's orders. Catherine is left to make her way home alone—a terrible breach of hospitality—but she arrives safely. She is moping for Henry when he shows up himself. General Tilney, it seems, had befriended Catherine because he falsely believed her to be an heiress he could marry off to his younger son. When he learned she had no great fortune, he sent her packing. By now, however, Henry has fallen in love with Catherine, and eventually they marry.

Persuasion (1818)

Eight years ago, Anne Elliot, the daughter of a baronet, was briefly engaged to an up-and-coming young naval officer, Frederick Wentworth. But her dead mother's friend, Lady Russell, persuaded Anne to break off the engagement because of Wentworth's uncertain career prospects. Now Anne's father, the vain spendthrift Sir Walter Elliot, has run up so much debt that he must rent out his estate and move into lodgings in cheaper

Bath. His tenants turn out to be Admiral and Mrs. Croft, Wentworth's sister and brother-in-law.

At twenty-seven, still in love with Wentworth and still regretting his loss, Anne is a depressed shadow of her pretty younger self. When her father and older sister go off to Bath, she temporarily stays behind, moving in with the family of her spoiled, lazy younger sister, Mary. Soon, Wentworth arrives on a visit to his relatives. He is handsomer than ever, and he has made a fortune in the Napoleonic Wars. He's ready to marry and settle down, and he begins flirting with Louisa Musgrove, whose brother Charles is married to Mary.

The whole party heads for the seaside town of Lyme, where they visit naval friends of Wentworth's — Captain Harville, his wife and children, and their friend Captain Benwick, who is grieving over the recent death of his fiancée, Harville's sister. As they walk on the Cobb, the stone sea-wall at Lyme, Louisa decides to jump down the steps into Captain Wentworth's arms. She falls and is seriously injured.

Anne moves on to Bath, where her father and older sister are enjoying the high society of the resort town. They have befriended a cousin, William Walter Elliot, who will inherit Sir Walter's title and estate, but who had become estranged from the family years earlier. Mr. Elliot begins to show a marked interest in Anne, whose looks and spirits are reviving. Anne has reservations about him, and her intuition is confirmed when an old school friend, the ailing and impoverished Mrs. Smith, provides her with evidence of Mr. Elliot's selfish and mercenary character.

Anne still expects to hear of Wentworth's engagement to Louisa, who is recovering from her fall. Instead, she learns that Louisa has become engaged to Captain Benwick, and she is still absorbing this surprise when Wentworth himself appears in Bath. Their paths cross repeatedly, and she begins to suspect that his love for her is returning.

Plans for Louisa's wedding to Benwick bring Captain Harville and the Musgroves to Bath, and Anne visits their inn. As Captain Wentworth writes a business letter, Anne and Harville chat about men and women and love, arguing good-naturedly over which sex is more constant. Wentworth overhears and, realizing that Anne is describing her own unwavering feelings for him, he writes her a passionate declaration of love. They meet on the street soon after she has read it, and she accepts his proposal. This time, with little delay, they marry.

A NOTE ON SOURCES

This book is a work of journalism, not a scholarly study of Jane Austen appreciation, and as such it is based primarily upon my interviews with Janeites and my observations at Janeite events. In the course of my research I did, however, consult a number of secondary sources — a small fraction of the many excellent books and articles that have been written about Jane Austen and her admirers.

For information on Jane Austen's life, I relied mostly on Claire Tomalin's biography, *Jane Austen: A Life* (New York: Knopf, 1997); on Austen's letters, edited by Deirdre Le Faye (Oxford: Oxford University Press, 1997); and on J. E. Austen-Leigh's *A Memoir of Jane Austen,* first published in 1870 and reprinted by the Oxford University Press in a 2002 edition, edited by Kathryn Sutherland, that includes an invaluable chronology of the Austen family.

Readers who want to know more about the reception of Austen's work and the phenomenon of Austen fandom have a rich array of sources from which to choose. Brian Southam's two-volume *Jane Austen: The Critical Heritage* (London: Routledge and Kegan Paul, 1979 and 1987) reprints key critical essays from the nineteenth and twentieth centuries and includes Southam's useful introduction; Laurence W. Mazzeno's *Jane Austen: Two Centuries of Criticism* (Rochester, NY: Camden House, 2011), summarizes major developments in the history of Austen criticism and brings the story up to the present. Kathryn Sutherland's *Jane Austen's Textual Lives: From Aeschylus to Bollywood* (Oxford: Oxford University Press, 2005) is a scholarly look at the transmission and transformation of Austen's texts; Claire Harman, in *Jane's Fame: How Jane Austen Conquered the World* (Edinburgh: Canongate Books, 2009), covers similar ground in a less academic style. Claudia L. Johnson's book *Jane Austen's Cults and Cultures* (Chicago: University of Chicago Press, 2012) looks at fans of Austen's work from the Victorian period through the years after World War II; the book amplifies elements of Johnson's article "Austen cults and cultures," in *The Cambridge Companion to Jane Austen* (Cambridge: Cambridge University Press, 1997). Juliette Wells, in *Everybody's Jane: Austen in the Popular Imagination* (London and New York: Continuum, 2011), examines how today's readers, writers, filmgoers, and literary tourists use and understand Austen. The scholarly essays in *Janeites: Austen's Disciples and Devotees* (Princeton: Princeton University Press, 2000), including the introduction by the volume's editor, Deidre Lynch, examine various facets of Austen appreciation over the centuries. Rachel M. Brownstein, in *Why Jane Austen?* (New York: Columbia University Press, 2011), combines close reading, cultural criticism, and memoir.

Everybody's Jane, by Juliette Wells, also provided me with helpful background on Alberta Burke and her Austen collection. I am indebted to Wells for the quotation from Alberta Burke's letter ("The J. A. collection is the perpetual pleasure of my life"), which can be found on page 43 in Wells's book.

Little or nothing has been written previously about most of my subjects. The notable exception is Sandy Lerner, and I relied on many books and articles for background on her life and career. The books I consulted included David Bunnell, *Making the Cisco Connection: The Story Behind the Real Internet Superpower* (New York: John Wiley & Sons, 2000); Ed Paulson, *Inside Cisco: The Real Story of Sustained M&A Growth* (New York: John Wiley & Sons, 2001); Stephen Segaller, *Nerds 2.0.1: A Brief*

History of the Internet (New York: TV Books, 1998); and Robert Slater, *The Eye of the Storm: How John Chambers Steered Cisco Through the Technology Collapse* (New York: HarperCollins, 2003). Among the most helpful of the newspaper and magazine articles I consulted were Robert X. Cringely, "High-Tech Wealth" (*Forbes,* July 7, 1997); Renee Tawa, "Lady Godiva" (*Los Angeles Times Magazine,* March 1, 1998); and Linton Weeks, "Network of One" (*Washington Post,* March 25, 1998).

The following quotations in my chapter on Sandy Lerner come from published sources:

"Do you think you're a bit eccentric?": Chris Wallace, "Power Player of the Week: Sandy Lerner," FoxNews, November 20, 2011

"It was not my intention to get rich": Cringely, "High-Tech Wealth"

"Len actually knew how to bathe": Segaller, *Nerds 2.0.1,* p. 241

"Sandy was born a barracuda": Slater, *The Eye of the Storm,* p. 81

"weird science": Cringely, "High-Tech Wealth"

"I'm just so fucking sick of it": Tawa, "Lady Godiva"

"I don't think there's anyone who's not on her side": Godfrey Smith, "Sandy Lerner: Underwriting Austen," *Sunday Times,* April 5, 2009

In two chapters, I changed some names in order to protect the privacy of people peripherally connected to the narrative. In Chapter 4, I changed Pamela Aidan's surname during her first marriage. In Chapter 7, I changed the names of Phyllis Ferguson Bottomer's students and of the participants in Christine Shih's bibliotherapy group.

ACKNOWLEDGMENTS

Do kind and generous people gravitate to Jane Austen? Or does reading Jane Austen inspire kindness and generosity? Whatever the explanation, the Janeites I met while researching this book were among the loveliest people I've ever dealt with. They picked me up at airports, served me home-cooked meals, showed me the sights of their hometowns, offered to treat me in restaurants, and graciously backed off when I explained that journalistic ethics required me to split the check — all while submitting uncomplainingly to hours of interviews about their lives, their work, and their love of Jane Austen. I wish this book could have included every Janeite story I heard, but even those I had to leave on the cutting-room floor helped me come to grips with our shared passion. Thank you to all who described their Janeite journeys to me. Special thanks to the women who make up the Central New Jersey branch of JASNA — my local! — especially our hardworking regional coordinators, past and present: Meredith Barnes, Joan Dow, Jennifer Fitzgerald, and Connie Paul. I've appreciated all your support and interest as this project took shape.

In the course of the three years I spent conceiving, researching, and writing this book, I incurred the usual array of debts. My agent, Jenni Ferrari-Adler, was an enthusiastic supporter of the project from the first, and my editor at Houghton Mifflin Harcourt, Nicole Angeloro, is both a sharp critic and a true Janeite. (I can imagine no higher praise.)

Jean Hanff Korelitz and Eve Niedergang gave me useful advice during my search for an agent. Jenny Allan, Catherine Crystal Foster, Jacqueline Knox, Eve Niedergang, Cynthia Yoder, and Amelia Zurcher read my book proposal, and in some cases also my manuscript, offering helpful comments. In particular, Jenny Allan, whom I met on the Republic of Pemberley, has been an indefatigable cheerleader every step of the way.

Useful contact information was supplied by Jenny Allan, Vicki Bendure, Lisa Brown, Marie Dalton-Meyer, Marsha Galdi, Sarit Kattan Gribetz, Cheryl Kinney, Stephen Lawrence, Michael McKeon, Barbara Moglia, Pamela Suggs, Allison Thompson, and Carol Zarda. Lacey Chemsak, Charles Ellis, Andrea Kaminski, and Kyle Standifer provided guidance in the perplexing realm of music licensing. Kate Dannals, Grant Justis, and Tara Olivero helped me access Goucher College's wonderful collection of JASNA papers. Rebecca Yaffe designed my website and gave me useful advice about the brave new world of social media.

I turned to many people for miscellaneous bits of information, from the inscription on the Chawton bells to the family background of the first Jane Austen sequel writer. Thanks to John Adey, John Bailey, Anita Fernandez-Young, Joanne Goodwin, Jane Booty Horn, Jeanne Kiefer, Helen Lea, Candace Lewis, Miranda Martin, Dale Miller, Lynn Oberlander, Tony Pears, Brian Ray, Michael D. Sanders, Jennifer Simone, Madelaine Smith, Rosalie Sternberg, Margaret Sullivan, Christine Tam, Elisabeth Trissel, Freydis Welland, and Elaine Yaffe. And an extra special thank-you to Debbie McNeil, for mailing me every one of her back issues of *Jane Austen's Regency World*.

Baronda Bradley, Beth Conklin, and the dynamic team of Claudia O'Brien and Lee Okster provided overnight hospitality during research trips, and I'm very grateful to them all. But I could never have taken those trips if my wonderful neighbors hadn't been around to pick up the slack while I was gone. Jacqueline Knox offered periodic child care, and Cynthia Yoder drove my daughter to Hebrew school more times than I can count. As they say, it takes a village to write a book.

Last, but never least, I must thank my family. My father, James Yaffe, first introduced me to the joys of classic English literature and remains one of the smartest readers I know. My mother, Elaine Yaffe, combines Mrs. Dashwood's empathy with Mrs. Morland's common sense.

My son, David, who seems to have given up his habit of shouting "Jane Austen was a man!" just to check if I'm paying attention, added *Pride and Prejudice* to his summer reading list at my suggestion and actually enjoyed it. (Should it worry me that he laughed so hard at Mrs. Bennet?) My daughter, Rachel, has watched just about every Jane Austen movie with me, and she's apparently forgiven me for yelling at her about the corset. They both tolerated my periodic absences and my long hours at the keyboard with exemplary patience and good cheer.

This book exists because my husband, Alastair Bellany, listened to my stories about the Republic of Pemberley, decided I should write a book about it all, and didn't stop nagging until I did. He is my first reader and my best friend. Although he lacks a landed estate, a naval commission, or a comfortable living in a nearby parish, he'll always be my idea of a Jane Austen hero.